Shaking the Pedestal

General Sir John Monash and the Battle of Hamel, 4 July 1918

Derek Clayton

Helion & Company

Helion & Company Limited
Unit 8 Amherst Business Centre
Budbrooke Road
Warwick
CV34 5WE
England
Tel. 01926 499619
Email: info@helion.co.uk
Website: www.helion.co.uk
X (formerly Twitter): @Helionbooks
Facebook: @HelionBooks
Visit our blog at http://blog.helion.co.uk/

Published by Helion & Company 2026
Designed and typeset by Mach 3 Solutions (www.mach3solutions.co.uk)
Cover designed by Paul Hewitt, Battlefield Design (www.battlefield-design.co.uk)

ISBN 978-1-804519-78-3

British Library Cataloguing-in-Publication Data.
A catalogue record for this book is available from the British Library.

Contents

The Wolverhampton Military Studies Series

Series Editor's Preface

As series editor, it is my great pleasure to introduce the Wolverhampton Military Studies Series to you. Our intention is that in this series of books you will find military history that is new and innovative, and academically rigorous with a strong basis in fact and in analytical research, but also is the kind of military history that is for all readers, whatever their particular interests, or their level of interest in the subject. To paraphrase an old aphorism: a military history book is not less important just because it is popular, and it is not more scholarly just because it is dull. With every one of our publications, we want to bring you the kind of military history that you will want to read simply because it is a good and well-written book, as well as bringing new light, new perspectives, and new factual evidence to its subject.

In devising the Wolverhampton Military Studies Series, we gave much thought to the series title: this is a military series. We take the view that history is everything except the things that have not happened yet, and even then, a good book about the military aspects of the future would find its way into this series. We are not bound to any particular time period or cut-off date. Writing military history often divides quite sharply into eras, from the modern through the early modern to the medieval and ancient; and into regions or continents, with a division between western military history and the military history of other countries and cultures being particularly marked. Inevitably, we have had to start somewhere, and the first books of the series deal with British military topics and events of the twentieth century and later nineteenth century. But this series is open to any book that challenges received and accepted ideas about any aspect of military history and does so in a way that encourages its readers to enjoy the discovery.

In the same way, this series is not limited to being about wars, or about grand strategy, or wider defence matters, or the sociology of armed forces as institutions, or civilian society and culture at war. None of these are specifically excluded, and in some cases, they play an important part in the books that comprise our series. But there are already many books in existence, some of them of the highest scholarly standards, which cater to these particular approaches. The main theme of the Wolverhampton Military Studies Series is the military aspects of wars, the preparation for wars or their prevention, and their aftermath. This includes some books whose main themes cover the technical details of how armed forces have worked, some books on wars and battles, and some books that re-examine the evidence about the existing stories, to show in a different light what everyone thought they already knew and understood.

As series editor, together with my fellow editorial board members, and our publisher Duncan Rogers of Helion, I have found that we have known immediately and almost by instinct the kind of books that fit within this series. They are very much the kind of well-written and challenging books that my students at the University of Wolverhampton would want to read. They are books which enhance knowledge and offer new perspectives. Also, they are books for anyone with an interest in military history and events, from expert scholars to occasional readers. One of the great benefits of the study of military history is that it includes a large and often committed section of the wider population, who want to read the best military history that they can find; our aim for this series is to provide it.

Stephen Badsey
University of Wolverhampton

Dramatis Personae

Command positions cited are as of 4 July 1918

Sir John Monash (1865–1931), Commander, Australian Corps

Born in Melbourne, he was educated at Scotch College and went on to graduate from the University of Melbourne with a Master of Engineering degree in 1893. He followed this with a Bachelor of Arts and a Bachelor of Law in 1895. He worked as a civil engineer on bridge and railway construction, played a major role in introducing reinforced concrete to Australian engineering practice, and eventually became president of the Victorian Institute of Engineers.

He joined the militia in 1884 and enjoyed regular promotion, commanding the 13th Infantry Brigade in 1912. He became a full-time army officer on the outbreak of the Great War and commanded 4th Brigade at Gallipoli. There, he acquired a reputation for his organisational abilities and careful preparation of battle plans. He was promoted to brigadier general in July 1915. After a brief spell at the Suez Canal, his command was transferred to the Western Front. On 10 July 1916, he was promoted to major general and took command of 3rd Division, leading them through the battles of Messines, Broodseinde and the First Battle of Passchendaele. The division spent the winter of 1917–1918 around Ploegsteert in Belgium before deployment to undertake defensive operations near Arras against the German Spring Offensive.

On 1 June 1918, he became a lieutenant general and took command of the Australian Corps. This promotion was contentious, drawing criticism from the future official historian Charles Bean and the journalist Keith Murdoch, both of whom were, however, said to be prejudiced against Monash's German-Jewish heritage. But for the success of the Battle of Hamel, and the backing of Douglas Haig, the Australian Prime Minister, Billy Hughes, might have been tempted to remove him from his command.

Monash's Corps then took part in the Battle of Amiens, following which Monash was knighted 'in the field' by King George V, becoming Knight Commander of the Order of the Bath. More success followed at Mont St Quentin and with the breaching of the Hindenburg Line.

While in London in 1919, Monash wrote *The Australian Victories in France in 1918*, a tome with which he unashamedly enhanced his own reputation.

He returned to Australia in December 1919 and, upon returning to civilian life, later became the head of the State Electricity Commission of Victoria, the vice-chancellor of the University of Melbourne, and president of the newly founded Zionist Federation of Australia.

Following his death from a heart attack on 8 October 1931, his funeral attracted an estimated 300,000 mourners.

Sir Henry Seymour Rawlinson (1864–1925), Commander, Fourth Army

Rawlinson was born in Dorset. His father, Sir Henry, 1st Baronet, was an army officer and celebrated Orientalist. Following his time at Eton, the young Henry gained a commission at the Royal Military College, Sandhurst, joining the King's Royal Rifle Corps in India as a lieutenant. He served in Burma during the 1886 uprising.

He returned to England following the death of his mother in 1889 and transferred to the Coldstream Guards, being promoted to captain in November 1891. He served in Sudan on Kitchener's Staff in 1898, and promotions followed: major in 1899 and brevet lieutenant colonel the same year. He served with distinction in the Second Boer War and was appointed Companion of the Order of the Bath, receiving the honour, after his return to England, from Edward VII in October 1902. He became commandant of the Army Staff College, with the substantive rank of colonel, in April 1903.

Rawlinson's career progressed: commander of 2nd Brigade in 1907, GOC 3rd Division in 1910. On the outbreak of war in 1914, he went to France as GOC 4th Division. He then, as temporary lieutenant general, took command of IV Corps, taking them through the 1st Battle of Ypres.

After a spell in England overseeing the training of 8th Division, he returned to the front as commander of the new Fourth Army in January 1916, and would play a major role in the conduct of the Battle of the Somme that year, advocating a 'bite and hold' approach, this putting him at odds with Douglas Haig.

In January 1917, Rawlinson was promoted to permanent general and briefly commanded Second Army. In February 1918, he became the British Permanent Military Representative to the Inter-Allied Supreme War Council at Versailles.

When Hubert Gough was sacked as commander of Fifth Army following the German March Offensive, Rawlinson took over command, taking most of his Fourth Army staff with him. Confusingly, Fifth Army was renamed Fourth Army on 2 April.

Rawlinson then led Fourth Army through the rest of the war, including at the Battles of Hamel, Amiens, and the Hindenburg Line.

After the war, Parliament awarded him the sum of £30,000 and raised him to the peerage as Baron Rawlinson of Trent. After a brief time as GOC Aldershot Command, he was made Commander-in-Chief, India in 1920.

Rawlinson died in Delhi, India, on 28 March 1925, following unsuccessful abdominal surgery. His body was returned to England for burial in his native Dorset.

Thomas Albert Blamey (1884–1951), Chief of Staff, Australian Corps

Originally a school teacher, he joined the military in 1906, graduating from the Staff College at Quetta, India, in 1913. He spent most of the Great War in staff appointments, with 1st Australian Division at Gallipoli and then as its GSO 2 on the Western Front. He became Chief of Staff of the Australian Corps in June 1918. He also served in the Second World War, being appointed Commander-in-Chief, Australian Forces, in March 1942. He retired to Melbourne after the war and became a field marshal in 1950.

Ewen George Sinclair-MacLagan (1868–1948), Commander, 4th Division

Born in Edinburgh, Scotland, MacLagan was commissioned into the Border Regiment as a second lieutenant in 1889. He served in India and then in the Boer War, where he was awarded the DSO. After a brief secondment to the Australian Army in 1901, he returned to England and, following a spell as major in the Yorkshire Regiment, he accepted, in 1910, the position of drill instructor at the Royal Military College at Duntroon, Canberra, returning to Australia as lieutenant colonel.

At the outbreak of the Great War, he commanded 3rd Brigade, 1st Australian Division, landing with them at Gallipoli in April 1915. The brigade then went into action on the Western Front at Pozières and Mouquet Farm in 1916. After a brief posting as commander of AIF depots in England, he was promoted to major general and took command of 4th Australian Division. He led it through Third Ypres, the German Spring Offensives, and ultimately the Hundred Days Offensives.

After the war, he returned to duty with the British Army and commanded the 51st Highland Division until his retirement in 1925.

Anthony Courage (1875–1944), Commander, 5th Tank Brigade

Courage was educated at Rugby School and the Royal Military College, Sandhurst. He was commissioned into the 15th King's Hussars in 1896 and then served with the Dorset Yeomanry in the Boer War, before returning to the Hussars and sailing with them to France in 1914 as part of the original BEF. He earned a Military Cross in 1915, was wounded at Second Ypres, and was appointed to the staff of GHQ in 1916.

In 1917 he was promoted to lieutenant colonel and commanded the 2nd Tank Brigade at Messines, Third Ypres and Cambrai. Then, as commander of 5th Tank Brigade, and attached to the Australian Corps, he was involved in the battles of Villers-Bretonneux, Hamel, Montdidier, Amiens and Hindenburg Line. He received a bar to his MC for his role at Hamel, and was also later awarded the DSO and Croix de Guerre.

Courage was appointed colonel of the 15/19th King's Royal Hussars in 1929. He retired from the army in 1932 and became chairman of the family business, the brewing company Courage & Co Ltd.

Charles Edwin Woodrow Bean (1879–1968)

Bean was born in Bathurst, New South Wales, and moved to England at the age of nine. He was educated at Brentwood School, Essex, Clifton College, Bristol, and Hertford College, Oxford, graduating with an MA in 1903 and a Bachelor of Civil Law in 1904. He returned to Australia and taught at Sydney Grammar School. He was admitted to the New South Wales Bar in 1905 and began a legal career as a barrister. In 1908, he abandoned the law for journalism. Work for the Sydney Morning Herald took him to the USA and back to England.

In September 1914, he was elected as the Official Correspondent to the Australian Imperial Force and went with them to Egypt, Gallipoli, and eventually the Western Front. He was opposed to the appointment of Monash as Australian Corps Commander.

After the war, in 1919, he was appointed the official historian, wrote the first six volumes of the *Official History of Australia in the War of 1914–1918* and edited the remaining six. The final volume appeared in 1942. He was involved in the founding of the Australian War Memorial and the Australian National Archives.

John Paton (1867–1943), Commander, 6th Brigade

Born in Newcastle, New South Wales, he joined the NSW Military Forces in 1887 as a second lieutenant in the 4th Infantry. He joined the AIF on 16 March 1915 as a lieutenant colonel, commanding the 25th Battalion. Having embarked for Gallipoli, he was there promoted to brigadier general on 15 October to command 7th Brigade.

His brigade arrived on the Western Front in March 1916, and on 5 November, Paton was wounded and evacuated to England, where he commanded 17th Brigade from May to July 1917. He returned to the Western Front to command 6th Brigade, taking them through the battles of Broodseinde, Passchendaele, and Hamel.

He returned to Australia in August 1918 and retired from the army in 1926.

James Harold Cannan (1882–1976), Commander, 11 Brigade

Born in Townsville, Queensland, he was educated at Brisbane Grammar School. Before the Great War, he worked in insurance.

He joined the Militia as a lieutenant in the 1st Queensland Regiment in 1903 and reached the rank of lieutenant colonel by 1914, commanding the 8th Infantry Battalion. He joined the AIF in September 1914 and took command of the 15th Battalion, taking this unit to Gallipoli. His battalion arrived on the Western Front in June 1916, and two months later, Cannan was promoted to brigadier general as commander of 11th Brigade. He was awarded the DSO in 1918.

Between the wars, he resumed his career in insurance before becoming Quartermaster General in 1940, serving in the south-west Pacific area. When he died in 1976, he was the last surviving Australian general of the Great War.

Charles Henry Brand (1873–1961), Commander, 4th Brigade

Born in Ipswich, Queensland, he became a teacher in 1887. In 1898, he was commissioned as a lieutenant in the Queensland Volunteer Infantry. He served in South Africa from 1899 to 1901 as a sergeant in the 3rd Queensland Mounted Infantry Contingent.

He then returned to teaching at Charters Towers State School. He was promoted captain in the Volunteer Infantry in 1903 and joined the permanent forces two years later, spending 1910–1911 in India as a general staff officer. He joined the AIF in August 1914 as a major. He became brigade major of 3rd Brigade, landing with them, via Egypt, at Anzac Cove.

On 20 May 1915, he was given temporary command of 8th Battalion. He was wounded the following day, but remained on duty, earning himself a DSO. The position became permanent in July, when he was promoted to lieutenant colonel. He took his battalion to the Western Front in March 1916, and in July, he succeeded Monash as GOC 4th Brigade. He was wounded again, by shell fire, in July 1917, but was back at duty 12 days later.

He commanded 4th Brigade for the rest of the war. He retired in 1933 with the rank of major general. The following year, he won a Senate seat for the United Australian Party, serving until 1947.

Evan Alexander Wisdom (1869–1945), Commander, 7th Brigade

Born in Inverness, Scotland, he emigrated to Australia in 1891 and became a gold prospector in Western Australia. He returned to Scotland in 1894, married Agnes Jackson a year later, and went back to Australia. He joined the Australian Militia as a lieutenant and was promoted to captain in 1903. By 1908, he was brigade major of the Western Australian Infantry Brigade.

It was about this time that he entered the world of politics and served as mayor of Cottesloe from 1908 to 1913. Between 1911 and 1917, he was a Liberal member of the Legislative Assembly.

During the Great War, Wisdom served at Gallipoli as brigade major of 5th Brigade, winning a DSO. On the Western Front, he became CO of 18th Battalion in February 1916 and led his men at Pozières that summer.

He then commanded 7th Brigade for the rest of the war, returning to Australia in December 1919. He served as Administrator of New Guinea from 1921 to 1933.

Walter Adams Coxen (1870–1949), Commander, 1st Australian Divisional Artillery

Coxen was born in Egham, England, but emigrated with his family to Australia at the age of 10. He was educated at Brisbane Grammar School and Toowoomba Grammar School. In 1893, he was commissioned into the Queensland Militia Garrison Artillery as a second lieutenant.

He was sent to England in 1897 to study at the Royal School of Gunnery and then trained with the Royal Artillery at Aldershot. He returned to Australia with the rank of captain in 1899, but was back in England in 1907 for training at the Royal Military Academy at Woolwich. He was promoted to major, returned to Australia in 1910, and soon attained the rank of lieutenant colonel.

In May 1915, he sailed from Melbourne to England with the 36th Heavy Artillery Group. After a brief spell in the British XVII Corps, he joined the Anzac Corps, supporting their attack at Pozières and winning a DSO.

In January 1917, he became a brigadier general and took command of the 1st Australian Divisional Artillery, a position he held for the rest of the war.

After the war, he was appointed Quartermaster General in 1925 and became Chief of the General Staff in 1930. His tenure was brief, as he retired the following year.

Harold Edward 'Pompey' Elliott (1878–1931), Commander, 15th Brigade

Born in West Charlton, Victoria, he grew up on the family farm. His father made a substantial sum of money prospecting for gold in Western Australia in 1894, selling his claim for £180,000 and a one-sixth interest. With the family financially secure, Elliott went to the University of Melbourne in 1898 to study law. He left in 1900, however, to serve as a subaltern in the Boer War. He returned to Australia to finish his degree and became a solicitor.

As a member of the Militia, he progressed through the ranks: promoted lieutenant in 1905, captain in 1909, major in 1911 and lieutenant colonel in 1913. At the outbreak of war, he joined the AIF and commanded the 7th Australian Infantry Battalion at Gallipoli. On the Western Front, as commander of the newly-formed 15th Infantry Brigade, he led his men at Fromelles, Second Bullecourt, Polygon Wood, Villers-Bretonneux, Hamel, Amiens and at the breaking of the Hindenburg Line.

Returning to Australia after the war, he was elected to the Senate in 1919, representing the Nationalist Party of Australia, and was re-elected in 1925. In 1926, he was appointed commander of 15th Brigade again and was finally promoted to the rank of major general the following year, taking command of 3rd Division.

Elliott suffered from diabetes, hypertension, and what would now probably be classed as post-traumatic stress disorder. He was admitted to hospital in February 1931 and, six weeks later, committed suicide by cutting himself with his shaving razor. He was buried on 25 March with full military honours, his coffin drawn on a gun carriage to Burwood Cemetery, Melbourne.

Charles Rosenthal (1875–1954), Commander, 2nd Division

Born in Berrima, New South Wales, he trained as an architect and became a draughtsman in the architectural division of the Department of Railways and Public Works in Perth. He later designed St Andrew's Church, Lismore, NSW, St Laurence's in Barraba and Holy Trinity in Sydney.

He joined the Victorian Militia Garrison Artillery in 1892 and was later commissioned second lieutenant in the Militia Garrison Artillery in Melbourne. He transferred to the field artillery in 1908 and became the commander of 5th Artillery Brigade. He joined the AIF in 1914 and sailed as lieutenant colonel commanding 3rd Field Artillery Brigade to Gallipoli. Twice wounded, he was evacuated to England before rejoining his unit in Egypt.

In February 1916, he arrived in France as a brigadier general, commanding the artillery of 4th Division. After the engagements at Pozières and Mouquet Farm on the Somme, he was wounded a third time in December 1916. In May 1918, he was promoted to major general and took command of 2nd Division. Wounded for a fourth time in 1918, he returned to duty in August and was involved in the Battle of Mont St Quentin. He returned to Australia in January 1920.

He served in the New South Wales Legislative Assembly from 1922 to 1925 and later in the New South Wales Legislative Council. He was twice president of the NSW Institute of Architects. During the Second World War, he was the administrator of Norfolk Island.

Joseph John Talbot Hobbs (1864–1938), Commander, 5th Division

Hobbs was born in London and was educated at St Mary's Church School, Merton, before joining the 1st Cinque Ports Artillery Volunteers in 1883. He emigrated to Western Australia in 1886 and established an architectural practice in Perth.

Soon after arriving in Australia, he joined the Volunteer Field Artillery in Perth and was commissioned in 1889. He rose to command the 1st (Western Australian) Field Battery in 1903 and, by 1913, was a colonel commanding the 22nd Infantry Brigade. He travelled to England four times to undergo intensive training in artillery practice, and when war broke out in 1914, he was given command of the 1st Australian Divisional Artillery.

After a spell at Gallipoli, he was promoted to brigadier general and, in March 1916, went to France, taking part in the capture of Pozières. In December that year, he took over command of 5th Division, his promotion to major general coming in January 1917.

The division fought at Polygon Wood in September, and then at Villers-Bretonneux in April 1918. Action at Hamel, Amiens and Mont St Quentin followed. He was knighted in January 1918.

Hobbs replaced Monash in command of the Australian Corps, when the latter was put in charge of demobilisation and repatriation of Australian troops, remaining in post until May 1919. After the war, Hobbs resumed his career as an architect and died of a heart attack at sea en route to the unveiling of the Villers-Bretonneux Memorial.

James Campbell Stewart (1884–1947), Commander 14th Brigade

Born in Belfast, Victoria, he was educated at Terang High School before starting a career in banking. Having moved to Melbourne, he joined the Victorian Scottish Regiment in 1901 and was commissioned in 1909.

Stewart enlisted in the professional army on 17 August 1914 and was appointed adjutant of 5th Battalion. Whilst acting battalion commander at Gallipoli, he was wounded by shrapnel and evacuated to Egypt. He returned to the peninsula and remained with 5th Battalion until the evacuation.

In February 1916, Stewart was appointed commander of 57th Battalion and was promoted lieutenant colonel the following month. Fortunate only to be placed in reserve at Fromelles, the battalion then fought at Polygon Wood in September 1917. He was promoted to command 14th Brigade in March 1918 and commanded them until the end of the conflict.

He commanded various brigades between the wars, but was rejected for AIF enlistment in the Second World War on age and medical grounds, but he still commanded the Melbourne Metropolitan Group, Volunteer Defence Corps from 1942 to 1945.

John Joseph Pershing (1860–1948), Commander, American Expeditionary Force

Born the son of a farmer near Laclede, Missouri. His great-grandfather, Frederick Pförschin, had emigrated to the USA from Alsace in 1749.

After completing High School in 1878, John became a teacher of local African American children. He also studied at the State Normal School (now Truman State University), graduating in 1880 with a BSc in Scientific Didactics. Two years later, he entered the US Military Academy at West Point. In 1886, he graduated 30th in his class of 77 and was commissioned as a second lieutenant. He served with the 6th Cavalry in New Mexico and took part in several campaigns against the Apache. He later fought the Sioux in South Dakota.

In 1891, he became professor of Military Science at the University of Nebraska-Lincoln, a position he held until 1895. Whilst there, he studied for a law degree, graduating in 1893.

In 1895, he took command of a troop of the 10th Cavalry, a regiment composed of African American soldiers under white officers. Whilst an instructor at West Point from 1897, his service with the 10th earned him the nickname 'Black Jack.'

He served in the Spanish-American and the Philippine-American wars before returning to the USA in 1903. After a brief spell as Assistant Chief of Staff of the Southwest Army Division in Oklahoma City, he was stationed as military attaché to Tokyo in 1905. This allowed him to serve as an observer during the Russo-Japanese War, and on his return to the USA later that year, he was promoted to brigadier general. He then served in the Philippines until 1913 as commander of Fort McKinley, near Manila.

Back in the USA in December that year, he took command of 8th Brigade and went with them to Fort Bliss, Texas, in April 1914. It was here that he received the devastating news that his wife and three young daughters had died in a fire at their home in San Francisco. Only his six-year-old son, Warren, survived.

In March 1916, Pershing led an expedition into Mexico to capture Pancho Villa. His men routed the revolutionaries, but failed to capture their leader.

When the USA declared war on Germany in April 1917, President Woodrow Wilson appointed Pershing as commander of the American Expeditionary Forces. He arrived in France in June that year.

The build-up of troop numbers in France was slow, and it was not until the summer of 1918 that they were ready to take an active role. Their first major battle was at St Mihiel in September, and this was followed by the Meuse-Argonne Offensive, where naïve tactics and logistical problems meant that the Americans suffered heavy casualties. The armistice came before the next substantial offensive, planned for 14 November, could take place. Controversially, he ordered his troops to continue fighting on 11 November, even though the armistice had already been signed, resulting in 3,500 American casualties on that day.

In recognition of his service, Pershing was promoted to General of the Armies of the United States in September 1919. In 1921, he became Chief of Staff of the United States Army. He published his memoir, *My Experiences in the World War*, in 1931.

George Windle Read (1860–1934), Commander, II Corps, US Army

Read was born in Iowa, USA, and graduated from the US Military Academy at West Point in 1883 as a second lieutenant. From 1889 to 1893, he was an assistant professor of Military Science at the University of Iowa. He then joined the 5th Cavalry Regiment in Texas, serving with them during the Spanish-American Wars in Cuba, New Mexico and the Philippines.

He was then on the Army General Staff from 1905 to 1909. After further service in Cuba, Puerto Rico and the Philippines, he attended the Army War College, graduating in 1914. As a lieutenant colonel, he took part in the Mexican Border War, including the Pancho Villa Expedition. Between 1915 and 1917, he was in Washington, DC, once more on the Army General Staff.

When the USA declared war, he went to France as commander of the 30th Infantry Division and was promoted to command II US Army Corps in June 1918.

After the war, he became commander of the Philippine Department before retiring in 1925.

George Bell Jr. (1859–1926), Commander, 33rd US Division

Bell was born in Baltimore, Maryland, the son of Brigadier General George Bell (1828–1907), a veteran of the American Civil War. George Jr attended West Point, graduating in 1880. In the 1890s, he was a professor of Military Science at Cornell University, where he also gained a law degree in 1894.

Having served in the Spanish-American Wars, he was promoted brigadier general in 1916. The following year, now a major general, he was assigned to command the 33rd US Division (Illinois National Guard) and sailed with them to France, leading them at St Mihiel and during the Meuse-Argonne Offensive.

After the war, he commanded the Sixth Corps Area, headquartered in Chicago, until his retirement in 1923.

Introduction

'There was ever more in him to be praised than to be pardoned.'[1]

On 21 June 1918, Lieutenant General John Monash – commander of the Australian Corps since the first of the month – submitted his plan for the capture of the village of Hamel to General Sir Henry Rawlinson, Commander Fourth Army BEF. The nature of the plan was heavily influenced by the input of Brigadier General Anthony Courage, Commander, 5th Tank Brigade. The assault was to be 'essentially a surprise tank attack' with no 'rigid creeping [artillery] barrage.'[2]

Four days later, at a conference at 4th Australian Division HQ, Monash's subordinates, led by the divisional commander, Major General MacLagan, 'gave short shrift' to the plan,[3] insisting that the scheme be fundamentally altered. Monash acquiesced, and it was Plan 'B' that was to prove so successful when the attack went in on the morning of 4 July 1918. In his recent book on the battle, Peter FitzSimons calls it 'a tactical masterpiece ... that changed the course of warfare and shortened the war.'[4]

1 Ben Jonson, *Timber*, (1641). The phrase originally referred to William Shakespeare.
2 C.E.W. Bean, *The Official History of Australia in the War of 1914-1918* (Sydney: Angus & Robertson, 1920–1942), vol.VI, p.253.
3 Bean, *The Official History*, p.254.
4 Peter FitzSimons, *Monash's Masterpiece. The Battle of Le Hamel and the 93 Minutes that Changed the World* (London: Constable, 2018), p.VII.

1

Preparations

> The true role of infantry was not to expend itself upon heroic physical effort, not to wither away under merciless machine-gun fire, not to impale itself on hostile bayonets, but on the contrary, to advance under the maximum possible protection of the maximum possible array of mechanical resources, in the form of guns, machine-guns, tanks, mortars and aeroplanes; to advance with as little impediment as possible; to be relieved as far as possible of the obligation to fight their way forward.[1]

One of Monash's first major concerns on becoming Corps Commander on 1 June 1918 was the manpower crisis facing the Australian formations. On 10 June, he penned an appeal to the men of Australia, exhorting them to enlist without delay:

> Since the opening of the German Offensive in March, every Division of the Australian Army in FRANCE has been engaged, and always with decisive success. The men of Australia, wherever and whenever they have entered this mighty conflict, have invariably brought the enemy to a standstill and have made him pay dearly for each futile attempt to pass them on the roads to AMIENS and the Channel Ports. Their reputation as skilful, disciplined and gallant soldiers has never stood higher throughout the Empire than it does today. Those who are privileged to lead such splendid men are animated with a pride and admiration which is tempered only by concern at their waning numbers. Already some battalions ... have ceased to exist as fighting units, and others must follow, unless the Australian Nation stands by us and sees to it that our ranks are kept filled. We refuse to believe that the men and women of AUSTRALIA will suffer their famous divisions to decay, or that the young manhood still remaining in our home land will not wish to share in the renown of their brothers in FRANCE. Nothing matters now but to see this job through to the end, and we appeal to every man to come, and come quickly, to help in our work and to share in our glorious endeavour.
>
> MONASH
> Lieutenant General.[2]

1 John Monash, *Australian Victories in France in 1918* (London: Hutchinson & Co., 1920), p.96.
2 Australian War Memorial (AWM): 3DRL 2316. Monash Collection 4 – 24 June 1918.

It was calculated that the Australian Corps (including all five divisions) was short of 8,255 men. Replacements available amounted to only 350 men at the base depot in Le Havre and 4,871 in England.[3] But Monash saw the need for 'a demonstration that there was some kick left in the British Army' and was keen that 'any such kick should be administered first at any rate by the Australians.'[4] He was mindful, however, of the need to minimise any subsequent casualties: 'any substantial losses would precipitate the time when the question of the reduction in the number of Australian divisions would have to be seriously considered.'[5] This would seriously affect his thinking. The following will serve as an example of the manpower deficiencies. The strength of 11th Australian Brigade on 22 June 1918 is shown in Table 1.

Table 1: 11th Australian Brigade, 22 June 1918

Battalion	Strength: Officers	OR	Deficiency: Officers	OR
41st	38	756	6	144
42nd	31	637	13	263
43rd	39	653	5	247
44th	44	856	-	44
Totals	**152**	**2,902**	**24**	**698**[6]

The chance to deploy the new Mark V tank was a possible and tempting solution to the problem, and Fourth Army had just received 144 of them. Monash and his Chief of Staff, Brigadier General Blamey, went to inspect these newly arrived monsters at Brigadier General Hugh Elles' invitation, and they were impressed by the scale of improvement on the old Mark IVs, which had let down the Australians so badly at Bullecourt the previous spring. The new Mark V was faster, with a top speed of 4.6 mph, much more manoeuvrable, needing only one man to steer it, and mechanically much more reliable. Substantial numbers of these tanks used in an attack might drastically reduce the number of casualties suffered by the understrength infantry battalions.

It remains unclear as to whether the idea for an attack on the village of Hamel was first proposed by Monash or Rawlinson. Monash wrote: 'I ... set about preparing a general plan for such a battle, which was to be my first Corps operation. Having mentioned the matter first verbally to Lord Rawlinson,[7] he requested me to submit a concrete proposal in writing.'[8] Rawlinson's diary, dated 18 June 1918, states: 'I went round the Australians today and suggested to Monash and McClagan [sic] an offensive with two Battalions of Tanks against the Hamel village and spur.'[9] MacLagan, commanding 4th Division, had previously proposed a scheme to capture Vaire Wood, but Monash had rejected it, fearing that the cost would be too high,

3 AWM: 361/2. Australian Corps General Staff Diary: Report by Monash to Rawlinson on Manpower Situation dated 22 June 1918. (Quoted in Bean, *The Official History*, vol.VI, p.252).
4 Monash, *Australian Victories*, p.44.
5 Bean, *The Official History*, vol.VI, p.252. Monash to Rawlinson 21 June 1918.
6 AWM: 3DRL 2316. Monash Collection. July 1918.
7 Rawlinson was not a Lord at this time.
8 Monash, *Australian Victories*, p.44.
9 Churchill College Archives (CCA), University of Cambridge, Rawlinson Papers: GBR/0014/RWLN 1/11 & 1/12. Diary entry dated 18 June 1918. Rawlinson's spelling was consistently inconsistent.

writing on 13 June 1918: 'I do not recommend that this operation be carried out at present.'[10]

Since then, however, the situation to the north of the River Somme had changed: the British 2nd Division had made advances eastwards along the crest near Morlancourt and Sailly-Laurette, effectively outflanking Hamel. This meant that German artillery batteries situated behind Accroche Wood (see Map 1) were now able to fire into the right flank and rear of the 2nd Division's new positions. Charles Bean wrote in his diaries:

Lieutenant General Sir John Monash, GOC Australian Corps (AWM)

> … the question is whether the Hamel fight is worth the cost…. Since [the] attack on the right [sic] of our line north of the Somme is so far in advance of our line to the south of it, that the Germans make its position most uncomfortable, shooting with whizz-bangs straight up the gullies at its flank. Cutlack[11] went over the top of the hill in front of Morlancourt the other day to reach one of the battalions of 7 Bde. As he came down the valley towards the Somme a whizz-bang shell passed his shoulder. A few seconds later another. He started to run – and before he reached safety he says that about twenty shells had been fired at him…. There have been a good many casualties in these gullies from the enfilade fire from behind Accroche Wood…. To stop those casualties and to give room for a massing a counter attack against Hill 104[12] and Villers-Bretonneux if ever they are once again taken by the Germans – this is the justification for the attack. And it is a very arguable reason.[13]

10 Bean, *The Official History*, vol.VI, p.243.
11 Frederic Morley Cutlack (1886–1967) served on the Western Front as a lieutenant during 1915–1916, and was attached to 3rd Division Headquarters as an intelligence officer in April 1917. In January 1918 he was recruited by Charles Bean as a war correspondent for the AIF. He was later the author of volume VIII of *The Official History* on the Australian Flying Corps.
12 Hill 104 is close to the current location of the Villers-Bretonneux Memorial.
13 AWM: 38. 3DRL 606/116/1. Records of C.E.W. Bean, Official Historian.

Monash listed the advantages and disadvantages of attacking Hamel, and these are recorded in the War Diary of the Australian Corps and dated 21 June 1918:

The advantages may be briefly summarised thus:

a) Straightening of our line.
b) Shortening of our line.
c) Deepening our forward defensive zone, particularly east of Hill 105 (sic: probably 104).
d) Improvement of jumping off position for future operations.
e) Advancement of our artillery south of the Somme.
f) Denial to enemy of observation of ground near Vaux-sur-Somme, valuable for battery positions.
g) Facilitating subsequent further minor advances North of the Somme.
h) Disorganisation of enemy defences.
i) Disorganisation of possible enemy offensive preparations.
j) Inflicting losses on enemy personnel and material.
k) Improvement of our observation.
m) Maintenance of our initiative on this Corps front.[14]

The list of disadvantages was much shorter: Monash mentioned the need to organise a new, 7,000-yard-long defensive system to secure the ground gained, but he was much more worried about the extent of the losses that might ensue, and with it the possibility of having to reduce the number of Australian divisions as a result.

It was surely this overriding anxiety, plus the desire to see how well the Mark V tank would perform under battle conditions, which led Monash to adopt the plan submitted by Brigadier General Courage the previous day. At his HQ at Bertangles, Monash had briefed Courage on 19 June, adamant that it would be a 'limited objective we are going for, and no consideration is going to prompt me to allow exploitation beyond the line chosen. On no account will an attempt be made to go chasing after the guns.'[15] Monash refused to consider Accroche Wood as a possible objective, even though it shielded many of the German artillery batteries. Such an enterprise would extend the scope of the advance by a thousand yards, and he did not want to overtax his troops, knowing that German resistance would, as ever, stiffen the further his men pushed them back. He also had to consider the fact that tanks do not operate at their best in wooded terrain: Vaire Wood was a valid objective, but Accroche Wood might just prove to be a wood too far. In any case, the Wolfsberg, the hill just to the east of Hamel village – and the eastern-most objective – overlooked Accroche Wood and effectively blocked the view from the wood to the river. If not untenable, the German artillery position would at least be rendered precarious.

According to the plan that Courage drew up, the attack would be 'primarily a tank operation.'[16] In a nutshell, the tanks would advance, capture the ground, while the infantry, following behind, would help to deal with strongpoints, mop up, and consolidate the ground captured. There would be no creeping artillery barrage, only a protective barrage covering the consolidation of

14 AWM: 361/2 War Diary Australian Corps General Staff.
15 AWM: D116 Records of C.E.W. Bean. 3 July 1918.
16 AWM: 26. 361/2 War Diary Australian Corps General Staff.

the final objective line. The artillery – other than counter-battery operations – would be employed firing on 'enemy centres of resistance' and other selected targets ahead of the first wave of tanks.[17] The proposal merits close examination.

Brigadier General Anthony Courage, GOC 5th Tank Brigade. (National Photographic Record)

To begin with, Courage defined the composition of a tank battalion: it comprised three companies of 12 tanks each, these being divided into four sections, each of three tanks. Taking into consideration what he saw as the main tactical areas that had to be captured – Vaire Wood and Hamel Wood,[18] Circular Post,[19] and Hamel village[20] – Courage estimated that a total of 45 tanks would be needed. In deciding on that number, he was influenced by two other factors: he observed that the only properly defined trench system was the former British line to the east of Hamel, the rest of the area being covered by shorter lengths of often unconnected trenches and machine-gun nests.[21] Possibly more influential were the verbal instructions from General Rawlinson that 'a sufficient number of tanks should be employed in order to save as many casualties as possible to the Australian Corps.'[22]

The tank force would be divided into three echelons. The 'Advance Section' would act as the name suggests, as a first wave, spearheading the assault ahead of the infantry. They were to:

> a) … protect the advance of the tanks following in the rear and the Infantry attached to the Main Body Sections.
> b) … move to the rear of the main Tactical points as quickly as possible in order to cut off the retreat of the garrison, and to prevent the enemy reinforcing these points. The effect of this manoeuvre will tend to demoralize the enemy.[23]

17 AWM: 26. 361/2 War Diary Australian Corps General Staff.
18 These were contiguous and can therefore be regarded as one entity.
19 More commonly referred to as 'Pear Trench.'
20 Note that at this stage the Wolfsberg was not specifically included in the list of tactical points to be captured, although it is clearly within the 'Blue Line' final objective on the accompanying map.
21 A glance at Map 1 however shows an almost continuous line forming the German front line to the west of Vaire Wood, stretching northwards as far as Pear Trench before echeloning back to the western outskirts of Hamel.
22 AWM: 3DRL 2316 Monash Collection, Doc. G26/16. Courage to Monash 20 June 1918.
23 AWM: 3DRL 2316 Monash Collection, Doc. G26/16. Courage to Monash 20 June 1918.

The Main Body Sections: with the infantry attached to these sections, they would 'lead the infantry to their objective, and give immediate protection by fire.'[24] This section would be approximately 50 yards behind the first wave. It was envisaged that this 50-yard gap would increase as the attack developed, the Advanced Section moving forward as quickly as possible.

The third 'Mopping Up' sections would follow on, replacing any tanks which had been put out of action and going to the aid of any infantry still held up by machine gun posts which had not been dealt with by the first two waves. The allocation of tanks to the various sections was as follows:

i) South of the Fouilloy – Warfusée road:
1 section of 3 tanks as Main Body Section.

ii) Vaire Wood and Hamel Wood Sector:
2 sections will act as Advance Section.
2 sections as Main Body Section.
1 section as Mopping Up Section.
Total: 1 Company + 1 Section or 15 Tanks.

iii) Circular Post Sector
1 Section as Advance Section.
2 Sections as Main Body Section.
1 Section as Mopping Up Section.
Total: 1 Company or 12 Tanks.

iv) Hamel Village Sector:
2 Sections as Advance Section.
2 sections as Main Body Section.
1 section as Mopping Up Section.
Total: 1 Company + 1 Section or 15 Tanks.[25]

Therefore, the Advance Section would total 15 tanks, the Main Body 21, and the Mopping Up Section nine.

With an attack frontage of around 5,500 yards, this would mean one Main Body tank to every 260 yards. The Advance Section would be sparser still, at 367 yards between tanks. Zero Hour had not yet been decided, but Courage assumed that it would be around dawn, adding that 'from a tank point of view, this should be fixed so as to admit of Tank crews being able to see their direction.'[26] Not an unreasonable demand.

Courage also recognised the danger to the tanks of direct enemy artillery fire: to obscure enemy observation, he recommended smoke barrages to the south of the main Villers-Bretonneux – Warfusée road and along the high ground north of the Somme, to the south of Morlancourt. Also, in order to drown out the noise of the tank engines during their approach,

24 AWM: 3DRL 2316 Monash Collection, Doc. G26/16. Courage to Monash 20 June 1918.
25 AWM: 3DRL 2316 Monash Collection, Doc. G26/16. Courage to Monash 20 June 1918.
26 AWM: 3DRL 2316 Monash Collection, Doc. G26/16. Courage to Monash 20 June 1918. Sunrise on 4 July 1918 was at 4:42 a.m.

aeroplanes 'with a noisy type of engine' should fly to and fro above the front lines.[27] Other low-flying aircraft would also watch for anti-tank guns being brought out into the open, and should bomb or strafe them as the opportunity arose.

Lieutenant General Monash estimated that this plan would require 7,500 infantry – one division plus a brigade. One half of the force would be employed in the advance with the Main Body of tanks; the rest would then take over and consolidate the positions won.

Detailed plans, dated 21 June, split the attack frontage into three sectors. The right, or southern, sector stretched from just north of the Villers-Bretonneux–Warfusée road to the Fouilloy–Warfusée road (see map: P.25 central to P.21.c.35.95).[28] Here, one company would act as 'tank escort', two half-battalions (less the aforementioned company) would make up the assault wave, with two further half-battalions acting as reserve or as carriers.

The centre sector, stretching from the Fouilloy–Warfusée road to a point 400 yards or so south of the Wolfsberg position (P.21.c.35.95 to P.10.d.60.25) would be manned by four battalions: one would go forward with the tanks to capture and mop up Vaire and Hamel Woods. Two battalions would constitute the second wave, tasked with capturing and consolidating the Blue Line final objective. The final battalion would be the reserve force, whose primary job would be to carry supplies forward.

The left sector, from the Wolfsberg as far north as the village of Bouzencourt, would also require four battalions: one to escort the main body of tanks with the aim of capturing and mopping up Hamel village, two to continue the advance to the Blue Line – including, therefore, the capture of the Wolfsberg strongpoint – and the fourth being the reserve.

Six battalions would remain in the original front line positions. Thus, divided into 'Assault Wave', the 'Supporting' wave and the 'Reserve' wave, their tasks were defined as follows:

> General Action of Infantry.
>
> a) The infantry detailed as escort to the Main Body Tanks will carry out the assault on the expected main centres of resistance and on machine gun nests, and will then remain with a proportion of tanks to complete the reduction and mopping up of such centres.
>
> b) Supporting wave will follow in rear of the Main Body Tanks, and on either flank of the Assault wave. Their role will be to push on and garrison and consolidate the ultimate objective – if necessary skirting any centres of resistance which may be holding out and following main body tanks to the ultimate objective.
>
> c) Reserve waves. The reserve wave will be used to carry as far forward as possible, if required for tactical action they would dump their loads and be used according to requirements.
>
> d) After the Support Wave has passed on towards the final objective, the Assault Wave will reorganise as soon as possible and become the Brigade Reserves of the respective brigades.[29]

27 AWM: 3DRL 2316 Monash Collection, Doc. G26/16. Courage to Monash 20 June 1918.

28 Appendix IV explains the contemporary map reference system.

29 AWM: 26 361/2 War Diary Australian Corps General Staff June 1918.

Distilled into one sentence, this meant that the tanks would capture the ground, the infantry would help to neutralise strongpoints, mop up, and occupy ground. With an inter-divisional relief planned for the period 28–30 June, Monash estimated that the attack could not go in any earlier than the first week in July. A period of training for the joint action of tanks and infantry would be essential.

Artillery preparation prior to the assault would begin in the days leading up to the attack, with a daily barrage along the whole Corps front simulating a 'defensive counter preparation' for varying periods of time.[30] It was expected, or at least hoped, that similar action on the day of the assault would therefore not arouse suspicion of an imminent attack. The daily barrages would include smoke and gas. On Zero Day, there would be smoke, but no gas. The Germans, used to the precedent, would don their gas masks. The Australians, however, would be free of any such restrictions.

Counter-battery work would be initiated, and any known trench mortar and machine gun positions would also be targeted. Some of the positions earmarked for 'annihilation and neutralization' on Z-Day would also receive periodic 'crashes by mixed calibres' in the days leading up to the attack.[31]

On Z-Day, the 'usual' volume of fire would commence before Zero Hour, helping to drown out the approach of the tanks. From Zero Hour onwards, 'centres of resistance' would be 'pulverized' and enemy artillery positions neutralized by gas, high explosive and shrapnel.[32] Smoke screens would be put in place as previously noted.

In addition, one or two batteries would be installed on Hill 104, near Villers-Bretonneux, from which they could employ direct fire against any possible German counterattack or help target hostile anti-tank guns. A total of 20 Stokes mortars and 72 machine guns would supplement the artillery contribution.

Brigadier General Blamey, on Monash's behalf, wrote to formation and unit commanders on 21 June, enclosing copies of the proposed plans of attack for their consideration. He suggested a conference on or about the 23rd to 'consider details.' The conference actually took place on 25 June, commencing at 10:30 a.m., at the Australian Corps HQ. Present were Monash, Blamey, Courage, Sir Archibald Montgomery (Rawlinson's Chief of Staff), MacLagan, Lavarack (GSO1 4th Div), Burgess (CRA 4th Div), Brigadier General Paton (GOC 6 Bde), Brigadier General Cannan (GOC 11 Bde), and Brigadier General Coxen (GOC 1st Australian Divisional Artillery).

Major General Ewen George Sinclair-MacLagan, GOC 4th Australian Division (AWM)

30 AWM: 26 361/2 War Diary Australian Corps General Staff June 1918.
31 AWM: 26 361/2 War Diary Australian Corps General Staff June 1918.
32 AWM: 26 361/2 War Diary Australian Corps General Staff June 1918.

Brigadier General Thomas Albert Blamey, Chief of Staff, Australian Corps. (AWM)

Brigadier General Walter Adams Coxen, GOC 1st Australian Divisional Artillery. (AWM)

Brigadier General John Paton, GOC 6th Brigade (AWM)

Brigadier General James Harold Cannan, GOC 11th Brigade. (AWM)

The idea of tanks leading the attack with no orthodox creeping artillery barrage horrified the majority of those present. 'In spite of strong advocacy by Courage and Montgomery, Monash's Chief of Staff, Brigadier General Blamey and the field artillery commander, Brigadier General Coxen urged their chief against such an experiment.'[33] MacLagan and his brigade commanders were of the same opinion, and Blamey produced a document outlining the pros and cons of the original plan:

1. Arguments in favor of Tank Method:-
   a) *Surprise* will be more likely.
   b) Wire will be automatically flattened by Advanced and Main Body tanks, *who move in front of all the Infantry.*
   c) More chance of making a large bag of prisoners, on account of the surprise encircling action of the fast Mark V tank.
   d) Great moral effect of a sudden attack with fast, powerful Mark V tank.
   e) The Infantry retain, to a certain extent, their power of manoeuvre, owing to the elasticity of the tank method.
   f) Tanks can see, whereas a barrage is blind. Therefore if tanks survive, they can deal more certainly with enemy resistance than can the barrage.

2. *Arguments against Tanks.*
   a) The inevitable uncertainty of the rank and file as to whether or not they will materialize. This is unfortunate, but is the result of experience with less effective tanks in days when their powers were not developed.
   b) The actual uncertainty, (apart from any question of prejudice among the rank and file), of their action, due to engine trouble, enemy action, and failure of personnel.
   c) Present lack of combined training between Infantry and tanks. (This can, of course, be remedied if time allows.)
   d) Difficulty of concealing movement of tanks, especially Advanced tanks, sufficiently long to enable the Infantry to avoid the enemy's defence barrage.
   e) The incompatibility of the Tank method with any form of Artillery barrage, owing to the difficulty of regulating the pace. The elasticity of the Tank Method is better suited to a freer operation than to one with a limited objective.

3. *Arguments in favor of Artillery Barrage Method.*
   a) Greater certainty, as it is less likely to be effected [sic] by failure of personnel.
   b) The Infantry rank and file know and trust it.
   c) The Infantry, by 'leaning on' the barrage, are guided to their objective and can overcome successive enemy defences by rushing them as the barrage lifts.
   d) This method allows the Infantry to move into 'No Man's land' before Zero Hour, and thus escape the enemy's counter barrage.
   e) For a limited objective, this method is a proved method and success can practically be guaranteed.

33 Bean, *The Official History*, vol.VI, pp.253–254.

4. *Arguments against the Artillery barrage Method.*
   a) It does not necessarily open paths through enemy wire.
   b) It is liable to leave enemy defended localities and 'nests' which must be dealt with by Infantry action or other means.
   c) It is rigid and practically cuts out Infantry manoeuvre.
   d) It is slower than a corresponding Tank operation.
   e) It militates against the capture of prisoners.
   f) It is a sure indication to the enemy of the scope of the operation and generally also of the objective reached by the Infantry.
   g) It is expensive as regards ammunition.[34]

The field artillery commander, Coxen, put forward perhaps the most telling argument: 'It's a purely limited attack that you are making. We know we can make an absolute certainty of it by relying upon artillery, and you can get the artillery lent you for it, so why not make it a certainty?'

Blamey's document ends with his conclusions:

> The Artillery barrage Method is the more certain. The Tank Method would be more of the nature of an experiment.
>
> The Tank Method offers greater chances of a sweeping success, but is somewhat 'chancy.' This might, to a certain extent, be remedied by practice between Infantry and Tanks.
>
> In view of the facts that the objective is limited, that there is no difficulty as regards ammunition, and of the great advantages to our defence, and subsequent offensive action, which would result from the capture of the objective, it is considered that the artillery barrage method is preferable.
>
> If it is decided to make Tank Action subsidiary to that of the Artillery barrage a method can be arranged by which the Infantry casualties can be reduced to a minimum, by using Tanks to 'Mop Up' localities and nests after the passage of the Artillery barrage.[35]

Faced with such opposition, Monash was forced to reconsider and swiftly backed down, accepting the arguments put forward by his generals. It was a logical decision: Blamey's rather convoluted document boils down to two salient points regarding the new 'experimental' attack method. Firstly, infantry advancing onto machine gun posts without a covering artillery barrage could prove disastrous. Secondly, tanks advancing without infantry support would be highly vulnerable to enemy anti-tank fire. Mutual support was the answer, with the added security blanket of artillery cover. The men were familiar with the creeping barrage method and trusted it. The addition of tank support would be a bonus rather than a risk. Paddy Griffith writes:

> … the tank was actually extremely vulnerable to enemy fire, particularly from field guns but also increasingly from armour-piercing machine gun rounds, special anti-tank rifles and even a whole new breed of contact mines. The tank needed protection from all these threats if it was to advance over open ground: or in other words its way had to be opened by

34 AWM: 26 361/2 War Diary Australian Corps June 1918. Document undated.
35 AWM: 26 361/2 War Diary Australian Corps June 1918. Document undated.

> infantry, aircraft or, especially, artillery.... Thus as late as August 1918 the manual SS214 was quite happy to concede that the tank was still in the process of being perfected in a technical sense, and that its role independent of infantry still lay very definitely in the future.[36]

With only 15 tanks in the proposed 'Advance Section' across such a wide frontage, even slight losses would have endangered the entire scheme, leaving the main body of tanks and the infantry at vastly increased risk. It was a gamble that Monash's subordinates were not prepared to take. The tactics were therefore fundamentally altered. Monash quickly formulated an amended plan and wrote to Rawlinson on 26 June, justifying the volte-face.

> With reference to my S/4671 of 21st instant I beg to submit for the consideration of the Army Commander a modification in the plan as originally proposed.
>
> The original proposal was to design the action on lines which would permit of the tanks effecting the capture of the ground, and the infantry to fill a subsidiary role in reducing centres of resistance and in consolidating the position. The ground was to be seized by a body of advanced tanks moving rapidly to the farthest objective. This modification consists primarily in doing away with the advanced tanks.[37]

Monash goes on to admit that the artillery barrage ahead of the advanced tanks might not be completely effective and would not prevent enemy anti-tank guns from coming into action, meaning that the tanks could well suffer 'a considerable number of casualties.' This would in turn mean that the main body of tanks and the infantry would be 'without any immediate protection, [and] would find themselves under heavy infantry, machine gun and trench mortar fire throughout the greater proportion of their advance.'[38]

It would appear that Monash is here faithfully representing the thoughts aired by his divisional and brigade commanders at the conference held on 25 June: whether he had genuinely seen and accepted the logic of their arguments or was still a reluctant convert remains open to debate. He concludes:

> It is therefore proposed to do away with the advanced tanks entirely. This involves a very considerable change throughout. This operation ceases to be primarily a tank operation. It becomes an infantry operation in which the slight infantry power receives a considerable accession by the addition of a large body of tanks.
>
> It becomes necessary to cover the advance of the main body of tanks and infantry by an artillery barrage moving at normal infantry rates.
>
> The rate of movement of the first elements to the most advanced objective is much less rigid, but the depth of the zone of penetration is completely and effectively dealt with by fire. The probability of the advance being held up is reduced thereby to a minimum.

36 Paddy Griffith, *Battle Tactics of the Western Front. The British Army's Art of Attack 1916-18* (London: Yale University Press, 1994), p.165.
37 AWM: 26 361/2 War Diary Australian Corps, June 1918.
38 AWM: 26 361/2 War Diary Australian Corps, June 1918.

It is considered that the proposed change goes a long way towards eliminating risk of failure.

J.M.

Lieutenant General, Commanding Australian Corps.[39]

Rawlinson approved the changes and informed Haig. Monash had already written to Rawlinson on 23 June asking that the proposed date for the assault be altered: it had been tentatively fixed for 2 July. After consultation with MacLagan, Monash asked for a two-day postponement to allow more time for preparation and training – the 11th Brigade, 'borrowed' from 3rd Division and considered by their divisional commander to be the best-suited to promulgate the attack, could not be ready before the 4th. Rawlinson agreed, and Z-Day was set for 4 July.[40]

Rawlinson, it seems, was not impressed by the hiatus at Australian Corps HQ, writing in his diary on 27 June that 'The Aust Corps are working out the details of their scheme but are not functioning very well and I am not altogether happy about the operation.'[41] He was concerned that MacLagan remained unconvinced about the inclusion of tanks in the plan, but as things settled, he was able to write the following day: 'I went out this morning to see the 4 Aust Divn practise with the tanks. McClagan [sic] has now got hold of the idea all right. I was afraid that he and Courage would not hit it off but they are all right now I think.'[42]

'Plan B' had therefore abandoned the idea of a tank attack supported by the infantry and had morphed into the exact opposite. Eleven battalions of infantry from four brigades would spearhead the assault, supported by 54 tanks. To the north of the Somme, three battalions of 15th Brigade (5th Division) would launch diversionary raids from their positions near Ville-sur-Ancre.

The 11 battalions involved in the main attack would be deployed as follows: four battalions of 11th Brigade (3rd Division) were tasked with capturing the village of Hamel and the heights of the Wolfsberg position to the east. On their right, four battalions of 4th Brigade (4th Division) would take Vaire and Hamel Woods before moving on to the Blue Line running south-west to north-east a thousand yards beyond them, but stopping short of Accroche Wood. Two battalions from 6th Brigade and one from 7th Brigade (2nd Division) would make limited advances on the southern extreme of the attack frontage, effectively forming a defensive flank across and to the north of the arrow-straight Villers-Bretonneux–Warfusée road.

The entire terrain targeted for capture would be swept by a substantial creeping artillery barrage. The artillery units of 4th Australian Division would be supplemented by others from various other formations,[43] bringing the total number of guns available to 326 field guns and 302

39 AWM: 26 361/2 War Diary Australian Corps, June 1918.

40 Some sources suggest that the 4 July date was chosen to please the American contingent who could then fight their first engagement on Independence Day. This is clearly untrue. It seems to have been a happy coincidence. The Australian *Official History* suggests that Rawlinson himself chose the 4 July to coincide with the American holiday, and Monash writes in his *Australian Victories in France 1918* that this was part of the reason for his choosing that date.

41 CCA: Rawlinson Papers. Diary entry 27 June 1918.

42 CCA: Rawlinson Papers. Diary entry 28 June 1918.

43 These include 47th Divisional Artillery, 4th Royal Horse Artillery Bde, 17th Divisional Artillery, 5th Australian Division Artillery, three brigades from 2nd Australian Division Artillery, 222nd Siege Battery Royal Garrison Artillery.

heavies.[44] This translates to 24 yards per gun on the start line, extending to 30 yards per gun on the final protective barrage line.

The field artillery was divided into four groups: Southern, Right, Centre and Left.[45] These coincided roughly with the frontages, respectively, of 6th and 7th Brigades, 4th Brigade and 11th Brigade, with Left Group deployed to the north of the river Somme, their task concentrating largely on known machine gun and trench mortar positions in that area. No infantry attack was scheduled for that portion of the front.

From Zero minus eight minutes until Zero, the 'usual' harassing morning fire, consisting of 90 percent high explosive (HE) and 10 percent smoke would be used to mask the noise of the tanks' engines as they approached the front line. At Zero, the creeping barrage proper would begin: the main barrage, fired by the 18-pounders, would fall on the start line, this situated 200 yards ahead of the infantry and tank jumping off line, remaining there for four minutes.[46] This would consist of 50 percent shrapnel, 40 percent HE and 10 percent smoke.[47] Two hundred yards further forward was the barrage supplied by the 4.5-inch howitzers, firing 90 percent HE with instantaneous fuses and 10 percent smoke. A third layer, another 200 yards to the east, would be laid down by the 6-inch howitzers. All three lines would creep forward at an initial rate of 100 yards in three minutes as far as the 'halt line', reaching this at approximately Zero plus 30 minutes. To give the infantry chance to either catch up, reorganise or consolidate, the barrage would rest there for 10 minutes before recommencing its forward movement, this time at a slightly slower rate of 100 yards every four minutes until it reached the protective barrage line (400 yards or so beyond the final Blue Line objective) and remain there until Zero plus 123 minutes, whereupon all firing would cease. During the 30 minutes that the 18-pounders were providing this defensive screen, the 4.5s would creep to and fro beyond it to a depth of 800 yards.

The 16th RHA Brigade, positioned on the high ground between the Somme and the Ancre rivers, would be engaged in firing on targets of opportunity, including roads and tracks and any traffic upon them, ahead of the creeping barrage, concentrating ultimately on the reverse slopes beyond the protective barrage and on Accroche Wood. Rates of fire were to be as follows:

18-pounders – three rounds per gun per minute, (one round per gun per minute on the Halt Line) and one round per gun per minute as a final protective barrage.

4.5-inch howitzers – two rounds per gun per minute (one round at the Halt Line) and one round on the protective barrage line.[48]

A rate of three rounds per gun would be maintained on the halt line where it traversed Hamel Wood and the village of Hamel itself.

The artillery barrage would be supplemented by 147 Vickers medium machine guns, 111 of these firing in enfilade from positions to the north near the Somme at Bouzencourt. This barrage would be provided by the 4th Machine Gun Battalion, commanded by Lieutenant

44 Around 200 of the heavies would be employed in counter battery work.
45 See Appendix I for details of the artillery units.
46 For lines and positions mentioned, see Map 1 and Field Artillery Barrage map below.
47 This would change to 75 percent shrapnel, 15 percent HE and 10 percent smoke after the Halt Line.
48 Simple arithmetic shows that around 1,500 shells were to fall on the German positions every minute.

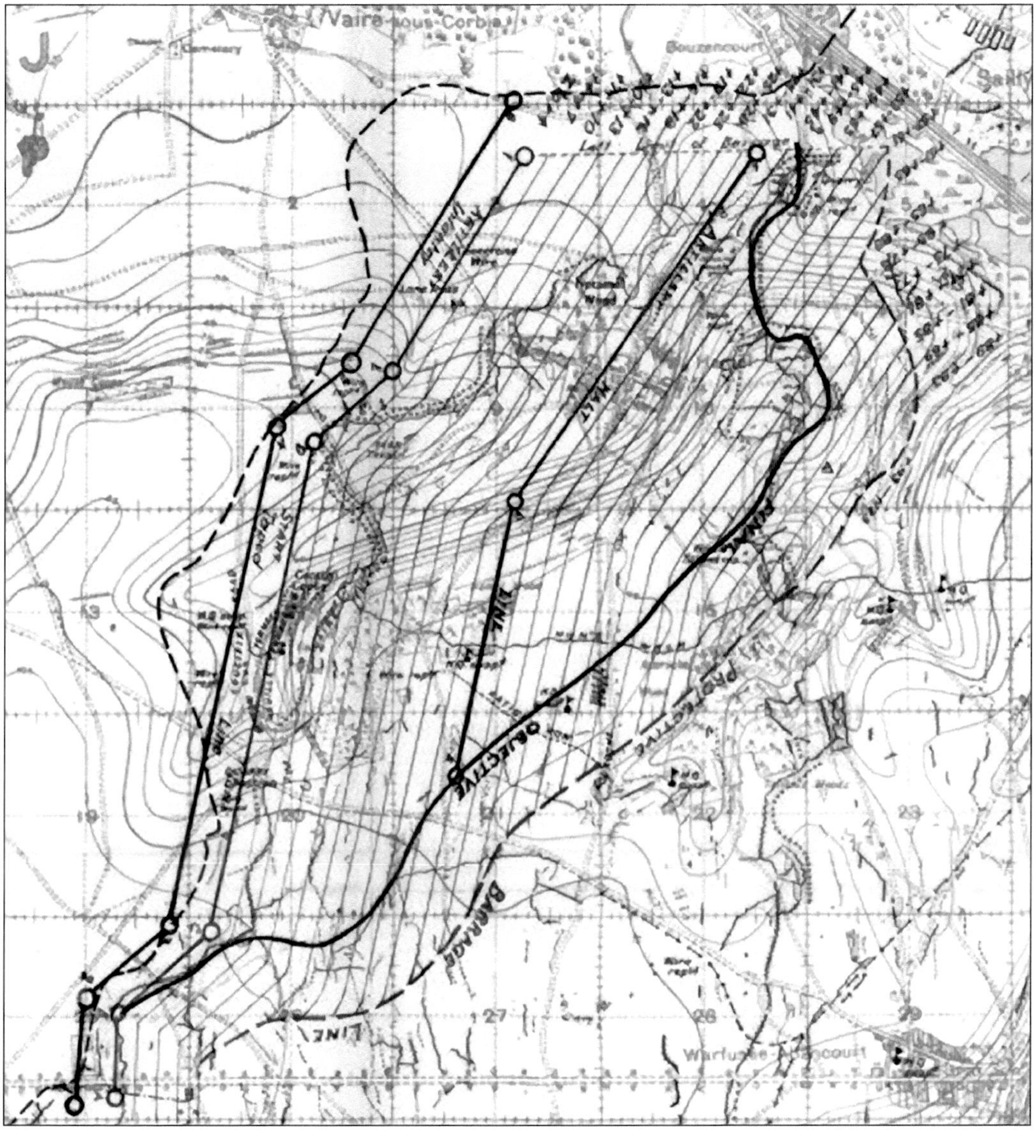

Field Artillery Barrage Map. (AWM)

Colonel Harry Murray VC, DSO & Bar, DCM. Each Vickers gun was supplied with 8,000 rounds, meaning that Murray's guns could send a total of almost 900,000 bullets over into the German positions. The remaining 36 guns would go forward with the infantry, ready to support the advance as and when necessary.

If all went to plan, the battle would be over in around an hour and a half. A simplified timetable for the attack was produced:

3:02 a.m.	Tanks start. Artillery harassing fire starts.
3:10 a.m.	Barrage opens.
3:17 a.m.	Infantry reach Pear Trench.
3:28 a.m.	Infantry reach Halt Line. Capture of Vaire and Hamel Woods completed.
3:51 a.m.	Barrage moves forward.
4:03 a.m.	Infantry reach Final Objective on left.
4:15 a.m.	Capture of Hamel Village completed.
4:35 a.m.	Infantry reach Final Objective everywhere.
4:43 a.m.	Protective Barrage reached by artillery everywhere.
5:13 a.m.	Protective Barrage stops.
6:10 a.m.	Ammunition dropping planes leave aerodrome.

Zero Hour was fixed at 3:10 a.m. This outline plan was delivered to brigades on 29 June, and brigadiers were invited to 'submit detailed plans as soon as possible.'[49] They would not have long. The plans were to be presented, discussed, ironed out and agreed upon at a conference held at Australian Corps HQ, the chateau at Bertangles, at 2:30 p.m. the following day, 30 June.[50] Monash arrived with a 130-point agenda covering seven pages to present to the 250 officers in attendance. With a scale model of the battlefield on the table in front of him, Monash's discourse ranged from the obvious: Zero Hour, assembly start-line, barrage rates, tank dispositions, to the obscure but still vital: darkness conditions preceding Zero Day, employment of 12-inch railway gun, spare barrels for machine guns, and Light Horse escorts for prisoners. He also had a handwritten note to himself defining the object of the conference: once all the points had been finally settled, there were to be absolutely no alterations allowed – all commanders needed to know exactly what everyone else was going to do. The conference lasted four hours and 20 minutes.[51] Plans were then disseminated down the chain of command in a series of further conferences at brigade and battalion levels.

There was also much to organise before Zero Hour: the amount of supplies needed to be brought forward required careful logistical planning:

> …half a dozen trains arriving at Amiens every night, 900 tons of supplies, equipment and ammunition of all kinds must be brought up eight miles to dumps behind the front line and concealed there. Some 160 tons of hay for the 20,000 transport horses, 100 tons of food per day for the men, and most importantly, 5000 tons of artillery shells must be stockpiled by Z Day. That's about 7800 wagonloads per night – no movement can take place in daytime lest Fritz spots it. The wagons, if placed in one column, would take up 15 miles of road. That's more than is available, so a tight timetable ensures there is no congestion. Monash is concerned that the roads won't be able to bear up. He has already stored 6000 tons of gravel along the roads, together with road repair crews. Nor can injured horses or broken wagons be allowed to impede the flow. Wheelsmiths, blacksmiths and veterinarians are also on hand

49 AWM: 4 1/48/27 War Diary 4th Australian Division General Staff June 1918. Div. Order No. 128.

50 Present would be: Monash, Blamey, GOC 4th Div, GSO1 4th Div, CRA 4th Div, AA & QMG 4th Div, GOC 4 Bde, GOC 6 Bde, GOC 11 Bde, CO 4th Aus Machine Gun Bn, GOC 5 Tank Bde, COs 8th and 13th Tank Battalions, OC 15th Wing RAF, OC 3 Sqdn AFC, OC No.1 Coy Special Bde Royal Engineers.

51 AWM: 3DRL 2316 Monash Collection July 1918.

along the main routes. Bridges too must be maintained. Stores of timber and detachments of engineers and carpenters camp by bridges to swing into action if a problem occurs. The whole thing is under the supervision of traffic police, standing at crossroads ensuring the long columns of wagons proceed at a standard three miles per hour.[52]

* * *

Two American divisions had been moved up into the area behind the British Third and Fourth Armies at Haig's request so that they would be available as a reserve force in case of a major German offensive. The 'doughboys' were recent arrivals in France: the 131st Regiment had arrived in Le Havre on the SS *Leviathan* on 30 May.

On 23 June, the American 33rd Division was in position at Molliens-au-Bois, and some units of their 66th Brigade began training with the Australian Corps. Rawlinson had not been impressed on his first visit to see the American troops, writing in his diary on 28 May: 'The men are… first class but the officers are far from good – a few may train on well, but the senior ones are poor stuff & must be changed before they can go fighting.'[53]

General George Windle Read, commander II Corps, US Army. (US National Archives)

He added on 14 June: 'There will be trouble with Pershing and DH.'[54] Ten days later, he visited General Read,[55] commander of the II American Corps, and described him as 'a nice, well-spoken old gentleman.'[56] It is unclear as to exactly when, but at some time during this period, Rawlinson came up with the idea of involving some of the American troops in the Hamel offensive. At a lunch with Haig and General Read on 29 June, he arranged 'to employ 6 American companies with the Austns in their attack.… It is an auspicious day for the attack being independence day.'[57] Read then authorised Major General Bell (33rd Division) to eventually send a further four companies to participate in the 'raid.' This made 10 in total from 131st and 132nd Regiments, one for each Australian battalion, these to 'participate in platoons or companies, each under the immediate command of its own officers.'[58]

52 FitzSimons, *Monash's Masterpiece*, pp.147–148.
53 CCA: Rawlinson Papers. Diary entry 28 May 1918.
54 John Joseph Pershing, Commander American Expeditionary Force. CCA: Rawlinson Papers. Diary entry 14 June 1918.
55 George Windle Read, Commander American II Corps.
56 CCA: Rawlinson Papers. Diary entry 24 June 1918.
57 CCA: Rawlinson Papers. Diary entry 29 June 1918.
58 AWM: 26.487.6. Historical Section A.W.C. Memorandum for Colonel Bach. *The Use of American Troops in Attack on Hamel July 4th 1918*, 3 November 1927.

Major General George Bell Jr, commander 33rd US Division (US National Archives)

The Australian *Official History* notes that the Australian battalions welcomed the addition to their numbers, which had been recently depleted by battle casualties and the influenza epidemic. With American companies numbering 250 men, using them in company strength would unbalance the structure of the Australian battalions: Captain Gale, commanding a company attached to the 42nd Battalion, recalled that he and Major Dibdin (acting CO of the 42nd Battalion) decided to place one American platoon with each Australian company.[59] This system seems to have been universally adopted. Even so, with American platoons numbering around 60 men, the situation still remained unbalanced; accordingly, 50 men from each American company were sent back to join the Australian nucleus party. Joint training commenced: at this point, Australian units were being rotated through the 5th Tank Brigade's training ground near Vaux-en-Amienois, with each battalion given the opportunity to work with the tanks and crews with whom they would operate on 4 July. 'The tank practices were regarded as vital by everyone from Rawlinson downwards, and not least by officers and men of the Tank Corps. These were enthusiastic believers in their machines and were determined to dispel the Australians' well-known objections, based on the performance of older tanks and less well trained and selected crews.'[60]

US troops rehearsing an attack with tanks. (Chicago States Publications Society)

59 Quoted in Bean, *The Official History*, vol.VI, pp.264–265.
60 Bean, *The Official History*, vol.VI, pp.267–268.

Monash described the exercises, with the advancing artillery barrage represented by a line of men carrying flags:

> Set-piece manoeuvre exercises on the scale of a battalion were designed and rehearsed over and over again; red flags marked enemy machine gun posts; real wire entanglements were laid out to show how easily the tanks could mow them down; real trenches were dug for the tanks to leap and straddle and search with fire; real rifle grenades were fired by the infantry to indicate to the tank the enemy strongpoints which were molesting and impeding their advance. The tanks would throw themselves upon these places, and, pirouetting round and round, would blot them out, much as a man's heel would crush a scorpion.[61]

The introduction of the Mark V tank was a real boost to the morale and confidence of the tank crews: the diary of the 13th Battalion Tank Corps compared it to its predecessor:

> The old Mk IV type had serious disadvantages. Its engine power on bad ground was insufficient and the clumsy secondary gears made turning slow and difficult, as well as requiring the services of at least two members of the crew in addition to the driver. This, in battle, became a heavy handicap upon the fighting powers of the tank. The Officer was hampered by the need to attend to brakes, and a gunner called upon suddenly to alter gears would lose the fleeting chance of firing at favourable targets. In the new Tank, these troubles largely disappeared. An engine of new design gave both greater speed and greater turning power, while a system of epicyclic gears made turning easy and under the sole control of the driver. The Officer was free to supervise his crew, the Gunner was free to use his weapon to the best advantage. Add that a greatly increased field of view was obtained by the addition of an observer's turret, and it will be understood that an immense advance in type had been secured.[62]

A Mark V Tank. (AWM)

61 Monash, *Australian Victories in France*, pp.49–50.
62 The National Archives (TNA): WO95/115/2 'The History of the 13th Tank Battalion' Chapter Three.

It was vital, of course, that tank crews and infantry would be able to communicate amid the noise and chaos of battle: tank commanders had been reminded that: 'It is the primary duty of Tanks to save casualties to the Australian infantry, and as this cannot be done so long as the Tanks remain in rear of them, Tank Commanders must do their utmost to get in between the Infantry and the Artillery barrage whenever possible.'[63] They were also reminded that: 'Tanks will come under the orders of Officers Commanding the Units to which they are attached for the operation.'[64]

A relatively simple system of communication was established: if the infantry were held up, they were to lie down and could call upon a tank for assistance, signalling to it by 'placing a steel helmet on top of the rifle – and will then indicate the position of the strongpoint by firing a phosphorous grenade in the direction.'[65] In turn, to signal to the infantry, tanks would carry three flags, these to be 'pushed out of the tank as required':

> Green and White (Diagonal) – 'All right – Come On'
> Red and White (Diagonal) – 'Broken Down'
> Red, White and Blue (Vertical) – denotes a British tank coming out of action.'[66]

Approval and enthusiasm for the Mark V tank were almost universal. Monash writes, perhaps with rather too much ardency:

> The fame of the Tanks and all the wonderful things they could do spread rapidly throughout the Corps. The 'digger' took the Tank to his heart, and ever after, each Tank was given a pet name by the Company of Infantry which it served in battle, a name which was kept chalked on its iron sides, together with a panegyric commentary upon its prowess.[67]

White, in his history of the 13th Battalion, is similarly effusive:

> Diggers and Tankmen were soon great pals and also treated their tanks as such: the monsters being given petnames, [sic] addressed kindly, admired loudly and, when occasionally scolded, scolded as one would scold a faithful dog. The Diggers climbed all over them, inside and out, rode across trenches and over walls and banks, and even drove them. 'They'll do us' was the general opinion.[68]

The war diary of the 4th Brigade HQ for 28 June 1918 takes a more sober, balanced view:

> Warm sunny day. Units training and refitting. One platoon per Battalion (100 all ranks) proceeded by motor lorry to Vaux-en-Amienois for training in conjunction with tanks.

63 TNA: WO95/114-3 War Diary 8th Tank Battalion. Appendices.
64 TNA: WO95/114-3 War Diary 8th Tank Battalion. Appendices.
65 AWM: 4 23/58/21 Part 1. War Diary 41st Australian Battalion.
66 AWM: 4 23/58/21 Part 1. War Diary 41st Australian Battalion. It was feared that Australian Infantry, faced with a tank moving towards them in a westerly direction, might mistake it for a German machine and fire at it. There is, however, no evidence of any German tanks being in the vicinity at the time.
67 Monash, *Australian Victories*, p.250.
68 Thomas A.White, *The History of the Thirteenth Battalion AIF* (Sydney: Tyrells, 1924), p.142.

> Army and Divisional Commanders present. The men were well pleased with what they saw, but still have doubts as to the value of tanks in attack.[69]

Rawlinson, after watching the exercises, was equally reserved in his judgment: 'I attended another demonstration with the Tanks at Vaux which went very well and at which Gen Bell Cmdng the 33 American Div was also present. I think we have now got the Australians to understand and appreciate the tanks.'[70]

The new plan of attack involved a force of 60 battle tanks from the 8th and 13th Tank Battalions, 5th Tank Brigade. On the right flank of the attack, 6th Brigade was allocated six tanks (two sections): these would accompany the infantry to the final objective, Blue Line, and cover them as they consolidated their newly-won positions. On the extreme right flank, the 25th Battalion of 7th Brigade, with the shortest distance to cover to their objective, would have to do without tank support. The 4th Brigade were given one company: 12 tanks. Six of them would help to clear and mop up Vaire and Hamel Woods. The remaining six would pass to the north and south of the woods – three to the north and three to the south – covering the flanks of the assault, before advancing to the Blue Line.

To the north, 11th Brigade would have 18 tanks (one company plus two sections). Six of these were tasked with clearing and mopping up Hamel village. The rest would skirt the settlement on their way to the Blue Line, including the capture of the Wolfsberg position. One company of 12 tanks would form the liaison unit positioned on the boundary between 4th and 11th Brigades. Three of these were given the special task of assisting in the capture of Pear Trench. Twelve tanks were positioned behind 4th and 11th Brigades, six behind each, forming the close support units. These would move forward behind the assaulting waves, filling in where necessary if tanks were put out of action as far as the halt line, and subsequently joining in the advance to the final objective.

Each 'fighting tank' would carry two boxes of small arms ammunition, Lewis gun drums and water for the infantry. In addition, four 'supply tanks' would each deliver a load of approximately 12,500 lbs to within 500 yards of the Blue Line within half an hour of its capture. The total of 50,000 lbs, at, say, a round figure of 40 lbs per man, would normally require 1,250 men to transport all this equipment forward.[71] All four tanks reached their destinations on 4 July.

Table 2. The Supply Tank Loads

Item	Tank No. 105	Tank No. 107	Tank No. 115	Tank No. 123
Coils of Barbed Wire	124	96	124	120
Screw Picquets (Short)	300	300	300	240
Screw Picquets (Long)	130	150	150	120
Corrugated Iron Sheets	45	30	26	52
Trench Mortar Bombs	150	150	150	150
Mills Bombs	240	-	-	-
Small Arms Ammunition (Rounds)	10,000	10,000	10,000	10,000
Drinking Water (Gallons)	100	100	126	100

69 AWM: 4 23/4/33. War Diary 4 Australian Infantry Brigade HQ.
70 CCA: Rawlinson Papers. Diary entry 30 June 1918.
71 TNA:PRO: WO95/112-1 War Diary 5th Tank Brigade July 1918 Appendix I.

The Royal Air Force and the Australian Flying Corps would also have their role to play. In the weeks running up to the attack, 'normal' activity was maintained: 3 Squadron Australian Flying Corps, for example, racked up over a thousand flying hours in their RE8 aircraft, completing 210 artillery patrols and having dropped 1,421 bombs on enemy positions. They had fired 57,260 machine gun rounds into German trenches and, perhaps most importantly, had taken 613 aerial photographs of the area. One aircraft of the squadron was given a very specific job: to over-fly the entire Corps area every day 'to note the extent to which our preparations can be ascertained from the air by hostile aircraft.'[72] There had been 14 air combats, of which four had had decisive results. Three officers had been killed,[73] with three wounded. Fourteen other ranks had also become casualties. One pioneering stunt was first tested by 3 Squadron AFC:

> 24 June. On this date experiments were carried out by Captain L.J. Wackett, Flight Commander of 'B' Flight, of dropping boxes of S.A.A. ammunition by parachute. The Army Commander, General Sir H.S. Rawlinson, Bart., GCVO, KCB, KCMG, was present. The boxes were attached to the bomb racks under the fuselage and making allowance for the wind, these were dropped onto the 'drome. The Army Commander seemed satisfied with the practicability of the scheme and decided to try the experiment on the first occasion that presented itself, the idea being to keep up a sufficient supply of ammunition to troops in the front line during an attack when supplies were apt to become short through enemy artillery barrages preventing the carrying of same.[74]

Captain L.J. Wackett, 3rd Squadron, Australian Flying Corps (AWM)

72 AWM: 4 1/48/28 Part 1. War Diary 4th Australian Division General Staff HQ. July 1918.
73 Second Lieutenant Sydney Jones, pilot, and Second Lieutenant Stanley Arthur Loram, observer, had been killed when their aircraft, A3817, crashed 10 minutes after take-off on 16 June. On the 28th, observer Lieutenant Arthur O'Connor Brook was killed when his aircraft was shot down during an artillery observation flight. The pilot, Lieutenant P.H. Kerr was wounded in the incident. All three are buried in Vignacourt British Cemetery, graves III.E.6, III.E.7 & IV.A.19 respectively. The War Diary and the CWGC give the 15th and 27th as the dates of death. The Flight Logs, however, clearly indicate the 16th and 28th. The author favours the Flight Log version.
74 AWM: 4 8/6/18 War Diary 3 Squadron AFC, June 1918.

An RE8 of 3 Squadron, AFC. (AWM)

For the day of the attack, five specific roles were assigned. Before Zero Hour, planes would fly up and down the line to mask the sound of the tank engines as they moved forward into their 'jumping off' positions. This task was given to the FE2bs of 101 Squadron RAF. In order to establish how far forward the infantry had managed to get, 'Contact' planes would fly over the battlefield, identifiable by two small, black flags, one foot square, attached to the rear edge of each tailplane, calling for flares at Zero plus ninety minutes by dropping a white flare and sounding a succession of Morse code 'A's on a klaxon. Infantry had been told that their answering flares should only be lit on the final objective, one every 15 yards.

'Counter-attack' planes, trailing a streamer from their right-hand wing strut, would fly over the battlefield at 3,000 feet throughout the day, looking for any evidence of an impending German counterattack. They would signal an SOS by wireless and by dropping a white parachute and smoke flares over the centre of the assumed attack. No. 9 Squadron RAF would drop ammunition for the infantry at five pre-specified points (see map). Infantry brigades would display a white 'N' on the ground, six feet in length, at those points. The aircraft would have the underside of each wing painted black for 2½ feet from the tip. Other aircraft would be assigned to bomb machine-gun nests, strong points, horse lines, possible assembly areas, and any other visible human targets.

The final piece in the jigsaw would be provided by the Royal Engineers. This was no starring role, as admitted by the author of the 4th Division Royal Engineers diary: 'The history of the operation is not an Engineer matter.... The formation of forward dumps of R.E. material was probably the most important part of the preparations.'[75] Five dumps were established, containing sandbags, screw pickets, barbed wire and so on. In addition to this, their duties consisted of maintaining the bridges across the Somme and the main traffic routes in the rear areas. After the attack, Royal Engineers dumps would be established further forward, new strongpoints dug and wired, and communication trenches created.

75 AWM: 4 14/10/30 Part 1. War Diary, HQ 4th Australian Divisional Engineers.

There were units of four German divisions deployed in defensive positions opposite the proposed attack frontage: the *Reserve-Infanterie Regiment 52, [RIR 52], 107. Division* was positioned between the Somme and the Ancre, facing what was to be a diversionary raid by the 55th, 58th and 59th Battalions of 5th Australian Division.

Defending the village of Hamel and the Wolfsberg were troops of *RIR 202, 43. Reserve Division*. To the south, was *13. Division*. Its *Infanterie-Regiment 55 (IR 55)* garrisoned Pear Trench and the northern part of Vaire Wood. The rest of the wood was held by *IR 13*, and between the southern boundary of Vaire Wood and the Roman road stood *IR 15*. The line was continued south of the road by *IR 137, 108. Division*.

On 22 June 1918, an Australian Corps intelligence report estimated the strength of the German forces facing them (excluding machine gunners and artillery) to be 2,790 men, with a further 2,860 available in reserve for counterattacks.[76] Bean, in the Australian *Official History*, however, suggests that this was an over-estimation: 'German companies were considerably weaker even than the Australian, averaging at this time (when influenza in its milder form was raging) about 50 rifles.'[77]

The main attack would, therefore, fall on the *43.* and *13. Divisionen*. The *43. Division* (*Generalmajor* Wilhelm Theodor Knoch), originally made up of troops drawn from regiments in the Guards Corps, now recruited men from the whole of Prussia. It had fought on the Western Front continually since 1914, apart from a brief period on the Eastern Front from June to November 1916. It had taken part in the Lys Offensive on 9 April 1918. A report on the perceived quality of the division in the 4th Australian Brigade diary of July 1918 states:

> The 43rd Division has always been considered a good fighting unit. It is drawn from the depots of guards regiments and consequently contains 'human material' of good quality. In the end of 1917 it was used as a special counter-attack division. Owing, however, to its many engagements and heavy losses, it has frequently been reconstituted.[78]

Generalmajor Rudolf von Borries, commanding 13th Division, German Army. (Public Domain)

76 AWM: 26 361/2 War Diary Australian Corps June 1918.
77 Bean, *The Official History*, vol.VI, p.313. The history of RIR 202 states that each of their battalions had between 60 and 80 men ill at any one time with Spanish Flu towards the end of June 1918. Dr Fritz Bergeder, *Das Reserve-Infanterie Regiment 202 auf den Schlachtfeldern des Weltkrieges 1914-1918* (Berlin: Verlag Tradition 1927), p.144.
78 AWM 4 23/4/34. War Diary 4th Australian Infantry Brigade.

A similar report in the 4th Australian Division war diary of June 1918 concludes that: 'it cannot now be considered a first class division'.[79] It had been in position in and around Hamel for a fortnight.

The *13. Division* (*Generalmajor* Rudolf von Borries), recruiting mainly from the Prussian province of Westphalia, had served on the Western Front since 1914, taking part in the initial German advance through Belgium and France. It also fought at Verdun, in the latter stages of the Somme in 1916, and spent much of 1917 on the Chemin des Dames ridge before taking part in the 'Michael' Spring Offensive of March 1918, where it suffered 40 percent casualties. The British *Official History* states that 'British intelligence estimated the Division to be first class.'[80] A 4th Australian Division Intelligence Summary was less sure:

> During 1915 the Westphalians distinguished themselves by excellent work on defences and fought tenaciously on all occasions. At Verdun and on the Somme too, the 13th acquitted itself well. Both in 1916 and 1917, however, desertions were not infrequent, these being mostly on the part of Poles and Alsatians, who are found in large numbers in the division. The division received a smashing blow on the Ailette in October 1917 and the drafts required to bring it up to strength again have not been put to the test. It is therefore not possible to estimate the value of the division at the moment.[81]

The *13. Division* had completed their move into the line at Hamel only on the night of 2/3 July.

The German trench system was far from complete. The woods and Hamel village were reasonably well fortified, as was the Wolfsberg, some 206 feet higher than the village, but the rest of the line was made up of strongpoints, including Pear Trench and Kidney Trench,[82] and of shallow and often non-continuous trenches. 'The wire was poor, there were no communication trenches[83] and no shell-proof dug outs in the foremost trenches.'[84] The Germans were, it seemed, in no real hurry to remedy the situation. An intelligence report for 11th Brigade states that:

> Up till recently the enemy has displayed little energy in the construction of forward defences opposite the Corps front, and as yet there are no signs of new work in the immediate back area at all.
>
> During the past few weeks, however, there are increasing indications that he intends to develop a complete two line system with the usual saps, dugouts, and communication trenches. In certain areas the work is nearing completion and a considerable defence scheme is evidently contemplated, the tendency being to link up the already existing chain of rifle pits and incorporate them in the trench lines.

79 AWM 4 1/48/27. War Diary General Staff Headquarters 4th Australian Division.
80 J.E. Edmonds (ed.), *History of the Great War Based on Official Documents by Direction of the Committee of Imperial Defence*, 1918 vol.III, p.198, fn. 3.
81 AWM: 4. Item 1/48, Roll 832. 4th Australian Division Intelligence Summary No. 304, 3 July 1918.
82 Both named for their shape when seen from the air. Pear Trench was known to the Germans as 'Nebelmulde', which translates roughly as 'Foggy or Misty Hollow.'
83 The exception was 'Hun's Walk', which extended back from Vaire Wood some 2,000 yards to the northern edge of Accroche Wood.
84 Edmonds (ed.), *History of the Great War*, 1918 vol.III, p.198.

From the report of patrols, there is no doubt that wire obstacles do exist, but they appear to be hastily improved and should not afford any great obstacle.[85]

* * *

Tuesday 2 July, two days before the planned assault, turned out to be 'a most highly inconvenient day' for Monash.[86] The Prime Minister of Australia, William Morris Hughes and the Minister for the Navy, Sir Joseph Cook – both unaware of the impending attack on Hamel – were on their way to a meeting of the Supreme War Council in Paris and decided, at very short notice, to visit the Australian Corps.

A swiftly organised timetable of events was drawn up, allowing the two dignitaries, by now apprised of the situation by Monash, along with their staffs and Messrs Murdoch and Glover, journalists, to meet and address as many of the units taking part in the attack as possible. A representative number of men from each unit to be visited was ordered to 'be assembled under cover of woods or trees, so as to reduce the risk of enemy observation from the air', with 'not more than 1,000 men to be assembled at any one spot.'[87]

In all, 14 separate visits were initially scheduled, each lasting between 15 and 35 minutes, starting at 9:40 a.m. and finishing at 6:45 p.m. Units of 11th, 4th and 6th Brigades were duly gathered and addressed, the day ending with a visit to 3 Squadron AFC and then dinner at Australian Corps HQ at Bertangles Château.[88] It is quite probable that these visits provided a morale boost to the troops, but with everything else going on, it was no doubt something that Monash could have done without.

* * *

The Prime Minister's visit turned out to be the least of Monash's worries that day. It seems that Generals Read and Bell, in initiating and organising the integration of the 10 companies of American infantry into the Australian units, had somehow neglected to inform General Pershing of their plans. Rawlinson wrote in his diary:

I got a message after tea to say Read wanted to see me at 9 pm so I went to the office after dinner to see him. He told me that Pershing had been inspecting the Divn in the Brit area and had definitely refused to sanction this employment of their American troops in the Aust attack.'[89]

Rawlinson initially told Read that he could withdraw six of the American companies, which were with the rear battalions, but not the four that had already gone up into the front line trenches. Pershing had previously, and vehemently, insisted that American formations and units

85 AWM: 4. 23/11/19. War Diary 11 Inf Bde June 1918 Appendices.
86 AWM: DRL 2316. War Letters of General Monash. Final Typed Copy 1934. Volume 11.
87 AWM: 3DRL 2316. Monash Collection July 1918.
88 More than one itinerary exists in the war diaries and the personal papers of participants. It is not possible to ascertain definitively which one, if any, was followed. The Australian Official History notes that one unit waited in vain for the Prime Minister to arrive, but does not say which one.
89 CCA: Rawlinson Papers. Diary entry for 2 July 1918.

should not fight under British or French command, but, once ready, as purely American formations. This principle could only be relaxed in case of emergency, and as Pershing – quite understandably – did not consider the attack at Hamel to constitute such an emergency, he concluded that 'the use of the Americans at this time was directly contrary to the arrangement.'[90]

Accordingly – but seemingly as a result of a slight misunderstanding – Australian units received orders on 3 July that only the six companies of American troops that had most recently joined were to be withdrawn immediately. The disappointment felt by the Americans was palpable: at the 16th Australian Battalion positions,

> they were dumbfounded.... The Officer in command of the Americans gave the 16th his men's best wishes and wished the battalion good luck. While he was speaking, the restraint with which his men held themselves was noticeable, and it could be seen that they were cut to the heart at the change of circumstances.[91]

General John Joseph Pershing, commander, American Expeditionary Force. (The Free Social Encyclopedia)

It soon became clear, however, that Pershing wanted all American troops withdrawn. The message was passed via Read to Rawlinson, who then telephoned Monash. By now, it was around 4:00 p.m. on the 3rd, and 'the time for getting the order to the infantry and making a second adjustment of the formations was dangerously short.'[92] When MacLagan found out, he was loath to make any further changes. Monash called what was, in essence, an 'emergency' meeting at MacLagan's HQ at Bussy-les-Daours at 5:00 p.m., with Rawlinson and his Chief of Staff, Montgomery, also present.

Monash, having acquiesced to the removal of the six American companies, decided that he would go no further: he told Rawlinson that it was very late in the day to implement any more changes, adding that if the Americans did not take part in the attack, he would be forced to cancel the whole operation. He therefore proposed to carry on with the assault, with the four remaining American companies taking part, unless Rawlinson gave him a direct order to the

90 Quoted in Bean, *The Official History*, vol.VI, p.277.
91 C. Longmore, *The Old Sixteenth. Being a Record of the 16th Battalion AIF during the Great War 1914-1918* (Perth: The History Committee of the 16th Battalion Association, 1929), p.180.
92 Bean, *The Official History*, vol.VI, p.278.

contrary by 6:30 p.m., after which time, with units by then already on their way to their battle stations, it would be too late to do anything anyway.

Rawlinson initially feared that inaction on his part at this juncture might ultimately cost him his job, but Monash stood his ground. Rawlinson reportedly retorted: 'You don't realise what it means – do you want me to run the risk of being sent back to England? Do you mean it is worth that?' 'Yes I do' said Monash. 'It is more important to keep the confidence of the Americans and Australians in each other than to preserve even an Army Commander.'[93] The Fourth Army commander spotted a solution to the dilemma: the buck was passed – if Haig did not cancel the attack before 6:30 p.m., (a deadline later extended to 7:00 p.m.), then all could proceed as planned.

Haig had been visiting Pershing in Paris that afternoon, and Pershing had told him that he considered his troops to be, as yet, insufficiently trained to take part in offensive action and had indicated his feelings to Rawlinson the previous day. When Haig offered to 'interfere in the matter',[94] Pershing declined, saying that as far as he was concerned, the matter was settled. When Rawlinson tried to contact Haig for a decision, it just so happened that the Commander-in-Chief was in a motor car on his way back to GHQ and unlikely to arrive there before the deadline.

Both Monash and Rawlinson were fully aware of Pershing's orders to withdraw *all* of his troops from the Hamel attack, and both sought devious means to circumvent them. Monash's behaviour towards Rawlinson in threatening to cancel the operation – saving his own skin but putting his superior's career at risk – must be regarded as devious at best, and (in Bean's eyes, see the *Official History*, p.279, fn96) his 7:00 p.m. deadline was a convenient falsehood. It is also possible that Rawlinson knew of his Chief's itinerary and was counting on his being uncontactable to exonerate him from having to make a decision. In the end, both got away with it because Haig decided to back his subordinate commanders. His diary entry for 3 July 1918 reads:

> Before dinner... Lawrence (my CGS) spoke to me regarding the Americans taking part in the Australian operations ... Some 6 companies had been withdrawn; about 4 could not be withdrawn; was the operation to be stopped in order to do so? I said 'No.' The first essential is to improve our position east of Amiens as soon as possible. The attack must therefore be launched as proposed even if a few American detachments cannot be got out before Zero Hour.[95]

Lawrence had, it seems, briefed his Chief to elicit the required response, and Haig, in any case, had no qualms about defying the American Commander-in-Chief.

The four American companies went into the attack on 4 July, split between the 13th and 15th Battalions of 4th Brigade and the 42nd and 43rd Battalions of 11th Brigade. The 11th Brigade diary bemoans the loss of the other American companies, this requiring them to launch the assault with around 2,200 men instead of nearly 3,000.

93 Quoted in Bean, *The Official History*, vol.VI, p.279.
94 G. Sheffield, & J. Bourne (eds), *Douglas Haig. War Diaries and Letters 1914-1918* (London: Weidenfeld & Nicolson, 2005), p.425.
95 Sheffield, & Bourne (eds), *Douglas Haig*, p.425.

Rawlinson's diary entry for 3 July describes his day as 'tiresome' and concludes: 'If Pershing goes on like this we will never win the war.'[96]

At around 3:00 a.m. on the morning of 4 July, Monash, unable at this stage to influence events and trusting that his planning would prove effective, was observed by Brigadier General Coxen pacing up and down nervously on the gravel drive in front of Bertangles Château. 'The stage was set, he was awaiting the rise of the curtain. Every now and again he would pause and look at his watch, awaiting zero hour.'[97]

96 CCA: Rawlinson Papers. Diary entry 3 July 1918.
97 AWM: 38 3DRL 606/276/1. Letter from Coxen to Bean, 1937.

2

The Right Flank: 6th & 7th Brigades

The front line of 6th and 7th Brigades – both 'lent' by 2nd Division (Major General Charles Rosenthal) to 4th Division for the attack – sat atop the Villers-Bretonneux plateau, astride the monotonously straight road that ran west-east along the ridge from Amiens through Villers-Bretonneux to Warfusée and beyond.[1] Stretching south-west to north-east, it therefore faced more or less south-east, before turning north to run down the slope to the west of Vaire Wood. The German line opposite ran north, perpendicular to the road before curving back to the north-east and then paralleling the Australian positions nearer Vaire Wood. Its convex nature meant that the width of No Man's Land varied from 500 to less than 100 yards. (See Map 2). Manning those trenches were the men of *Infanterie-Regiment 15,* part of *13. Division*. The defensive positions were far from favourable, and the regiment was also under-strength:

> The regiment's position was scantily constructed and full of gaps, particularly in the main resistance line. It could not stand up to long artillery bombardments or resist a strong infantry attack. The number of fighting troops was very limited, as few drafts had arrived and the developing influenza epidemic had caused substantial losses.[2]

The job of the Australian brigades here was to form a defensive flank, preventing any German counter incursion from the south. This task was entrusted to three battalions. For those on the extreme right, 25th Battalion (Lieutenant Colonel William MacIntyre Davis) and to their left, 23rd Battalion (Lieutenant Colonel William Brazenor), this involved no more than capturing and holding the German front line trench. For 21st Battalion (Major Alfred Effingham Reed), to the north, the objective lay well beyond it, just under 1,000 yards away at its maximum, facing almost due east, but with the right-hand company echeloned back, facing south to maintain touch with 23rd Battalion. The brigades' advance would not take them beyond the artillery halt line.

1 This is the modern-day D1029.
2 Gustav Riebensahm, *Infanterie-Regiment Prinz Friedrich der Niederlande (2. Westfälisches) Nr. 15 im Weltkriege 1914-18* (Minden: Selbstverlag des Bundes ehemaliger Angehöriger des Infanterie-Regiments Nr. 15, 1931), p.346. Translated from the original German by the author.

The 25th Battalion placed two companies in the front line: B Company on the right, and D Company on the left, with C Company in support, leaving A Company in reserve, well back in the Villers Line trench, where battalion HQ was also situated. The battalion's total fighting strength at this time amounted to no more than 12 officers and 237 other ranks.[3]

In addition to the regular artillery barrage from both medium and heavy guns, the 6th and 7th Brigades assault would be supported by the 35 Vickers medium machine guns of 2nd Battalion, Australian Machine Gun Corps, 19 of which were covering the 25th Battalion's attack, spraying over 253,000 rounds over the heads of the advancing troops into the enemy rear areas, and on the 25th Battalion front, by eight 3-inch Trench Mortars of the 7th Australian Light Trench Mortar Battery. Six of these, under Lieutenant W.L. Miller, deployed directly behind the 25th Battalion jumping off positions, would bombard the German front line from P25.d.35.25 to P25.b.2.0 (the north-south section), with two of these 'paying particular attention' to the German strong point located just south of the main road,[4] before lifting 100 yards at Zero plus four minutes. Two more, under Corporal W.T. Whiley, from positions further to the south (O.36.a.95.30), would launch 250 rounds onto the orchard in square O.36.c., 'prevent[ing] M.G. fire from thence on to right of attack from Zero to Zero + 30 mins.'[5]

Four-inch Stokes mortars would put down a smoke screen along the main road from Zero to Zero plus 120 minutes, and to help protect the right flank from enfilade fire and possible counterattack, heavy mortars were to target strategic points further to the south. As previously mentioned, however, 25th Battalion would go into the attack without tank support.

A 'contact' aircraft of the Australian Flying Corps would fly over the objective at Zero plus 90 minutes and call for ground flares to be lit by the infantry by dropping a white flare and sounding a succession of Morse code 'A's on a klaxon. During the night of 3/4 July, allied aircraft had circled over the German trenches, dropping flares and machine-gunning the enemy positions. On the morning of the 4th, the bleary-eyed German garrison had enjoyed little, if any, rest.[6]

The spearhead companies, B and D, were in position in the front line at 2:30 a.m. on 4 July, 40 minutes prior to zero, with the necessary gaps in their own wire already cut. They were each to advance 'in two waves on a two-platoon frontage, with 50 yards between waves.'[7] Each man carried 250 rounds of small-arms ammunition, two hand grenades (designated Rifle Grenadiers would carry six), 24 hours' rations, and every second man had either a pick or a shovel, with a ratio of one pick to three shovels.

C Company would move forward in support and would act as carrying parties. Two platoons of A Company would form a fourth wave and move forward to be used if necessary as reinforcements in the attack. Later, they were to dig a communication trench from the old front line where 'Albert CT' meets it, to the captured objective.[8]

The artillery opened up with some harassing fire along the German front line as planned, eight minutes before Zero, and at 3:10 a.m., as the barrage proper fell on the objective, the men

3 AWM: 4 23/42/35. 25th Battalion War Diary, July 1918.
4 AWM: 4 13/120/4. 7th Australian Light Trench Mortar Battery War Diary.
5 AWM: 4 13/120/4. 7th Australian Light Trench Mortar Battery War Diary.
6 Riebensahm, *Infanterie-Regiment 15*, p.346.
7 AWM: 4 23/42/35. 25th Battalion War Diary, July 1918.
8 On the night of 2/3 July, the first 100 yards of this new communication trench was dug out into No Man's Land, leaving about 150 yards to be completed after the objective was captured.

of B and D Companies filed out through the gaps in the wire, calmly opened into extended order, and then began the advance, following the barrage as closely as they dared. The barrage proved to be very effective, a number of Germans being found dead in their trenches, killed by shrapnel.

The right-hand company had to deal with the German strong point next to the main road. The prolific machine gun and rifle fire from this position and the German artillery counter barrage wreaked havoc among the advancing Australians: amongst the B Company dead were ginger-haired 4789 Private Edwin 'Bluey' Dixson, hit by shell fragments in the chest and head, along with 5351 Private George Edward Hooke, also a victim of shell fire, and 6545 Lance Corporal Herbert Evans, a former schoolmaster from North Queensland, killed by machine gun fire. All three died within yards of each other as they crossed No Man's Land.[9]

The grave of Private George Edward Hooke, 25th Battalion. (Author)

The grave of Private Alexander McDonald Cossar, 25th Battalion. (Author)

The machine gun nest also accounted for 6302 Private Alexander McDonald 'Tiny' Cossar, B Company, whose body was later found lying beside a dead German soldier near the main road.[10]

9 As reported by Stretcher Bearer 4976 Pte H. Bang, 25th Bn, in the Red Cross Report, AWM: 1DRL/0428. Dixson, Hooke and Evans are all buried in Crucifix Corner Cemetery, graves IX.A.6, IX.A.1 and VII.C.13 respectively.

10 Cossar is also buried in Crucifix Corner Cemetery, grave IX.A.2, next to Hooke. In the Red Cross Report, 'Tiny' is described by Sergeant Ham, rather implausibly, as being four feet tall.

The grave of Private Edwin Dixson, 25th Battalion. (Author)

The grave of Second Lieutenant Cecil George Toft, 25th Battalion. (Author)

The situation had become critical: soon, only nine men from the two leading platoons were left to capture the strong point. With his officer, Second Lieutenant Cecil George Toft already dead,[11] Lance Corporal Robert James Richardson helped Lance Sergeant Charles George Ham to rally the few survivors and then turned his Lewis gun on the German position, silencing one machine gun and allowing his comrades, led by Sergeant Ham, to storm the redoubt.[12]

With the shorter distance across No Man's Land to cover, D Company was able to report at 3:35 a.m. that the German front line trench had been captured. They had met with stiff opposition, but not, it seemed, until they actually entered the German line, where 'several hand-to-hand struggles took place, and several enemy were killed by bayonet thrusts.'[13] It was reported that Lieutenant Auchterlonie was the first man into the enemy trench, where he accounted for two of the defenders with his pistol and then organised clearing parties to work along the trench on either flank.[14]

11 Toft occupies grave IX.E.19 in Crucifix Corner Cemetery.
12 For this action, Ham received a DCM, and Richardson the MM.
13 AWM: 4 23/42/35. 25th Battalion War Diary, July 1918.
14 Lieutenant Cecil Arthur Auchterlonie was recommended for the MC for this action. He earned a Bar to his MC later that month, but was sadly killed in action on 10 August 1918, aged 22. His two brothers were also killed in action: Sergeant Bertrand Innes Auchterlonie, 15th Bn, was killed on 8 August 1915, age 21, at Gallipoli and is commemorated on the Lone Pine Memorial. Lieutenant

Lieutenant Cecil Arthur Auchterlonie MC, 25th Battalion. (AWM)

Two other soldiers in D Coy were also commended for their bravery and initiative: although he had already been wounded three times before Zero, Lance Corporal Valentine led his section into the attack, using his Lewis gun to good effect, both during the advance and while the newly-captured position was being consolidated. It was only at this point, once the position was secure, and when ordered by his platoon commander, that he went back to receive medical attention.

Just further to the north, on the extreme left flank of D Company's attack, Private Mackay, himself slightly wounded, took charge of his section when his section leader was hit, and, firing his Lewis gun from the hip, successfully led 'his' men onto the objective, all the time managing to maintain touch with the battalion on his left (23rd Battalion).[15]

The 7th Brigade war diary asserts that:

> The advance was so rapid that our troops reached the objective before the enemy infantry were aware that an attack was in progress.
>
> Prisoners captured stated that they did not think that Infantry could advance so close to a protective barrage as our men did. Notwithstanding the above, however,... a machine gun [just to the north of the main road] caused a number of casualties before it was put out of action.[16]

The diarist then incorrectly claims that 'the right company [B Company] met with practically no opposition at all.'[17] Casualty figures already mentioned above clearly refute this statement.

Consolidation and 'reversing' the newly-won position were now the immediate concerns. The 25th Battalion war diary reports that:

> The Old German Trench was in excellent condition and in a very short time fire-steps were constructed in the parados and men well established. On the Right... the assaulting troops constructed 3 Platoon Posts connecting up with our old front line at P 31.a.20.70. At night these posts were extended and improved and two further posts dug.[18]

Archibald Vivian Auchterlonie, 25th Bn, was killed, age 23, on 20 October 1915, also at Gallipoli, and is buried in Embarkation Pier Cemetery, Special Memorial A 31.

15 1120 L/Cpl William A. Valentine and 2700 Pte Arthur William Mackay were awarded the MM for these actions. The by then Cpl Mackay was awarded a Bar to his MM for his actions during the Battle of Amiens on 9 August 1918. Valentine was also later awarded a Bar to his MM.

16 AWM: 4 23/7/35. 7th Infantry Brigade War Diary July 1918.

17 AWM: 4 23/7/35. 7th Infantry Brigade War Diary July 1918.

18 AWM: 4 23/42/35. 25th Battalion War Diary, July 1918.

The trench mortar crews of 7th Australian Light Trench Mortar Battery had not had a good day of it: their actions were praised by the infantry, one report stating that 'the trench Mortar shooting was very satisfactory and of great assistance especially in the attack on the strongpoint',[19] but at Zero plus two minutes, one of the mortars of the most northern group situated behind the 25th Battalion front suffered an unexplained premature burst which killed two of the crew and wounded a third.[20] The battery's diary also complains about the projectiles they were using: the shells with blue cartridges and blue rings produced a 'terrific flash' when a rapid rate of fire was needed.[21] This, in the semi-darkness of the early morning, attracted the attention of the German artillery, meaning that the mortar positions were under constant, heavy enemy bombardment throughout the operation. The group firing on the orchard to the south was forced to move their position further up the trench at 7:00 a.m., 'owing to very heavy enemy artillery fire on the mortar positions',[22] which sadly resulted in the death of Corporal Whiley, who was commanding this group.[23]

The grave of Private James Troy Cable, 7th Australian Trench Mortar Battery. (Author)

The grave of Private George Thomas Lawson, 7th Australian Trench Mortar Battery. (Author)

19 Quoted in AWM: 4 13/120/4. 7th Australian Light Trench Mortar Battery War Diary.
20 1764 Private James Troy Cable and 20968 Private George Thomas Lawson are buried in Crucifix Corner Cemetery, graves III.B.19 and III.B.22 respectively. The wounded man was Cpl G.V.M. Fowler.
21 AWM: 4 13/120/4. 7th Australian Light Trench Mortar Battery War Diary.
22 AWM: 4 13/120/4. 7th Australian Light Trench Mortar Battery War Diary.
23 2289 Cpl William Thomas Whiley is buried in Adelaide Cemetery, grave III.L.12.

The Germans were not finished, however. Fighting in this sector was not over. It took only a short while for the Germans to reorganise and react to the Australian incursion, and at 4:20 a.m., a counterattack to regain the strong point by the main road was launched. It was a two-pronged assault: a number of attackers moved up the trench from the orchard to the south, while another group advanced along the main road. The nine men defending the position sent up an SOS signal, and the resulting artillery and trench mortar fire managed to keep most of the German force at bay. Some got within grenade-throwing range, however, and it looked at one point as if they would force the tiny garrison out and recapture the strongpoint. Lieutenant Auchterlonie realised just how precarious the situation had got, and promptly sent a platoon from D Company under Sergeant Denny to reinforce the position. 'This he did with great initiative, recapturing the position and establishing a block in the trench. Later the enemy made a second bombing attack on the post, but owing to Sgt DENNY'S prompt action and the splendid guidance of his men the enemy was unable to make any progress.'[24]

This turned out to be the German's last throw of the dice in that sector. The next parties to approach the trench, in twos or threes, and in one case 10, came over to surrender 'from distances up to 350 yards from our objective.'[25] Two Vickers machine guns had gone forward with the attacking troops, and these were positioned on either side of the main road, the one to the north covering the road itself, the other covering the southern approaches. These, along with rifle and Lewis gun fire, prevented any further German incursions. The expected appearance by a contact aircraft never materialised: the war diary of 7th Brigade records an aircraft circling over Villers-Bretonneux, sounding its klaxon for a few minutes at around 4:30 a.m., but the 25th Battalion's flares remained unlit.

The battalion war diary asserts that during the attack, 92 German prisoners had been taken, and about 50 German dead were counted in their sector. Initial estimates put the 25th Battalion casualty count at two officers and 19 other ranks killed, with one officer and 71 other ranks wounded.[26] Although these figures may appear to be 'light' at first glance, they amount to a not insignificant casualty rate for the battalion of 37 percent.

* * *

The 6th Brigade's frontage comprised 21st and 23rd Battalions, deployed left and right, respectively. The 23rd Battalion lined up in their jumping off positions with D Company on the right (Lieutenant Hodgson), B Company in the centre (Captain Hinchcliffe), and A Company (Captain Moss) on the left, but positioned behind B Company and the right-hand company of 21st Battalion on their left. The attack frontage would expand from 1,000 yards at Zero to almost 2,000 yards on the objective, so A Company would therefore move forward to fill in the space on the left as the advance developed. C Company, in support, would act as 'carriers' for the attacking companies.

24 Quoted from 5319 Sgt Roland James Denny's citation for his action for which he received a Bar to his MM. He had won his first MM on 4 & 9 October 1917 during the attack on Zonnebeke, Belgium.

25 AWM: 4 23/42/35. 25th Battalion War Diary, July 1918.

26 Commonwealth War Graves Commission figures up to and including 6 July confirm 26 fatalities for 25th Bn.

B and D Companies would advance in a single wave with a line of skirmishers out ahead, followed by a line of sections in file, 20 yards behind them. Three tanks – one section of C Company, 13th Tank Battalion – would be 'employed on the Battalion front after the gaining of the objective, and also to assist the infantry in dealing with any opposition that may be met: in this case the tank would precede the infantry in continuation of the attack.'[27]

Twenty-six Vickers machine guns and eight trench mortars would supplement the artillery barrage, and at Zero plus 30 minutes, brigade snipers were to be sent forward to establish five double posts within each attacking battalion's positions.

All troops were in position 45 minutes before Zero. Captain Lionel Short, C Company, wrote home to his 'dear Edith' on 8 July, recounting his experiences of the Hamel attack. He begins: 'It has been a time of utmost excitement.' His platoon was acting as carriers of ammunition and water to Captain Moss' A Company on the left flank of the battalion front. He continues:

> We had arranged to go over together. You can picture an absolutely still fine night with the dawn just breaking as the barrage opened. We had been laying out in the crops for an hour with two companies on the tape and Moss in rear ready during the advance to fill in a gap that would be caused by the spreading out in fan formation of the two front companies.
>
> My men had a very strenuous job. The heavy ammunition and water tins had to be brought along trenches for about a mile. Telephone wires ran across in maddening repetition so that the men's rifles slung over their backs were caught in the entanglement. I thought we would never reach the J.O.T. [Jumping Off Tape] and the minutes flew by. One could not hurry or the men would be lost far behind. It was necessary to halt continually and get the word passed back 'rear closed up.' Still we did get there. I found Moss sitting with his runner and stretcher-bearers in a shell hole. I reported all O.K. for the next movement.

Captain Lionel Gordon Short (Second from left), 23rd Battalion. (AWM)

27 AWM: 4 23/40/34. War Diary of 23rd Battalion, Battalion Order No. 123, 3 July 1918.

> You have never waited for a barrage to open, so have not experienced the absorbing anxiety of those minutes. Everything was as still as death with the intermittent brilliancy of the Huns flares. He fired no rounds. Every minute or so Moss would say: 'Shortie, what's the time?' I would say 'ten to three' and so on. Suddenly at 3 a.m. our guns opened up with harassing fire on every battery gun of the enemy. The intense subdued excitement seemed to radiate through the air. And at 3:10 a leaping line of flame burst on the enemy trenches. The scene was enthralling and tremendous. The din nigh-well intolerable.[28]

The artillery barrage included smoke shells falling just in front of the enemy front line trench, which, according to a captured German officer, successfully 'deceived the Enemy as to the movement of the Attacking troops.'[29]

As the men advanced and fanned out onto the objective, gaps were inevitably created: D Company veered to the right as it tried to maintain touch with 25th Battalion; similarly, B Company found that both of its flanks were briefly 'in the air.' On the left, A Company successfully filtered into the gap, meeting very little resistance as they reached the objective. Captain Short confirms this:

> Everyone was making for their objective and the first German trenches. On our bit of sector he put up no fight. When we reached the front line every live Hun was out in a state of terror, like rabbits frightened to death. They wore no equipment and carried no rifles or gas helmets. They must have been sleeping or chatting when our barrage fell on them. After that, their minds must have been a blank. Yet their machine guns were untouched and determined men could have given us a very rough time.[30]

Captain Moss had successfully led his men onto the objective, taking 60 prisoners in the process. He then reconnoitred 200 yards further forward, under fire, and subsequently moved the line to a more commanding position.[31]

Short goes on to tell of the death of an officer of C Company, Second Lieutenant Breen. In Short's version, Breen threw a grenade, but a German picked it up and threw it back, killing the unfortunate Australian. The Red Cross report on Breen contains various versions of events, each slightly different.[32] It was a tragic end for the former A Company sergeant who had won the MM at Westhoek, Belgium, on 21 September 1917 and had just returned to the battalion from officer training, having gained his commission on 1 June 1918.

28 AWM: 2018.19.46. Letters of Captain Lionel Gordon Short, 23rd Battalion.
29 AWM: 4 23/40/34. War Diary 23rd Battalion.
30 AWM: 2018.19.46. Letters of Captain Lionel Gordon Short, 23rd Battalion.
31 Captain Richard George Moss was awarded the MC for his actions on 4 July. He went on to command the 37th Battalion as lieutenant colonel in the inter-war years.
32 Australian Red Cross Society Wounded & Missing Enquiry Bureau files 1914-1918. 1DRL/0428: Second Lieutenant Gordon Breen MM. 23rd Battalion. There are eighteen 'eye-witness' versions of events. All differ slightly. The four most-commonly-offered alternatives are: 1) Breen threw a grenade at what he thought was a dug out, but it turned out to be a water-proof sheet, from which the bomb rebounded. 2) He lifted the cover of what he thought was a dug out, but this turned out to be a shallow scrape in the side of the trench. His grenade therefore exploded very close to him. 3) He threw the grenade into a dug out, but it rolled back out. 4) He hit the wooden frame of a dug out entrance with his throw and the grenade bounced back. Whichever is true, he was killed by his own grenade. He is buried in Villers-Bretonneux Military Cemetery, grave X.E.5.

Above: Second Lieutenant Gordon Breen, C Company, 23rd Battalion. (AWM)

Right: Breen's Headstone. (Author)

Both B and D Companies encountered more determined resistance from the defenders, each, once on the objective, having to bomb their way southwards along the German trench to gain touch with the units on their right. The actions of two individuals, both resulting in gallantry awards, will serve as examples of the nature of the fight. As was often the case at this stage of the war, it was the German machine gunners who continued to put up the most stubborn resistance.

Lieutenant Sydney Hodgson, commanding D Company, was awarded a Military Cross for his actions on 4 July. His recommendation reads:

> During the attack at VILLERS BRETONNEUX on 4.7.18 this Officer led his Company with dash. Immediately on leaving the J.O.T. he was severely wounded, but went on. He was again wounded on reaching the objective, but finding the enemy on his flank had not been mopped up he organised and led a bombing section, cleared the gap and joined up with the flank unit. He remained on duty for some time under heavy fire until the enemy resistance was overcome and completed the consolidation of the new line before being evacuated. Lieut. HODGSON displayed great courage and grit.
>
> (Signed) C.H. BRAND, Brigadier General Commanding 4th Australian Division.'

Lieutenant Summers had also led his platoon onto the objective, but their advance had been held up briefly by machine gun fire from a German strong point: Summers and his men stormed the position, capturing two machine guns and fifteen prisoners, he himself having shot five of the enemy.[33]

33 Lieutenant Walter Olveston Summers was also awarded the MC for his actions on 4 July. He survived the fighting, but was sadly killed in an accident on 28 December 1918 when the 23rd

With the Australians now firmly established in the German front line trench, some survivors of the garrison attempted to retreat through the tall crops growing in the fields behind their trenches. 'The active use of Lewis guns by HOSING FIRE' brought many of them down as they did so,[34] but it was clear that the cover provided by the crops allowed a substantial number to evade both the tanks and the Australian bullets.

Two of the tanks supporting the attack in this sector (from C Company, 13th Tank Battalion) caught up with the infantry on the objective line and then continued forward to deal with enemy posts beyond the German trench. Second Lieutenant Dower's machine, a female tank of No. 12 Section, after dealing with a number of machine gun posts in front of B Company's positions, became ditched. His crew, along with a group of German prisoners gathered by Dower himself, set about digging the tank out.

Ahead of D Company, one German machine gun nest, about 50 yards from their right front, was proving particularly troublesome. Lieutenant Berry's tank was diverted southwards to deal with it: 'Berry,… finding that the Infantry were embarrassed by a post in front of the objective, led his tank on foot to attack it. He shot with his revolver the crew of a machine gun which he captured and carried back himself to his tank.'[35]

It would appear that the third tank deployed in this sector (Second Lieutenant Hulton) was delayed by mechanical problems and was only able to return 'home' once the Company Engineer, Second Lieutenant Kay, had brought forward a spare part and effected a repair under constant shell fire. Each tank carried forward two boxes of ammunition, filled Lewis gun magazines and tins of drinking water for the infantry. All three tanks were able to return to the rallying point early that evening.

The next task for the infantry was to consolidate the captured trenches. B and D Companies had captured almost undamaged trenches and were therefore able to construct fire steps in the German parapet quite rapidly. A Company formed a series of half-platoon posts along their sector. Lewis gun posts were pushed out along the whole line, about 50 yards in front of the objective, and by 4:00 a.m., two Vickers machine guns had been brought forward and a post established at P.26.b.3.8. (See Map 3). The enemy made no attempts to hinder this work, and one company was able to move the existing German wire across the trench and reposition it to their advantage. York Street communication trench was also successfully extended – dug to a depth of three feet – to meet the new front line. Ammunition was dropped from an aircraft within a 'few yards of our trench.'[36]

The only apparent disappointment that morning was the performance of the light trench mortars: the 23rd Battalion after-action report states that 'Although [eight] 3' Stokes mortars

Battalion were in Belgium. 'He was dedetonating two nose caps when by some means one exploded, killing Lt Summers instantly.' AWM: 4 23/40/39 War Diary 23rd Battalion, December 1918. He was buried in Haies Communal Cemetery, Nalinnes. His body was exhumed on 24 November 1964 and he was reburied in Cement House Cemetery, grave XX.A.20. Somehow in the move, his date of death was wrongly transcribed as 29 December.

34 AWM: 4 23/40/34. War Diary 23rd Battalion.

35 TNA: WO95/115/2. 'History of the 13th Tank Battalion.' Chapter 4. Second Lieutenant T. Dower received an MC for his actions on 4 July 1918. Berry did not. Dower was wounded and taken prisoner on 8 August 1918, the first day of the Battle of Amiens. Berry was killed on the evening of 4 July by a bomb dropped by a German aircraft on the Tank Battalion's rallying point at around 10:30 p.m. Three more officers and three other ranks were also killed in the incident. (See below).

36 AWM: 4 23/40/34. War Diary 23rd Battalion.

were engaged on portion of enemy trench not covered by Artillery fire,... they did not get on to Target.... Stokes mortars were, owing to impossible view of target, unable to register and had work by Map reference only.'[37] As mentioned above, however, the silver lining to this cloud was the fact that the undamaged trenches could be reversed and consolidated very quickly.

The operation had resulted in 80 to 90 prisoners being captured, along with three heavy and 11 light German machine guns. It was estimated that between 60 and 80 Germans had been killed, most of them in the corn fields as they tried to escape.

No counterattacks were attempted by the Germans in this sector, and Lieutenant Colonel Brazenor, accompanied by Lieutenant Lowe, who had acted as liaison officer with 21st Battalion during the attack, was able to make 'an extended reconnaissance' of the captured area the same morning.[38] Another incursion into No Man's Land, under sniper and machine gun fire by the CO the following day, led him to push the newly-won positions out a further 200 yards, again with no reply from the Germans. These acts, combined with his prominent leadership displayed during the initial assault, earned Brazenor a Bar to his DSO.

Initial casualty figures for 23rd Battalion – reported on 6 July – are too low: they enumerate one officer and nine other ranks killed, with four officers and 61 other ranks wounded. Commonwealth War Graves Commission records show 18 fatalities for the battalion up to and including 6 July.

* * *

On the left flank of 6th Brigade, the 21st Battalion had, at least on paper, the most difficult task assigned to the brigade: a 1,000-yard advance due east, crossing two German trench lines before establishing themselves in a third, with one company forming a south-facing defensive flank in order to maintain their link with 23rd Battalion on the right. (See Maps 2 & 3.)

The battalion lined up with A Company (Lieutenant W.H. Roberts) on the right – and thus responsible for the defensive flank – C Company (Captain M.B. Kelly) in the centre, and D Company (Captain P.T. Hurrey) on the left. The attack was to be made in two waves: the first deployed in two lines, 15 yards apart; the second would start off in artillery formation, extending into lines when the company commander deemed it necessary. Both waves would make for the final objective.

B Company (Lieutenant H.N. Garton) were in support: they were to follow the second wave as closely as possible as far as the trench system in square P.20.d. (see map), carrying ammunition, grenades, tools, water and stretchers. They were to form a defensive flank facing north should the attack on their left by 13th Battalion (4th Brigade) prove unsuccessful.

At 10:30 a.m. on 3 July, the 21st Battalion commanding officer, Lieutenant Colonel Duggan DSO, who had been taken ill during the previous night, was evacuated to the rear battalion HQ at Lamotte. Major A.E. Reed took over command. Using his surname as the code word, the battalion was able to wire Brigade HQ at 2:55 a.m. on the 4th, to confirm that all units were assembled on the jumping off tapes. These tapes were actually just behind the Australian front line trench, in order to keep the waiting infantry far enough back from the artillery start line.

37 AWM: 4 23/40/34. War Diary 23rd Battalion.
38 AWM: 4 23/40/34. War Diary 23rd Battalion.

The men would cross the trench on duck boards and then negotiate the gaps that had been cut in their wire before deploying into their battle formations.

Three tanks from 13th Tank Battalion were making their way forward to support the attack. One of them would go forward with B Company, ready to replace either of the front two should they become casualties. Twenty-two machine guns and eight trench mortars would add their weight to the artillery barrage.

Confidence was, it seems, high: in a document entitled 'Notes to Accompany 21st Aust. Bn Order No. 155', issued on 3 July and compiled by the battalion adjutant, Lieutenant J.L. Watt, the last paragraph reads: 'A complete German Rifle and Equipment is required for the War Museum. All ranks are also reminded that souvenirs – either our own or the enemy's – will be gladly received at this depot. These articles are placed to the credit of the Battalion.'[39]

At 3:02 a.m. precisely, the harassing fire from the artillery fell on the German positions. Major Reed, in his after-action report, hints that this was perhaps too intense as it solicited an early response from the enemy, who almost immediately sent up SOS signals, concluding that 'it is doubtful whether it would be wise to adopt this system in future operations.'[40] The German artillery response – which was not heavy – fell largely behind the advancing Australians. The German front-line garrison had demanded a counter barrage from their artillery, but this was 'extremely limited, as they were still in the process of completing the relief.'[41]

So, at 3:10 a.m., as the artillery barrage proper began, 'the waves got away in splendid style.'[42] The German response turned out to be very limited: 'The two leading waves did not encounter any serious opposition when passing the enemy trenches in P.20.a and d.... Very little enemy wire was encountered.'[43]

On the right flank, A Company 'made a fair start' and 'we got over our old front line and through our wire without any bother.'[44] The attack had clearly surprised the German garrison: Roberts continues the narrative: 'From then on the advance simply developed into following up the barrage and clearing up the two German trenches between us and our objective, and a few odd small shelters – most of which proved to be full of Germans. Excepting for slight machine gun fire, 'A' Company met with no resistance.'[45]

The advance was so swift, and enemy retaliation so weak, that most of the A Company men swept on past their objective 'and had excellent sniping of the enemy as he moved back',[46] Lewis gun fire proving particularly effective. The officers soon recalled their perhaps over-eager charges onto the objective line and, after advanced Lewis gun posts had been sorted out, consolidation could begin.

The assault had not been totally trouble-free: 150 yards into No Man's Land, at the first German outpost line, two Germans surrendered to Private Gilbert and two of his colleagues. As Gilbert went forward to accept the surrender, one of the Germans threw a grenade,

39 AWM: 4 23/38/35 War Diary 21st Battalion.
40 AWM: 4 23/38/35 War Diary 21st Battalion, Appendix No. 9, 'Report on Offensive Operations carried out on 4.7.1918.'
41 Riebensahm, *Infanterie-Regiment 15*, p.346.
42 AWM: 4 23/38/35 War Diary 21st Battalion.
43 AWM: 4 23/38/35 War Diary 21st Battalion.
44 AWM: 4 23/38/35 War Diary 21st Battalion, Report by Lieutenant W.H. Roberts, OC A Coy.
45 AWM: 4 23/38/35 War Diary 21st Battalion, Report by Lieutenant W.H. Roberts, OC A Coy.
46 AWM: 4 23/38/35 War Diary 21st Battalion, Report by Lieutenant W.H. Roberts, OC A Coy.

wounding him in the abdomen. His comrades promptly shot the two Germans, and Gilbert was evacuated to No. 47 Casualty Clearing Station. Unfortunately, Gilbert's wound was pronounced inoperable, and he succumbed to his wounds later that day.[47]

Once it became clear that the Australians had no intention of advancing any further, German snipers became active, particularly on the right flank. One unfortunate victim was one of A Company's Lewis gunners, Lance Corporal Oke: he was helping to consolidate the newly-won trench and 'placed his hand on top of his shovel to have a spell in a resting attitude' and he was looking over the parapet when he was hit in the head and killed instantly.[48]

The grave of Private David Charles Gilbert, 21st Battalion. (Author)

CSM George Campbell Hunt DCM, 21st Battalion. (AWM)

47 AWM: 4. 1DRL/0428. Australian Red Cross Society Wounded and Missing Enquiry Bureau Files. Reported by 6477 Pte W.H. Chapple. 6808 Private David Charles Gilbert is buried in Crouy British Cemetery, grave III.B.8

48 AWM: 4. 1DRL/0428. Australian Red Cross Society Wounded and Missing Enquiry Bureau Files. 3979 Lance Corporal Norman Richard 'Okey' Oke is buried in Crucifix Corner Cemetery, grave IX.A.23. Buried alongside him are 6131 Pte Frederick Smith, grave IX.A.21, 153 Sergeant Major George Campbell Hunt DCM, IX.A.22, and 6821A Pte John Thomas Hart, IX.A.24, all of whom were originally buried together in a single grave in a shell hole near where they fell.

The graves of Private F. Smith, Company Sergeant Major G.C. Hunt, Lance Corporal N.R. Oke, Private J.T. Hart, all 21st Battalion. (Author)

A sniping duel soon developed; 4446 Private Johanson and his mate – and fellow sniper – 4357 Private Jack Arthur were firing at the enemy positions when a German sniper hit Johanson in the head. Arthur carried his comrade back so that he could be evacuated by a couple of stretcher bearers, but Johanson died of his wound. Arthur returned to his position and continued firing. He claimed four hits and was later recommended for the MM.[49] Trench Mortars were brought up, and several shells were lobbed onto the known German sniper positions, bringing a halt to this deadly game.

The enemy was still initially in possession of the small trench system immediately to the south of A Company's positions (Square P.26.b.), but after about 30 minutes, the Germans withdrew, and a block was established in the communication trench leading to it. It seems likely that this German position had been held by *Sergeant* Harre and his men of *1. Kompanie*, *IR 15*, who had been sent forward as the Australian attack developed. 'After steadfast resistance, he was encircled by superior forces, [and] overpowered.'[50] A similar fate awaited a platoon led by *Feldwebel-Leutnant* Möller,[51] this unit being echeloned to the rear on the right flank: they 'held out for some time, but [were] eventually forced to withdraw as [they] were threatened with encirclement on the right.'[52] A patrol under Second Lieutenant Weir was sent down to inves-

49 4446 Pte Gustaf 'Gus' Johanson, born in Norway, has no known grave and is commemorated on the Villers-Bretonneux Memorial.
50 Riebensahm, *Infanterie-Regiment 15*, p.347.
51 A rank given only to depot or garrison troops.
52 Riebensahm, *Infanterie-Regiment 15*, p.347.

tigate the system, and a wounded German officer and one other rank were found and brought back. According to Lieutenant Roberts, A Company sent back around 30–35 prisoners, and suffered a total of 18 casualties, four killed, 10 wounded, and four missing.

The men of C Company, in the centre of the battalion line, having waited patiently and silently on the jumping off tapes for 45 minutes, encountered only enemy wire as they crossed the first two German trench lines. Captain Kelly reported 'no opposition' and having taken 'a few prisoners',[53] his men were able to bypass a number of unmanned machine gun nests. Machine gunners in the third German line had time to man one of their guns before the Australians arrived. The smoke/gas ruse had clearly worked here, as it was noticed that the machine gun crew were wearing gas masks. They did not hold C Company up for long: one machine gunner was killed, two were wounded, and three taken prisoner as the position was 'soon overcome.'[54] The final objective was occupied, and consolidation began. A block was quickly constructed in the communication trench that snaked off to the east, and a patrol sent along it later found a '*Minenwerfer*' position with four guns, about 500 yards from their new line. The patrol bagged 15 prisoners, but were unable to retrieve the guns straight away, as German snipers were active in the area.

Two Vickers machine guns and two Stokes mortars were quickly brought forward and positioned in the 'new' front line. Aeroplanes from 3 Squadron made two successful ammunition drops by parachute just behind the objective line,[55] and the two tanks that had accompanied the advance had continued onwards and were by now patrolling between the objective line and the line of the protective artillery barrage. One of these, clearly exceeding his brief, was seen later heading in the direction of Warfusée, some 1,000 yards further on, engaging any enemy posts that they encountered. 'Apparently he enjoyed himself thoroughly out there and ultimately returned safely.'[56]

Captain Kelly reported only light casualties – six men wounded and three missing. At 4:16 a.m., he was able to telephone battalion HQ and report 'All C Coy Officers OK. Very few casualties. In a good trench on objective and consolidated. Am getting in touch with both flanks.'[57]

On the extreme left of 6th Brigade's frontage, D Company of 21st Battalion were disturbed just before Zero by some of their own artillery shells falling short. Luckily, they fell just behind their lines. As soon as the barrage lifted, 'their' tank advanced ahead of the infantry, 'close up to, and in the barrage.'[58]

Once more, the Germans put up very little resistance. Indeed, 'numerous posts [were found] deserted.'[59] Only once did a German machine gunner remain at his post, and his bravery cost him his life. As consolidation of the final objective began, the tank patrolled ahead of the new

53 AWM: 4 23/38/35 War Diary 21st Battalion. Report by Captain M.B. Kelly, OC C Coy.
54 AWM: 4 23/38/35 War Diary 21st Battalion. Report by Captain M.B. Kelly, OC C Coy.
55 Probably RE8 B6462, with pilot Lt R. Neall and observer Lt S. Chandler at around 7:00 a.m., and RE8 B5098, with pilot Lt G. Milner and observer Lt A. Porteus somewhere between 9:30 and 10:00 a.m.
56 AWM: 4 23/38/35 War Diary 21st Battalion. Appendix No. 9, 'Report on Offensive Operations carried out on 4.7.1918.'
57 AWM: 4 23/38/35 War Diary 21st Battalion.
58 AWM: 4 23/38/35 War Diary 21st Battalion. Report by Captain W.H. Taylor OC D Coy. The original Officer Commanding D Coy, Captain P.T. Hurrey, was wounded during the advance and Capt. Taylor took over.
59 AWM: 4 23/38/35 War Diary 21st Battalion.

front line, 'silencing strong points' almost as far as Accroche Wood.[60] A German account referring to the tanks and the general Australian advance puts a different slant on events:

> A tank suddenly appeared to the rear of No. 1 and No 3 Companies and fired into their positions from behind. The *Batl.-Tambour* [Battalion Drum-Major], *Vizefeldwebel* Schumicki, as cool-headed as he always was, let it approach to within 30 metres and then fired at it with his anti-tank rifle, whereupon it disappeared.... The majority of No 3 Company had not let the tank distract them from the advancing infantry, and scrambled up the embankment and met them, along with No 1 Company, with well-aimed rifle fire. At this, Tommy [sic][61] disappeared into shell craters and the high crop. The enemy attacked again, but was repulsed in like fashion and withdrew to our abandoned main resistance line.[62]

The only other hindrance to D Company's advance came, it seems, from a group of about 20 American soldiers attached to 13th Battalion on the left, who strayed across into 21st Battalion territory and 'caused a certain amount of crowding',[63] arriving on the objective mixed up with the Australians. The doughboys were only too happy to help D Company with the consolidation of the new front line before returning to 'their' sector later in the day.

Private Karl Sainsbury Rochstein, 21st Battalion. (AWM)

During consolidation, work was hampered by German sniper fire coming from a communication trench. Corporal Garland, No. 1 in his Lewis gun team, rushed out under fire with his gun and forced the snipers to withdraw. He continued to pursue them and killed or wounded several of them as they fled.[64]

B Company, the designated 'carriers', in support but keeping well up with the units in front, were overtaken by the tanks as they

60 AWM: 4 23/38/35 War Diary 21st Battalion.
61 The German account repeatedly refers to the attacking troops as 'English.'
62 Riebensahm, *Infanterie-Regiment 15*, p. 347. This account, in common with others referred to in later chapters, gives the impression that a deeper Australian advance had been thwarted, the Germans being unaware of the limited nature of the Australian plan. It tells of a command post at the crossroads of the Warfusée to Fouilloy and Hamel to Marcelcave roads being held courageously by runners, orderlies and communications personnel gathered together under Captain Preuschen. This post was beyond the Australian's final objective line.
63 AWM: 4 23/38/35 War Diary 21st Battalion. Report by Captain W.H. Taylor OC D Coy.
64 1545 Corporal Eugene Loftus Garland was recommended for the MM. Unfortunately, engaged in a similar operation on the following day, he was wounded in the abdomen and evacuated to No. 47 Casualty Clearing Station, where he died on 6 July. He is buried in Crouy British Cemetery, grave III.D.20. The MM was awarded posthumously.

approached the first German line. The tanks fired along the trench 'crushing all the spirit that the enemy may have had to fight.'[65]

One platoon – No. 8 – was left behind here to consolidate the trench line and establish machine gun posts. Unfortunately, a dozen or so Germans who had been 'missed' by D Company on the left flank 'started to bomb and snipe at us.'[66] Witnessed by Lieutenant Garton, commanding the company, Private J.M. Stewart immediately grabbed his rifle and ran forward alone, firing at this enemy group. He shot a couple of them and drove the rest back slightly. Within minutes, a group of his comrades had also advanced and surrounded the by now bewildered party of Germans, forcing them to surrender.[67] By the time Lieutenant Garton caught up with his front line platoons, they had already deposited their loads on the final objective and returned to the German second line – their objective – and were beginning to dig in. For the rest of the day, their work was disturbed only by a short spell of desultory shelling in the afternoon.

The advance of 21st Battalion had been rapid. With a telephone line having been successfully run out to the final objective, the first reports that it had been taken and that consolidation had begun reached battalion HQ just before 4:00 a.m. Major Reed's initial after-action report did not give an exact number of prisoners taken, stating merely that 'a considerable number were captured.' Many of them, coming from *IR 13, 15* and *137* 'appeared to be very young.'[68] Casualty figures were unsurprisingly low: six other ranks killed, with three more dying of their wounds, two officers and 43 other ranks wounded, four injured, and eight unaccounted for.[69]

Lieutenant H. Edwards DCM, MM, MC, 21st Battalion. (AWM)

Reed was later awarded the DSO for his leadership on 4 July. Second Lieutenant R.L. Weir received an MC, as did Lieutenant H. Edwards DCM MM. DCMs were awarded to 1742 Corporal G.W. Torney and 837 Private A.J. Dunn. Eleven members of the battalion received the MM.

The after-action report in the 6th Brigade war diary, sounding perhaps slightly disappointed, states that:

65 AWM: 4 23/38/35 War Diary 21st Battalion. Report by Lieutenant H.N. Garton, OC B Coy.
66 AWM: 4 23/38/35 War Diary 21st Battalion. Report by Lieutenant H.N. Garton, OC B Coy.
67 718A Pte J.M Stewart was awarded the MM for his actions.
68 AWM: 4 23/38/35 War Diary 21st Battalion. Appendix No. 9, 'Report on Offensive Operations carried out on 4.7.1918.'
69 AWM: 4 23/38/35 War Diary 21st Battalion. Appendix No. 9, 'Report on Offensive Operations carried out on 4.7.1918.' Commonwealth War Graves Commission figures for 21st Battalion, 4 – 6 July 1918, show 16 fatalities.

> There was too little fighting for many of the enemy to be killed and the number of German corpses lying in the captured ground after the attack was probably between 60 and 90.
>
> On the right a large number of Germans who had either escaped from the front line when it was attacked or had been in supporting positions behind it, were observed to run Eastwards into our barrage, after it had passed over them, before the German second line had been reached on the left. A large number of casualties must have been suffered by them, not only from Artillery, but also from rifle and L.G. fire. Later the same thing happened on the left when the final objective was reached there.[70]

Brigade casualty figures for the day were given as one officer killed, and six wounded, 16 other ranks killed, and 101 wounded.[71]

C.E.W. Bean, in the Australian *Official History*, goes perhaps a little too far when he describes the advance of 6th Brigade thus: 'Here progress assumed the ease of a field day.'[72] It was, however, over quite quickly: 'On the whole of the southern flank the final objective was attained before the barrage reached its ten-minutes halt line.'[73]

70 AWM: 4. 23/6/35 Part 1. War Diary 6 Brigade, Appendix X, 'Preliminary Report on Operations of 6th A.I. Bde on 4-7-1918.'
71 AWM: 4. 23/6/35 Part 1. War Diary 6 Brigade, Appendix X, 'Preliminary Report on Operations of 6th A.I. Bde on 4-7-1918.' CWGC figures show one officer fatality and 33 other ranks. Two officers and 24 other ranks from 25th Battalion, 7th Brigade, can be added, giving an overall total for the right flank attack of 3 officers and 57 other ranks.
72 Bean, *The Official History*, vol.VI, p.297.
73 Bean, *The Official History*, vol.VI, p.299.

3

The Attack of 4th Brigade

If, at the start of July 1918, a soldier had had the temerity to stand on the parapet of the Australian front line trench in broad daylight somewhere near the centre of 4th Brigade's frontage, he would have had a panoramic view, from his elevated position near the Vaire to Villers-Bretonneux road, of almost the entire battlefield. Between 2,000 and 3,000 yards away, directly in front, ran the ridge, the spine of which marked the brigade's final objective. It ran roughly south-west to north-east, gradually diminishing in height as it stretched northwards, before climbing again, this time more abruptly, to the heights of the 'Wolfsberg' behind Hamel village. Its capture would allow the Australians to overlook German positions in Accroche Wood and beyond. Directly in the way, however, stood what was left of Vaire Wood,[1] with the German front line, including the 'Kidney Trench' redoubt, just to the west of it.

The assumption that fighting *through* the wood would prove to be a relatively slow and arduous process led to the development of a plan of attack that would see the wood enveloped in a double pincer movement to the north and south, requiring the central battalion of the brigade to advance as far as its eastern edge and no further. This task was allotted to the 16th Battalion. On their right, to the south, 13th Battalion would squeeze through the narrow gap between the brigade boundary and the southern edge of the wood before performing a tricky manoeuvre that would then enable them, after the artillery pause, to fan out and occupy the final objective as far north as 'Hun's Walk.' (See Map 4). On the left, to the north, 15th Battalion would move down into the valley, having eliminated the German strongpoint at Pear Trench, skirting the northern edge of the wood and thence up the gentler slope to the objective line. The 14th Battalion would be in reserve and carry stores and supplies forward as required, before digging a support line 500 yards behind the final objective. The 16th Battalion, having completed its task, would then be withdrawn to the original Australian front line. On paper, it all looked very simple: 'the 4th Australian Infantry Brigade will capture VAIRE and HAMEL WOODS and consolidate on the spur East of those woods.'[2]

What is clear from the brigade war diary is that the men would not be short of essential battle supplies: on 1 July at the Rear Brigade Headquarters, they were issued – across the brigade

1 Vaire and Hamel Woods are contiguous. For ease of expression, the author will use 'Vaire Wood' to indicate this entire wooded area unless circumstances require a more accurate nomenclature.
2 AWM: 4 23/4/34 Part 1. War Diary 4th Infantry Brigade.

– with 350,000 rounds of small arms ammunition, in excess of 10,000 grenades of various sorts, along with the 900 picks, 900 shovels and 7,000 empty sandbags vital for consolidation. In addition, two supply tanks, one for 13th Battalion, the other for 15th Battalion, would bring up barbed wire, screw pickets, corrugated iron, water, trench mortar bombs and more ammunition. A further 200,000 rounds, 4,500 grenades and more barbed wire, pickets and sandbags were to be carried forward by the men of 14th Battalion.

These figures do not include the extra small arms ammunition carried in the fighting tanks or dropped by parachute by 9 Squadron RAF. Each infantryman would go into the attack carrying 220 rounds, two grenades, one pick or one shovel, and three sandbags.

On 1 July 1918, 4th Brigade's total strength was reported as 178 officers and 3,490 other ranks.[3] Only 13th and 15th Battalions retained a number of attached American troops, the majority having been withdrawn (including all of those with 16th Battalion)[4] at the last minute on General Pershing's orders. The loss of these men was felt by both nationalities: 'Received order during morning to send the two Companies of AMERICANS back to reserve. The GOC UNITED STATES ARMY being unwilling for them to take part in active operations. Most of the AMERICANS very hurt at having to go back, but there was no help for it.'[5]

The attack of 4th Brigade was, of course, to be supported by tanks: a total of four sections from B Company (Major G.A. Grounds DSO), 8th Tank Battalion, were allocated to this frontage. One section (No. 5 Section under Lieutenant I.C.A. Glanville MC) would be attached to 15th Battalion and would skirt Vaire Wood to the north and 'protect them by keeping down enemy fire from the wood – to cut off and isolate the wood, and then push on with the Infy to Blue Line.'[6] One tank from this section was tasked with working along 'Hun's Walk', denying its use to the enemy.[7] No. 8 Section under Captain Edwards would complete a similar manoeuvre to the south of the wood with 13th Battalion. The initial advance by the tanks was not entirely smooth:

> As we raced forward, the moon not having come out, it was quite dark. One tank went straight down a 10 foot drop which in the dark the driver could not see and the back of his driver's seat hit him in the middle of his back making him hors de combat, so much so they had to remove him from driving and laid him at the back of the tank till the engagement ended.[8]

In the centre, 16th Battalion would be accompanied by two sections of tanks (No. 6, Captain W.H. Viveash and No. 7, Captain E.A.H. Jones). They were to assist in the capture and mopping up of Vaire Wood and were then to remain in place 'until the Infy are firmly established.'[9] To assault the front line German trench system in front of Vaire Wood, two tanks would work

3 AWM: 4 23/4/34 Part 1. War Diary 4th Infantry Brigade.
4 On 1 July, two companies – G and H – of the 131st Regiment of 33rd Division had joined the 16th Battalion.
5 AWM: 4 23/33/32 Part 1. War Diary 16th Battalion. 3 July 1918.
6 TNA:PRO WO95/114-3. War Diary 8th Tank Battalion.
7 Hun's Walk is a German Communication Trench leading back from Vaire Wood to Accroche Wood. See Map.
8 Bovington Tank Museum: E2102.4678. Private papers of Sergeant Edwin Bond, 8th Tank Battalion.
9 TNA: WO95/114-3. War Diary 8th Tank Battalion.

around each flank and then turn either north or south to get between the trench and the wood, the remaining two attacking frontally.

Pear Trench was singled out for special attention. One section of A Company, 8th Tank Battalion (No.1 Section, Captain C.E. Scott) would 'subdue' this strongpoint before continuing to the Blue Line with the infantry, along with the rest of A Company (Major E.D. Blackburn DSO MC).[10]

An additional nine tanks would move forward along the northern brigade boundary, ready to assist – one section to 'accompany liaising infantry and assist liaising sections in mopping up trenches and M.G. posts',[11] the other two sections would be 'nominally in reserve to replace casualties prior to Zero',[12] but in reality they joined the attack on the Blue Line.

'Preliminary Instructions' were issued to the tank crews on 1 July 1918, stating that:

> It is the primary duty of tanks to save casualties to the Aust. Infantry and as this cannot be done so long as tanks remain in rear of them, Tank Commanders must do their utmost to get in between the infantry and the Artillery barrage whenever possible.
>
> Opportunities will occur to do this, and Tank Commanders must keep a sharp look out for any point where the Infantry are held up or the barrage appears to be running away from them.

The following advice was also added: 'Belts of wire should be crossed as nearly as possible at right angles, and on no account must tanks be 'swung' when halfway through, otherwise they may become completely enveloped.' Paragraph 12 states: 'In the event of infantry being held up, and requiring assistance, they will signal to Tanks by placing a steel helmet on top of the rifle – and will then indicate the position of the strongpoints by firing a phosphorous grenade in the direction.'[13]

At 2:59 a.m. on 4 July, with all tanks having been at their assembly points since the night of 2/3 July and having moved up to their forming up lines between 23:45 p.m. and 1:15 a.m. the following night, 'all tank engines were swung up punctually and at 3.2 a.m. every tank started [forward] without exception.'[14]

* * *

The men of 16th Battalion (Lieutenant Colonel E.A. Drake-Brockman) lined up on a battalion frontage of around 800 yards in two waves on the assembly tapes – 150 yards from the Zero artillery barrage line – as follows: right to left were A Company (Major R. Harwood), then C Company (Captain F.F. Woods), B Company (Captain H.A.F. Wilkinson) and finally D Company (Captain W.J.D. Lynas MC & 2 Bars).

As they lay there, aircraft were buzzing overhead and dropping bombs on enemy positions, this to disguise the noise of the tanks' approach. As the planes had been doing this on and off

10 TNA: WO95/114-3. War Diary 8th Tank Battalion.
11 TNA: WO95/114-3. War Diary 8th Tank Battalion.
12 TNA: WO95/114-3. War Diary 8th Tank Battalion.
13 TNA: WO95/114-3. War Diary 8th Tank Battalion.
14 TNA: WO95/114 – 5. 8th Tank Battalion War History, p.36.

for a fortnight, the enemy seemed unaware that anything out of the ordinary was about to take place. Would the element of surprise be maintained? 'It seemed, however, to the diggers of the 16th… that every German in France must be able to hear the clanging and grinding of these fearsome engines of war as they made their way on to the line of assembly.'[15]

Lieutenant Colonel Edmund Alfred Drake-Brockman, CO 16th Battalion. (AWM)

The Vaire Wood sector was defended by the men of *Infanterie Regiment 13, (1. Westfälisches).* On a 1,200-metre frontage, they occupied three defensive lines: one to the west of Vaire Wood; the '*Hauptwiderstandslinie*' (main line of resistance) running south-west to north-east just to the east of it; and the support line just to the west of the Hamel to Marcelcave road, the latter being beyond the Australians' final objective. *IR 13* had relieved *IR 419* during the nights of 1/2, 2/3 and 3/4 July. 'The relief was barely complete when… a surprise attack was directed against the regiment.'[16] The *1. Bataillon* held the front line, with *3. Bataillon* in support and *2. Bataillon* back in reserve near Proyart.

The full fury of the artillery barrage fell at Zero: 'So far as the Front of the Battalion was concerned, the Barrage was generally speaking good. There were a few cases of short shooting and a few casualties were inflicted, but nothing beyond what is normally expected on these occasions.'[17]

It was possibly one of these high explosive 'shorts' that blew Captain Lynas off his feet as he stood on the jumping off tape, ready to lead D Company forward into the attack. Lieutenant Klopper rushed across from the neighbouring platoon to assist his company commander, but, bleeding profusely from two wounds, Lynas refused to go back or even have his wounds treated. D Company's first wave had been 'thrown into some confusion by this shelling, [but he] set a magnificent example of coolness and unconcern under shell fire, despite the fact that he was… evidently suffering pain',[18] and restored some semblance of order before leading his men into the attack.

Accounts of the 16th Battalion assault are both scarce and brief: in the battalion war diary, the CO's 'Narrative of Operations' devotes only 15 lines of typescript to the actual attack and is short on detail:

15 Captain C. Longmore, *The Old Sixteenth. Being a Record of the 16th Battalion AIF during the Great War 1914-1918* (Perth: History Committee of the 16th Battalion Association, 1929), p.181.
16 Carl Groos & Werner von Rudloff, *Infanterie-Regiment Herwarth von Bittenfeld (1. Westfälisches) Nr. 13 im Weltkriege 1914-1918* (Oldenburg & Berlin: Verlag Gerhard Stalling, 1927), p.306.
17 AWM: 4 23/33/32 Part 1. War Diary 16th Battalion.
18 AWM: 4 23/33/32 Part 1. War Diary 16th Battalion. Report by Second Lieutenant Taylor.

> Strong resistance was experienced in the first system of trenches on the west side of VAIRE Wood. This however was quickly overcome and a number of prisoners and machine guns captured. Numerous centres of resistance and machine gun nests were encountered in both VAIRE and HAMEL Woods and on the outskirts of these woods. All these posts were however readily dealt with by Infantry and Tanks… The whole of VAIRE and HAMEL Woods were mopped up and some 400 prisoners, 23 machine guns and 3 Minenwerfers were collected within an hour and a half of the commencement of the operation.[19]

Captain William James Dalton Lynas, 16th Battalion. (AWM)

The account of this part of the battle in the German regimental history is equally brief: 'The forward companies of *1. Bn IR 13* (2., 3. and 4.), whose numbers had been seriously weakened during the previous few days by the current influenza epidemic, put up a courageous defence, but were, after heavy fighting, overrun by superior forces.'[20]

To add detail, from the Australian point of view, it is necessary to examine the very few extant scribbled messages sent back during the operation, Red Cross reports, and recommendations for gallantry awards.

On the right of the battalion frontage, A Company, led by Major Ross Harwood, seems to have completed their task with very little trouble: two accounts of the actions of individuals will serve to demonstrate the kind of tactics used.

Major Ross Harwood, 16th Battalion. (AWM)

19 AWM: 4 23/33/32 Part 1. War Diary 16th Battalion. Appendix 2, 'Narrative of Operations carried out on the 4th July 1918.'

20 Groos & von Rudloff, *Infanterie-Regiment 13*, p.307.

Private Jack Johnston (7564) was advancing through the southern sector of Vaire Wood when a German machine gun nest that had been missed by the creeping barrage was brought into action:

> This nest was holding up and causing casualties to the Battalion on our right [13th Battalion]. JOHNSTON immediately appreciated the situation; screened the post with No. 27 Smoke Grenades, and then promptly rushed it; followed by several of his men; capturing three machine guns and killing and capturing the whole of the crews. He personally killed at least five enemy.[21]

Tasked with maintaining touch between A and C Companies, 1977 Sergeant Jack Butler led his men through the wood 'quickly suppressing any opposition by the use of rifle, bombs and bayonet.'[22] Both of the above were awarded the Military Medal for their actions that day. Another MM went to stretcher bearer 7314 Private Randall James Trigwell:

> One of our men was struck by a phosphorous shell. TRIGWELL at once rushed to his assistance, although it necessitated penetrating the barrage: regardless of his own safety, he attended to the casualty, removed his clothing which was on fire, and subsequently carried him back to the Aid Post. He was himself severely burnt from contact with the phosphorous… He was evacuated later in the day suffering very seriously from his burns.[23]

The grave of Corporal Alexander Paterson Scott, 16th Battalion. (Author)

A Company came through the battle with 14 men wounded, including Lieutenant Broadbent, and only one fatality: 7191 Corporal Alexander Paterson Scott.[24]

A scribbled report, bordering on illegibility and timed at 4:05 a.m., was received at battalion HQ confirming that A Company was 'right out on our objective…. Am patrolling wood.'[25] It also reports that 13th Battalion was passing through to continue the attack.

On A Company's left, C Company (Captain Woods), were to lose 11 men killed during

21 AWM: 4 23/33/32 Part 1. War Diary 16th Battalion. Recommendations for Awards.
22 AWM: 4 23/33/32 Part 1. War Diary 16th Battalion.
23 AWM: 4 23/33/32 Part 1. War Diary 16th Battalion.
24 Scott is buried in Villers-Bretonneux Military Cemetery, grave XII F 7.
25 AWM: 4 23/33/32 Part 1. War Diary 16th Battalion. The officer's signature is unfortunately illegible.

their attack, by far the highest company casualty rate in the battalion. They came up against strong opposition from the German garrison in the German trench line west of Vaire Wood. Platoons met with mixed success, depending upon whether they found gaps in the enemy wire or came up against an intact section. In the first wave of the assault, Lieutenant Minchin entered the first German trench line, killed one officer and several men, capturing a machine gun, a Minenwerfer and 20 prisoners in the process. He then encountered a machine gun nest near the southern end of the copse in front of Vaire Wood and 'led his men in an impetuous charge. Some six of the enemy were killed, two of whom Lieutenant MINCHIN himself accounted for. The balance of the crews, also the guns were captured.'[26]

To the north, a Lewis gun section was struggling against uncut wire. This gave the Germans time to get a machine gun in Kidney Trench into action and inflict casualties on the unfortunate section. One of those killed there was C Company's commander, Captain Woods,[27] but it is likely that his wounds were caused by a German shell. The same shell accounted for five other men.[28] Also killed, a little further to the north, was Second Lieutenant Blee.[29]

Captain Frederick Frank Woods, C Company, 16th Battalion. (AWM)

Wood's headstone. (Author)

26 AWM: 4 23/33/32 Part 1. War Diary 16th Battalion. Recommendations for Awards. Lieutenant James Basil Minchin was awarded a bar to his Military Cross.

27 Captain Frederick Frank Woods, C Coy, born in Surrey, England, died of his wounds later that day in 13th Australian Field Ambulance having suffered wounds to both thighs. He is buried in Daours Communal Cemetery Extension, grave III D 37.

28 8070 Pte Joseph Beaver (Villers-Bretonneux Military Cemetery, XIII F 6), 3416 Pte Hugh Buckingham XII.F.5, 7140 Pte Colin Charles Storey (XII F 6), 3056 Pte Charles John Taylor (XII F 3) and 1457 CSM Harold Goldie Blinman (Daours Communal Cemetery Extension, III D 36).

29 Second Lieutenant Horace Edgar Blee. It is unclear whether he was killed by a shell or

Second Lieutenant Horace Edgar Blee, 16th Battalion. (AWM)

Blee's headstone. (Author)

This whole incident was witnessed by Lance Corporal Axford, a member of an adjacent platoon.

> Axford, with great initiative and magnificent courage, at once dashed to the flank, threw his bombs amongst the machine gun crews; followed up his bombs by jumping into the trench, and charging with his bayonet. Unaided he killed ten of the enemy and took six prisoners; he threw the machine guns over the parapet and called out to the delayed platoon to come on. He then rejoined his own platoon and fought with it during the remainder of the operations.[30]

Close to where Axford performed his heroic deed, the oldest man in the battalion, 64-year-old Private Charlie Hubbard, was severely wounded, hit by bullets in the back and neck. Paralysed, he fell to the ground.[31]

machine gun fire: there are conflicting reports in the Australian Red Cross files. Blee had joined the battalion as a private and had just returned from officer training in England. He is buried in Daours Communal Cemetery Extension, grave III D 38, alongside Captain Woods and CSM Blinman. The three men, buried together, had all been company sergeant majors together in 16th Battalion.

30 AWM: 4 23/33/32 Part 1. War Diary 16th Battalion. Recommendations for Awards. 3399 Lance Corporal Thomas Leslie Axford MM was awarded the Victoria Cross.

31 6830 Private Charlie Hubbard, an unmarried former miner, had lied about his age when he enlisted in late February 1917. He survived his wounds – the paralysis proved to be temporary – and returned

With Woods, the company commander, out of action, it fell to Lieutenant Minchin to take over. He successfully led C Company on to their final objectives and sent back a hand-written confirmation of their success to battalion HQ: 'C Coy completed task & mopped up wood. Captain Woods wounded & other casualties light. Awaiting orders at near edge of wood.'[32]

Minchin's excellent leadership and bravery had not gone unnoticed, as evidenced by the account already cited. This was backed up by Axford, a member of his own platoon, who wrote:

> Further on in the wood, we ran up against another machine gun post, and he personally led a few men and captured the guns and killed about six. I have been with the battalion since its arrival in France and in all the attacks the battalion had made. This piece of work is the bravest I have witnessed.[33]

Lance Corporal Thomas Leslie Axford, VC, MM. (AWM)

B Company's advance into Vaire Wood went very much to plan. Their commander, Captain (Hon. Major) Wilkinson, was first into the enemy defences and quickly realised the importance of securing the long communication trench known as Hun's Walk (See Map 4). He ordered bombing sections to work their way along it until they reached the eastern edge of Hamel Wood, a distance of about 1,000 yards. At one point, Wilkinson personally led a small group of his men in an attack on a German machine-gun nest that was threatening the advance of D Company on the extreme left of the battalion frontage, these having faced strong opposition and subsequently lost the barrage. Wilkinson captured two machine guns, killing or capturing the crews. By 4:05 a.m., he was able to send a written message back to HQ by runner, stating: 'Have reached P.15. c. 1.8 – without any casualties so far as known at present. Sent back about 20 prisoners – captured 2 Machine Guns. All OK.'[34]

B Company came out of the battle with 12 casualties, only two of them fatal.[35]

to Australia after the war. He died in November 1934, aged 81.

32 AWM: 4 23/33/32 Part 1. War Diary 16th Battalion.

33 AWM: 4 23/33/32 Part 1. War Diary 16th Battalion. Recommendations for Awards.

34 AWM: 4 23/33/32 Part 1. War Diary 16th Battalion. Recommendations for Awards.

35 5332 Pte Joseph Leonard Hennerty and 7753 Pte Thomas Henry Hill are both buried in Villers-Bretonneux Military Cemetery, graves XII B 4 and XIII E 1 respectively. According to the Red Cross report, Hennerty, 28, having advanced some 2,000 yards into Hamel Wood, got entangled in the German barbed wire and was then hit in the stomach by a rifle bullet. He was carried back to 13th

The grave of Private Joseph Leonard Hennerty, 16th Battalion. (Author)

The grave of Private Thomas Henry Hill, 16th Battalion. (Author)

Captain Lynas, commanding D Company on the left flank, later acknowledged that: 'it was entirely due to his [Wilkinson's] dash in leading his Company into the enemy front line system that we were enabled to come forward… without severe casualties.' With regard to the capture of Hun's Walk, Lynas continues: 'This communication sap and fire trench completely commanded the flank of my advance and it speaks for his dash and courage in negotiating same for me to state that I had no opposition at all from either this sap or the double junctions of sunken roads half way through the wood.'[36]

D Company was led forward by the already wounded Captain Lynas: he tried to keep his men as close to the creeping barrage as he could, but as mentioned above, the uphill slog through Vaire Wood saw them lag behind. As they continued into Hamel Wood, Lynas was wounded again, but once more refused treatment. Approaching the edge of the wood, they encountered a German company HQ dugout, which was stubbornly defended by a group of stretcher bearers, orderlies, and part of a reserve platoon. Lynas signalled to a tank for assistance, but before it could arrive on scene, someone lobbed a phosphorous grenade into the dugout: several of

Australian Field Ambulance but died about two hours later. Hill, 29 years old and born in Abbott's Bromley, Staffordshire, England, was a Lewis gunner and suffered a head wound just before reaching the western edge of Vaire Wood.

36 AWM: 4 23/33/32 Part 1. War Diary 16th Battalion.

the German garrison were killed, and the survivors immediately surrendered.[37] The company captured between 150 and 200 prisoners, along with eight machine guns and four Minenwerfers. Lynas was awarded the DSO for his outstanding leadership that day.[38] He was awarded the decoration during a battalion inter-company cricket match on 30 July, 'the recipient being loudly cheered.'[39] The company suffered 13 casualties on 4 July, only one of them fatal.[40] The battalion had completed its mopping up of Vaire Wood, and the companies were ordered to return to their original front and support line trenches, reaching them by just after 5:00 a.m.

The grave of Corporal George Ball, 16th Battalion. (Author)

The tactics employed had proven to be largely effective: leaning closely on the creeping barrage enabled German positions to be captured quickly, and Lewis gunners firing from the hip as they advanced added very effectively to the firepower of the platoon as they drove the enemy from their lairs, rather like a line of beaters going through a grouse wood. Two examples of award recommendations will demonstrate both aspects.

Two almost identical recommendations are recorded in the battalion war diary for 7811 Private Henry Howard Richardson and 7129 Private Eugene Oswald Roder:

> He is always well in the lead keeping close up to the barrage. When the barrage 'lifts' occurred, he was always the first to rush the enemy encountered. On several occasions he was so quickly into the enemy posts, and kept the crews of enemy machine guns so busy defending themselves from his personal onslaught, that they had no chance of getting their guns into action. He personally bayonetted several, and enabled his comrades to mop up the balance with a minimum of loss to our own troops.[41]

37 AWM: 38 3DRL606/190/1 Official History, 1914-18 War: Records of C.E.W.Bean, Official Historian. Diaries and Notebooks. Notebook 1915,1918, and Bean, *The Official History*, vol.VI, p.292.
38 Captain William James Dalton Lynas, born in Auckland, New Zealand, had previously earned the Military Cross with two Bars: at Pozières in August 1916; at Mouquet Farm later that same month; and near Hamel in June 1918. He survived the war.
39 AWM: 4 23/33/32 Part 1. War Diary 16th Battalion.
40 650 Corporal George Ball MM, 28 years old, is buried in Villers-Bretonneux Military Cemetery, grave XII A 5.
41 AWM: 4 23/33/32 Part 1. War Diary 16th Battalion. Recommendations for Awards.

Longmore sums up the tactic in his battalion history: 'When the German front line was seen through the smoke, the method was to throw bombs and after a short pause to allow for the burst, to rush it with the bayonet.'[42] Both men were awarded the Military Medal.[43]

The second example is Lewis gunner 7082 Private William Henry Taylor, who also received the Military Medal:

> He is No.1 of a Lewis Gun Crew. During the advance through Vaire Wood he behaved with great daring. He was constantly well in advance of his crew, firing his gun from the hip, and causing many casualties to the enemy. At one point the advance was temporarily held up by an enemy post. He rushed the post, killed the crew, captured the gun and enabled the advance to continue.[44]

Many of the Germans encountered were wearing gas masks, having fallen for the Australian ruse set up over the previous few days, and this, according to Lieutenant Colonel Drake-Brockman 'made the task of dealing with them very much easier.'[45]

No. 6 Section of B Company, 8th Tank Battalion, under Captain Viveash, had also played a significant part in the advance, tackling machine gun nests in the German front line positions, and in response to the infantry requesting assistance by firing their No. 27 grenades, 'on at least two occasions.'[46] Longmore, in 'The Old Sixteenth', reports that: 'The tanks did splendid work. Hopping off with the infantry, they cruised up and down close to, and sometimes in the barrage, machine gunning strong points, dispersing groups of the enemy, and generally preparing the way very effectively for the men behind them.'[47]

Advancing through the wooded areas was of course problematic for the tanks, but they were able to penetrate the woods by using the rides: 'excellent aeroplane photographs of Vaire Wood (oblique) were obtained shewing that the main ride was sufficiently good for tanks. It proved so and tanks passing up this ride were quite sufficient to clear out the enemy.'[48]

The 8th Tank Battalion war diary makes a clear distinction between the ordinary German infantry and their machine gun crews: the former all too often 'surrendered as soon as a tank made its appearance'; the machine gun crews were a different matter – 'enemy machine guns were captured and there are several instances of tanks going over MG & crew to silence it.'[49] The battalion's war history paints a similar picture:

> During the action… Tank Commanders found that in most cases the moral effect of the tank was sufficient to cause complete surrender with the exception of the machine gun

42 Longmore, *The Old Sixteenth*, p.183.
43 Richardson, sadly, did not live to receive his honour. He died of wounds, age 40, on 11 August 1918, as a lance corporal, having been shot in the head on 8 August, the first day of the Battle of Amiens. He is buried in Terlincthun British Cemetery, grave II B 4. Roder survived the war.
44 AWM: 4 23/33/32 Part 1. War Diary 16th Battalion. Recommendations for Awards.
45 Quoted in Bean, *The Official History*, vol.VI, p.291.
46 AWM: 4 23/33/32 Part 1. War Diary 16th Battalion. 'Narrative of Operations carried out on the 4th July 1918.'
47 Longmore, *The Old Sixteenth*, p.182.
48 TNA: WO95/112-5. 8th Tank Battalion War Experiences, p.35.
49 TNA: WO95/112-5. 8th Tank Battalion War Experiences, p.35.

Vaire Wood oblique aerial reconnaissance photograph. (AWM)

> crews, who showed extraordinary courage and tenacity, and refused to surrender, being completely wiped out or run over by the tank. There are innumerable cases of tanks running over and crushing MG emplacements and crews.[50]

The 16th Infantry Battalion, their day's work finished by 6:00 a.m., the wood having been thoroughly cleared and the men safely back in their original trenches, had suffered, according to the war diary, 15 men killed, and 59 wounded, including Lieutenants Broadbent, Day and Kerr.[51] Many of these were 'incurred by that bugbear of attacking infantry – the short firing gun in the battery or brigade of artillery.'[52] But for this and the isolated incident suffered by the C Company commander and his men, the figures are remarkably low. They had captured 55 machine guns, 12 trench mortars and around 400 prisoners.

* * *

On the right, or southern brigade boundary, 13th Battalion (commanded by 23-year-old Lieutenant Colonel Douglas Gray Marks) had the challenging, if not slightly daunting, task of

50 TNA: WO95/114-5. 8th Tank Battalion War History, p.36.
51 Commonwealth War Graves Commission records put the final fatality count, including two who died of wounds on 5 July, at 18: two officers, five NCOs and 11 Privates.
52 Longmore, *The Old Sixteenth*, p.183.

skirting the southern edge of Vaire Wood on a very narrow frontage before executing some tricky manoeuvres allowing them to fan out, filling the space behind the wood and re-organising during the artillery pause before continuing the advance to the Blue Line. 'The men of the extending companies had been told to take their tactics from Rugby football, looking upon Vaire Wood as a scrum, their task being to double round it like the scrum half-back and make for the corner 500 yards to the north, where they would turn east and advance in line again.'[53]

Lieutenant Colonel Douglas Gray Marks, CO 13th Battalion. (AWM)

Lieutenant Colonel Marks decided to hold a conference for his officers at battalion HQ at 4:00 p.m. on 2 July. There, following a 36-point agenda, he briefed his commanders on the details of the forthcoming attack. His main concern was the formation that geography would force his men to adopt:

> Having only a frontage of 400 yards for the initial attack, my main difficulty was in devising a formation which would carry the Companies destined for the left, the furthest objective past VAIRE WOOD, without being engaged. It was finally decided that one Company [D Company], less a Platoon detailed to dig a strongpoint under Engineers' supervision, should form the first wave and be allotted an intermediate objective,[54]... the remaining three Coys forming: two having each two platoons in line as second wave and each with two platoons in lines of sections following; and finally one Coy following in section columns in rear of the left of the other two.[55]

These formations would include the welcome addition of six officers and 222 other ranks of A Company,[56] 132nd Regiment, United States Army, one platoon attached to each company of the 13th. They would be accompanied by three tanks of No. 8 Section, B Company, 8th Tank Battalion, under the command of Captain W.M. Edwards. Two of the tanks would skirt the southern boundary of Vaire Wood, with the third following the Warfusée to Fouilloy road. Each tank carried a member of 13th Battalion acting as a scout.

53 Bean, *The Official History*, vol.VI, p.293.
54 D Coy would dig in along a line P21. a. 00.65 to P21. a. 25.30. See Map.
55 AWM: 4 23/30/45 Part 1. War Diary 13th Battalion.
56 It is apparent that some men from G Coy, 132nd Regiment also took part in the attack, as this company suffered 11 fatalities on 4 July. L and M Coys also suffered one fatality each. See Abel Davis, *The Story of the 132nd Infantry A.E.F.* (Luxembourg: 1919).

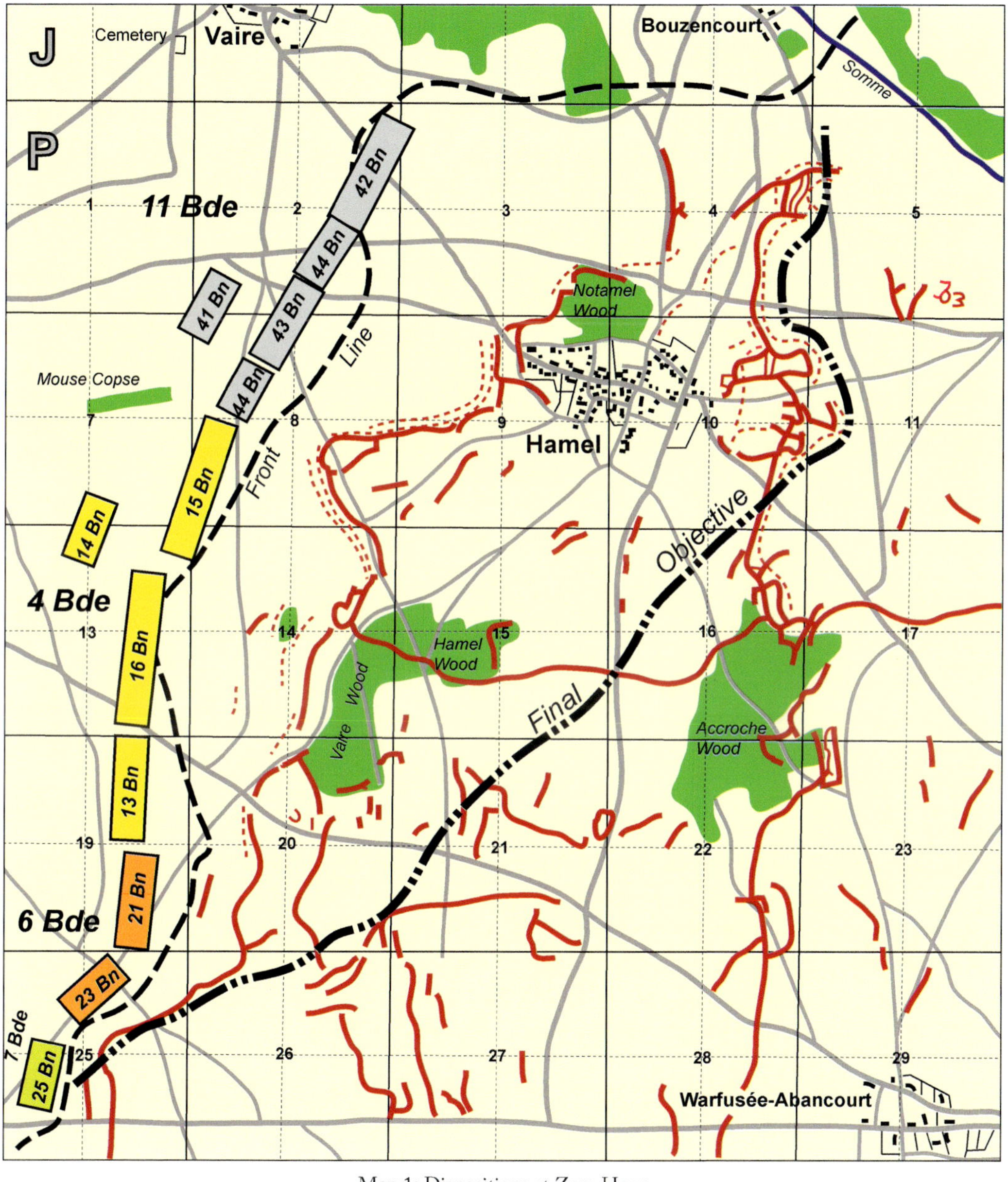

Map 1: Dispositions at Zero Hour.

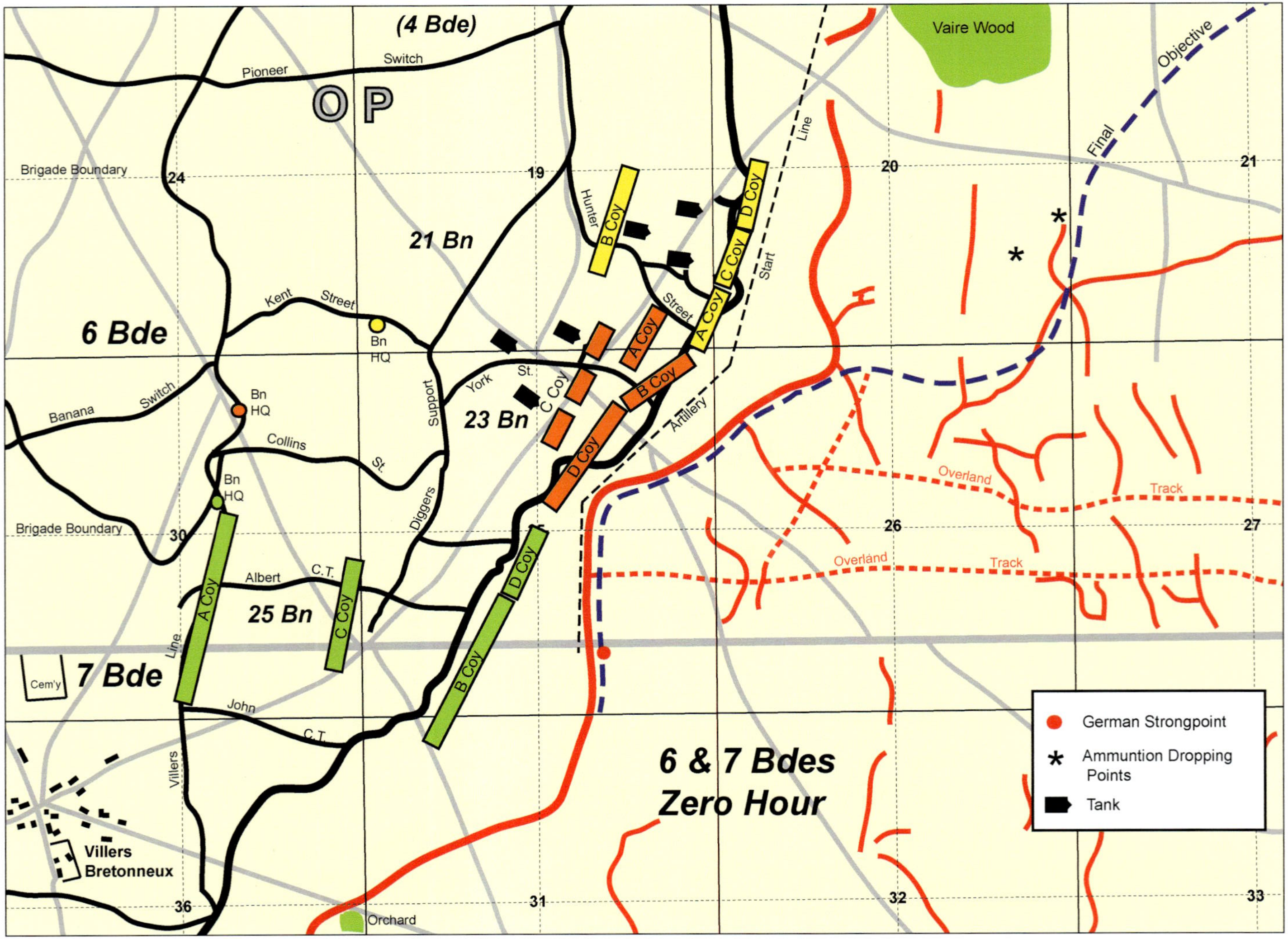

Map 2: 6th and 7th Brigades' attack.

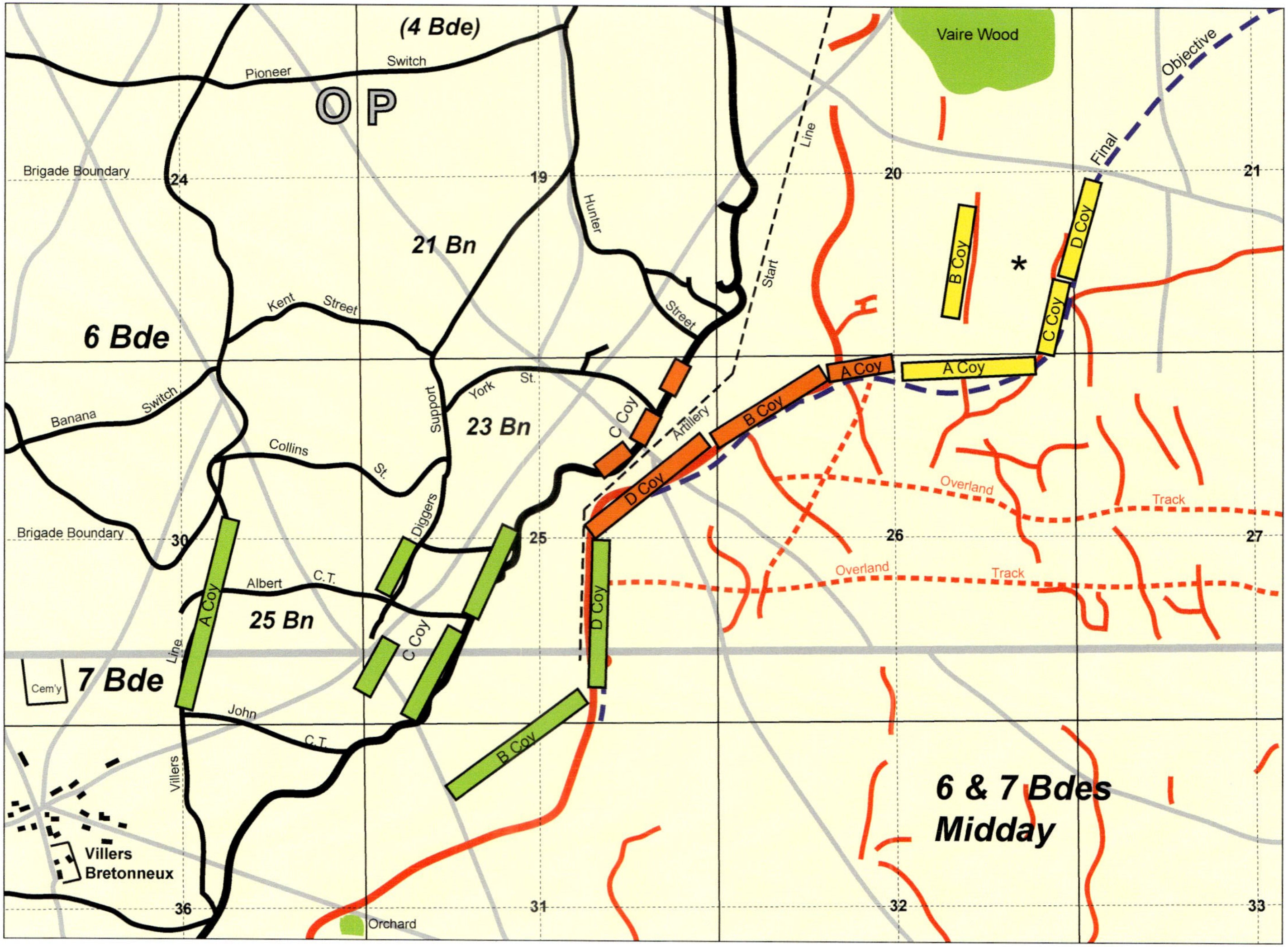

Map 3: 6th and 7th Brigades at midday.

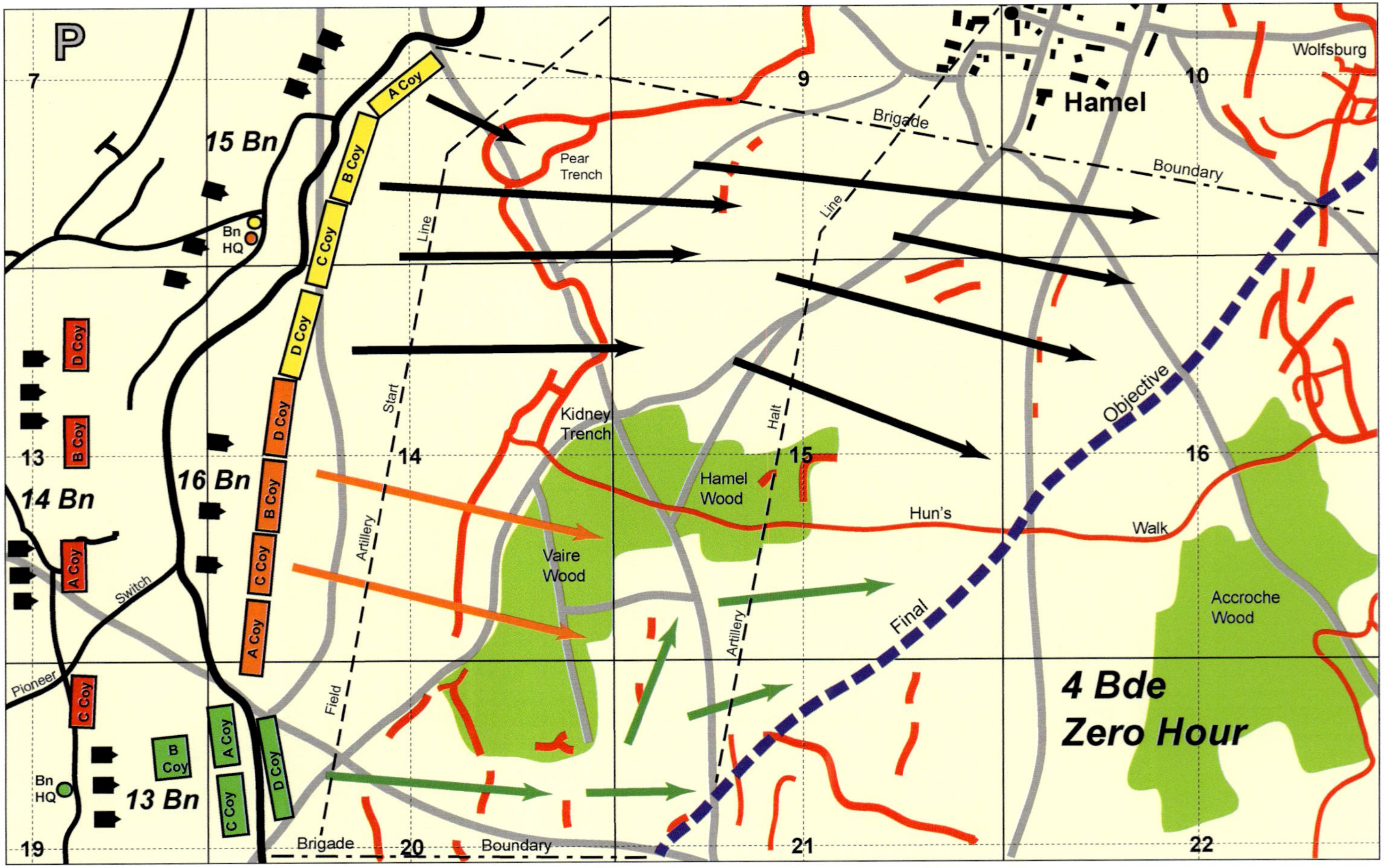

Map 4: 4th Brigade's attack.

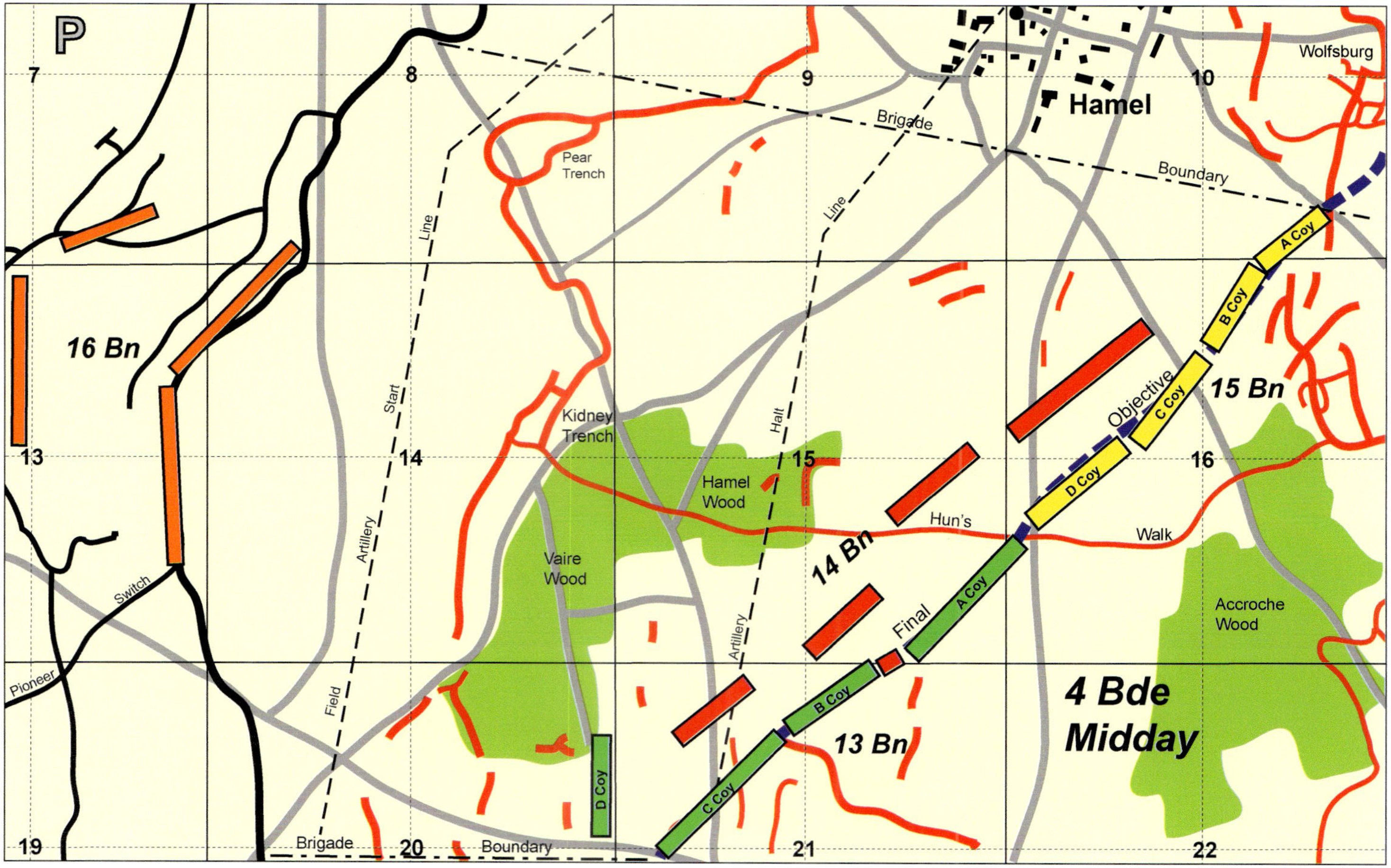

Map 5: 4th Brigade at midday.

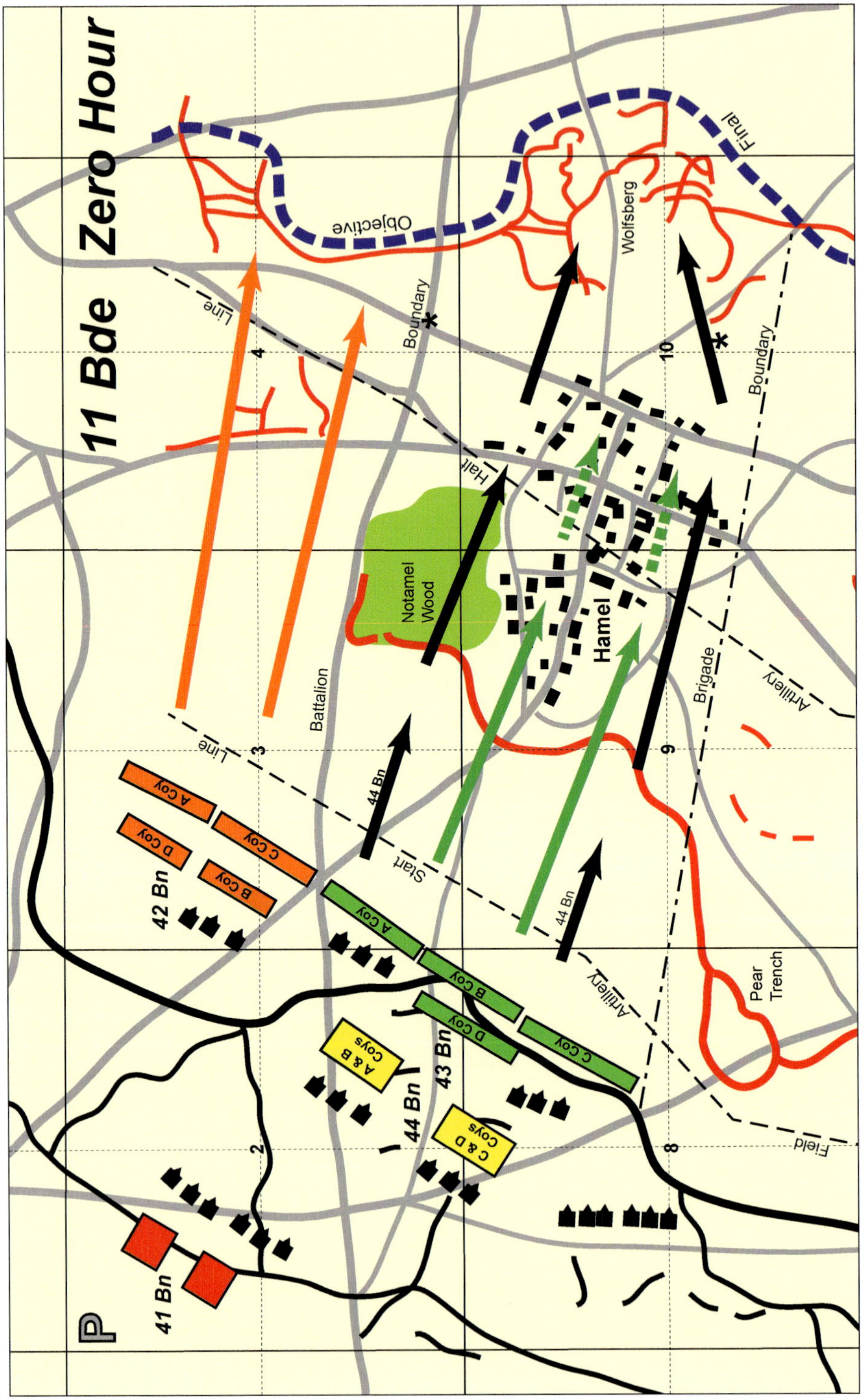

Map 6: 11th Brigade's attack.

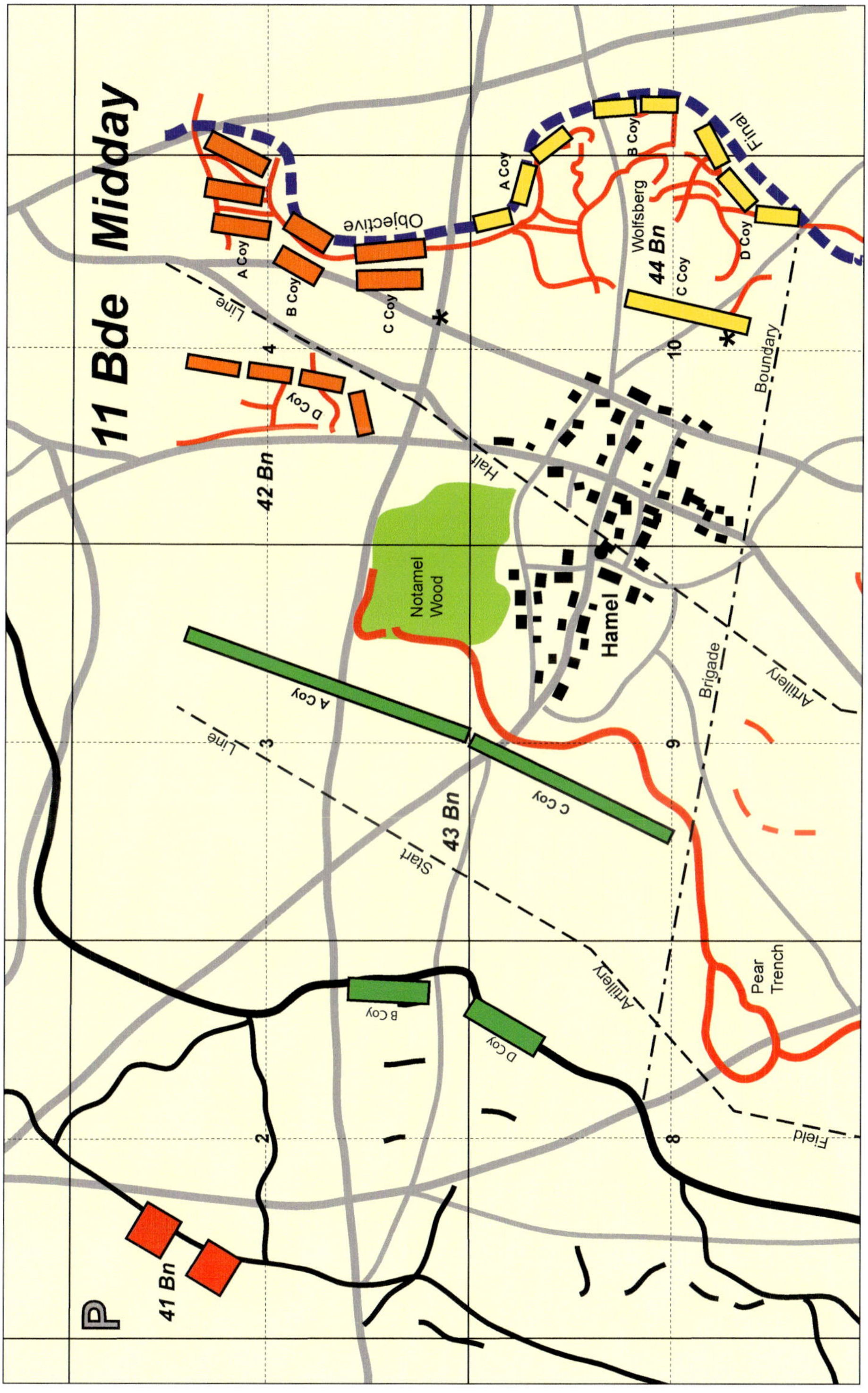

Map 7: 11th Brigade at midday.

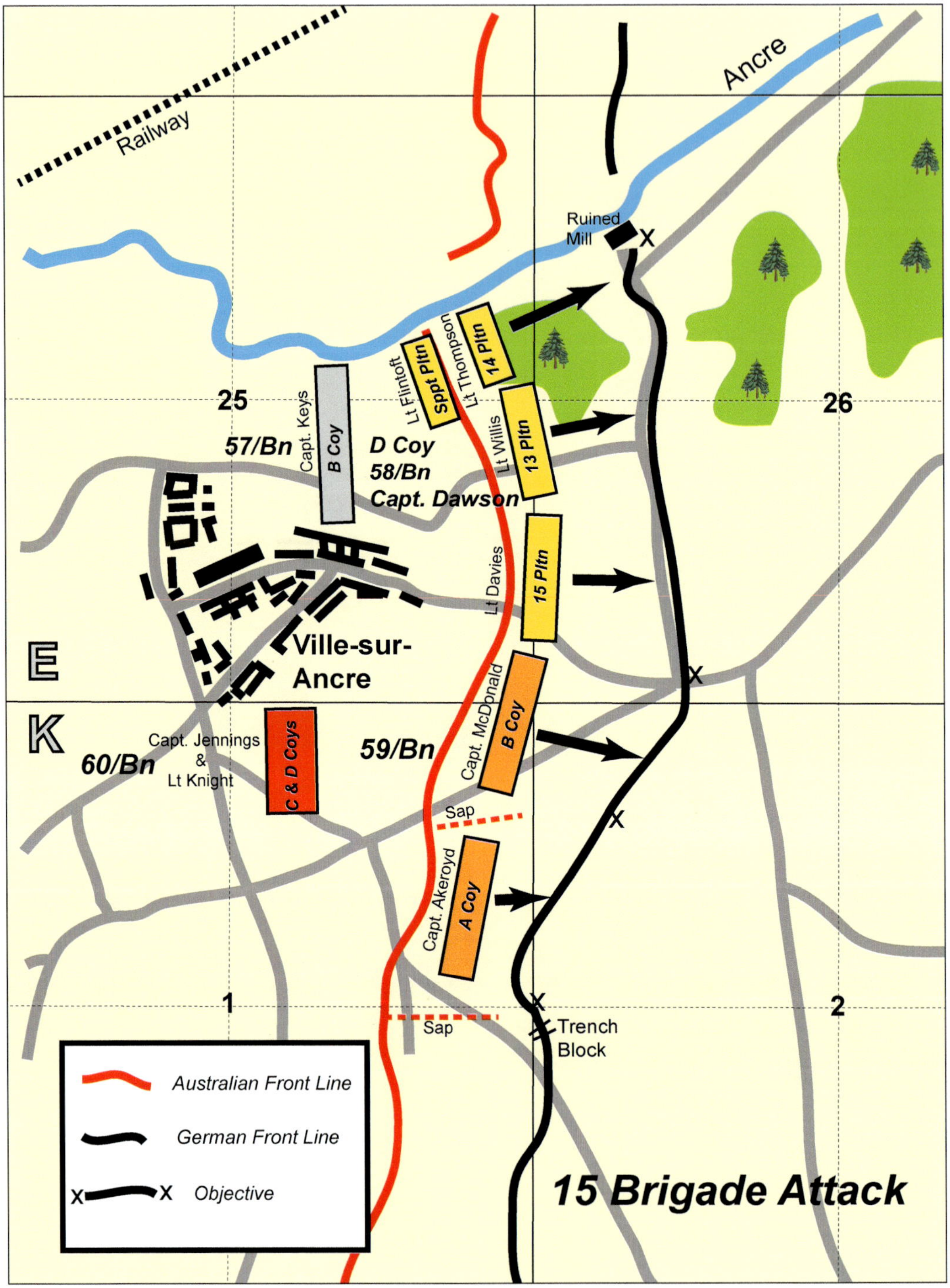

Map 8: Diversionary attack by 15th Brigade.

Every man in the battalion was issued with a message map,[57] and every officer and NCO also had an air reconnaissance photograph. 'Material for the operation was available in such quantities as we have never seen before.'[58] The company strengths on 2 July are detailed on Table 3.

Table 3. 13th Battalion company strengths[59]

Company	Officers	O/R	US Officers	US O/R
A Company	4	106	1	52
B Company	4	98	2	52
C Company	4	109	1	52
D Company	4	93	1	51
HQ	7	122	1	4
Total	**23**	**528**	**6**	**211**

Ten officers and 110 other ranks were left at the Transport Lines. Each company contained four Lewis gun sections, each comprising two teams of six men, operating as follows:

> No.1 carried and fired the gun.
> No.2 carried the spare parts bag and one pannier of four magazines.
> Nos. 3 – 6 carried one pannier and a pick or shovel each.

Each gun, therefore, had 20 magazines available. At eight per company, and four more attached to HQ as a reserve to replace casualties or damaged guns, this meant that 13th Battalion went into battle with 36 Lewis guns; a formidable level of firepower.

So, with D Company (Captain Geary) in front, spread across the 400 yards battalion frontage, A and C Companies (Captains Marper and McKillop) left and right forming the second wave and B Company (Lieutenant Merifield) ready to follow behind A Company, all were in position on the jumping off tapes at 2:15 a.m., a nervous 60 minutes was spent lying out in the open, hoping that the German garrison opposite was unaware of the impending mayhem.

> At 3.2 a.m. the usual morning heavy fire was opened on the enemy and smoke shells were again used with the heavy stuff in order to lead Fritz to put on his gas helmets. We had been sending gas over mixed with smoke many times lately in order to lead him to believe that 'where there was smoke there was gas.' But no gas went over this morning for our own troops were going into the area. Still Fritz got the 'wind up', put his masks on and thus inconvenienced himself considerably.[60]

Eight minutes later, during which time the tanks were lumbering forward as fast as they could from their jumping off positions to get in line with the infantry, the main barrage came down with a stupendous crash, the 18-pounder shells falling just 200 yards in front of the tapes. The men

57 A map of the battlefield with a message template printed on the reverse.
58 AWM: 4 23/30/45 Part 1. War Diary 13th Battalion. 'Report on Operations Vaire Wood – 4.7.1918.'
59 AWM: 4 23/30/45 Part 1. War Diary 13th Battalion.
60 White, Thomas, *The History of the Thirteenth Battalion AIF* (Sydney, Tyrell's Ltd., 1924) p. 143.

of D Company immediately started to crawl forward to within 60 yards of the curtain of fire. The rear companies also edged forward a little with the intention of getting clear of the area where an enemy SOS barrage might be expected to fall as soon as possible. One or two rockets bursting into twin red flares were seen arcing high into the sky above the German lines, but these were way over to the left, possibly in front of 15th Battalion positions. The German artillery response was, in any case, negligible.

Sergeant James Lihou DCM & Bar, MM, 13th Battalion. (AWM)

The tanks caught up with the infantry with impeccable timing – just at the first artillery barrage lift at 3:14 a.m. – and the forward German posts on the road running north through square P.20.a. taken, it seems, by surprise by the speed of the Australian advance, were overrun and captured with little difficulty. Prisoners began to file back, and by 3:37 a.m., a telephone message received by Lieutenant Colonel Marks announced that an advanced battalion HQ had been established in the quarry at P.20.a.9.4. (See map). This quarry had been cleared in exemplary fashion, using by-1918-standard platoon tactics: Sergeant James Lihou, firing his Lewis gun from the hip, poured a stream of bullets into an enemy post, 'whilst a bombing party crept around the flank to destroy it.'[61] Lihou was recommended for the award of the DCM for his exploits that day.[62]

Captain Geary's D Company continued the charge against seemingly limited German opposition. McKillop's C Company did encounter more serious opposition as it crossed the Hamel road, and a few casualties were later caused by 'shorts' from their own 18-pounders, including some from the American contingent who were chasing the barrage rather too enthusiastically. When he saw that a group of Americans were getting mixed up in the barrage, which had halted for 10 minutes, Sergeant Roach, IX Platoon, in charge of a section adjacent to the American soldiers, whose officers had become casualties and were apparently unaware of the artillery halt, 'gallantly rushed forward though he must have realised his own danger, and succeeded in turning back the party. Unfortunately, in the performance of this most courageous act, Roach was seriously wounded.'[63]

61 Peter Pedersen, *Battleground Europe: Hamel, Somme* (Barnsley: Pen & Sword, 2003), p. 81.
62 Sadly, 5713 Sergeant James Lihou DCM & Bar MM was killed in action on 18 September 1918. He is commemorated on the Villers-Bretonneux Memorial.
63 AWM: 28 1/236. Recommendation file for honours and awards, AIF 1914-18 War. 7063 Sergeant Michael 'Mick' Joseph Roach died of wounds at the 47th Casualty Clearing Station [CCS] on 5 July 1918, age 23, and is buried in Crouy British Cemetery, grave III.D.1.

The grave of Sergeant Michael Joseph Roach, 13th Battalion. (Author)

The tank on the right flank, No. 9044,[64] commanded by Captain William Edwards, advanced along the road near the brigade boundary, and received a direct hit from one of these 18-pounder 'shorts' – in this case a high explosive shell – and was put out of action, five of the crew being wounded. Sadly, the 13th Battalion scout who was riding with the tank and helping to direct it from his position in the conning tower, Private Thomas Parrish, was killed, having suffered devastating wounds to his head and neck.[65] The tank was halted and evacuated. Whilst outside, one of the crew, Sergeant Bond, received shrapnel wounds to the arm, requiring his evacuation to a dressing station.

D Company reached its intermediate objective and began digging in. So that they could be recognised as 'troops to be leapfrogged, they had their helmets streaked with red.'[66] A telephone message received at 4:00 a.m. at battalion HQ confirmed their position and that 'all area in rear had been mopped up.'[67] Fifteen minutes earlier, battalion HQ had been informed that all companies had cleared the wood and were 'shaking out' into their new extended lines during the artillery halt.[68]

By now deprived of its supporting tank, C Company pressed forward, swinging their left wing forward as they approached the Blue Line. A strong German machine gun post challenged their forward momentum as they closed on their objective, and a number of casualties were sustained before it was suppressed and captured. Just as this line was reached, Private John Rogers took a machine gun bullet in the stomach and died about 30 minutes later in a shell hole before stretcher bearers could get to him.[69] With the machine gun post eliminated,

64 A 'male' tank. Male tanks were equipped with two 6-pounder guns. 'Female' tanks were equipped with machine guns only: usually six Hotchkiss guns, with the tank carrying 282 belts of ammunition, which, at 50 rounds per belt, gives a total of 14,100 rounds.

65 3770 Private Thomas Parrish, age 20, is commemorated on the Villers-Bretonneux Memorial. His brother, 4866 Private Joseph Parrish, 4th Australian Machine Gun Battalion, age 21, had died of wounds the previous week, on 27 June. He is buried in Terlincthun British Cemetery. Both brothers had been born in Wales.

66 White, *The History of the Thirteenth Battalion*, p.144. In Lieutenant Colonel Marks' briefing notes from 2 July, point 29 states that D Coy's helmets would be marked with white paint. The Americans' helmets were adorned with blue paint.

67 AWM: 4 23/30/45 Part 1. War Diary 13th Battalion.

68 Ibid. The ten-minute artillery halt was timed to begin at 03:38.

69 85 Pte John 'Jockey Jack' Bowen Rogers, a jockey from Melbourne, 5 ft 5in tall and 23 years old, was buried in Villers-Bretonneux Military Cemetery, grave VIII. C. 3.

and three guns captured, they began to consolidate their gains on the ridge of the spur, but the Germans – men from *11. Kompanie IR 13* – made several attempts at dislodging them by launching bombing raids up the trench running through square P.21.b., but these were all repulsed and a number of prisoners taken. It was during this counterattack that the commander of *11. Kompanie*, *Leutnant* Clasen, was killed.[70]

A Company, as it shifted direction and moved north behind Vaire Wood, came under serious machine gun fire from a concealed position: these machine gun nests, forming part of the *Hauptwiderstandslinie* and manned by two platoons of *1. Kompanie IR 13* under *Leutnant* Rosenbaum,[71] threatened to stem the Australian tide. Captain Marper rushed the strongpoint and shot three of the enemy with his revolver and captured the gun. It is probable that 284 Private Reginald Gordon Leeder had become a victim of that machine gun, shot in the chest as he advanced. Leeder had been court-martialled twice in 1917, reduced from sergeant to private, and had entered No. 1 Military Prison on 20 June that year. His sentence was subsequently suspended and he rejoined 13th Battalion on 27 May 1918.[72]

Private Reginald Gordon Leeder, 13th Battalion. (AWM)

Also killed there was Private William Pike, 24 years old, hit by machine gun bullets in the thigh and chest. He succumbed to his wounds about half an hour later, after having given his wallet, containing a letter he had written the night before, and his notebook, to Private Jamieson, who sent them back to Pike's mother, who lived in Newtown, New South Wales.[73]

As the artillery barrage began to move forward again after its 10-minute halt, A Company was completing its second 'wheel', this time to face east, when it was confronted by another

70 Groos & von Rudloff, *Infanterie-Regiment 13*, p.307. Clasen was the only officer fatality suffered on 4 July by *IR 13*.
71 Groos & von Rudloff, *Infanterie-Regiment 13*, p.307.
72 Leeder is commemorated on the Villers-Bretonneux Memorial.
73 2632 Pte William Thomas Pike is commemorated on the Villers-Bretonneux Memorial.

enemy trench 'so well camouflaged that it had not been seen by airmen or on photo.'[74] White describes how this strongpoint was dealt with:

> Two machine guns in the trench, firing point blank into 'A' [Company] threatened to hold them back. [Captain] Marper again immediately, quite regardless of himself, rushed across the swept area to attract the attention of a tank, and in doing so was severely wounded in the chest and arm. He remained to see the tank lumber over the top of the stubborn enemy and, spinning like a top, crush the guns and crews into nothing.[75]

Captain George Marper DSO. (Sheffield & District Wine, Beer and Spirit Trade Association)

Only once he was satisfied that his company was once more advancing as planned behind the moving barrage did Marper hand over command to Lieutenant 'Tommy' Dwyer. Dwyer himself, along with Lieutenants Nugent and Smith, was also soon wounded, but Dwyer carried on, receiving the MC for his actions. The citation reads:

> In the attack on VAIRE WOOD E. of CORBIE on 4th July 1918, this Officer's Company Commander became a casualty while attacking a strong point. Though himself wounded in the leg he took over command and led the Company forward to its final objective. Throughout the consolidation he moved about amongst his Company with cool cheerfulness and said no word of his wound until his leg became so stiff and he had to be carried away.[76]

It fell to the only unwounded officer left in A Company, Lieutenant McRae, to take over command, and he was able to report the company on the final objective and in touch with 15th Battalion on the left at 4:18 a.m. Marper received the DSO.[77]

B Company, as per the plan, followed in the rear of A Company, and did not encounter any real opposition until they approached the final objective, where two platoons were required to fill the gap between A and C Companies. The rest of B Company was called forward onto the Blue Line at 6:00 a.m., when readjustments to the company frontages were made. Casualties

74 White, *The History of the Thirteenth Battalion*, p.145. This, according to a captured German sketch map, preserved in the 13th Battalion war diary, was just in front of the *Hauptwiderstandslinie*, running from the most southern part of Hamel Wood to the Warfusée–Fouilloy road.
75 White, *The History of the Thirteenth Battalion*, p.145. Bean's Notebooks, AWM: 38 3DRL606/190/1, suggest that the tank crushed one of the machine guns and its crew, whereupon the crew of the second gun surrendered.
76 AWM: 28 1/236 Recommendation file for honours and awards, AIF 1914-18 War.
77 Marper survived his wounds and in September that year married Miss Emily Bennett in Sheffield, England. He had known Emily as a youth before the war in Sheffield, where he was born on 27 March 1891. The bullet that had lodged in his chest, just above the heart, was operated on, removed, and kept by Marper as a souvenir. He went on to have two children, born 1919 and 1924. Emily died in 1960. Marper died on 3 October 1973, aged 82.

in B Company were accordingly not heavy, but included their commander, Lieutenant Merifield, who was wounded, and Second Lieutenant Hall was killed.[78]

Even as they consolidated their positions and tanks patrolled the ground ahead of them, the odd stubborn German machine gun hidden in the crops could pose a problem. One such, in front of B Company, was becoming 'a nuisance to the boys', so Corporal 'Bluey' Fairbairn and Corporal Cima decided to go out and deal with it. They had gone about 100 yards when the German machine gunners spotted them and opened fire: Cima was wounded in the face, and Fairbairn was killed outright.[79]

The grave of Corporal Norman Stanley Bathurst Fairbairn, 13th Battalion. (Author)

The American troops of A Company, 132nd Regiment, attached to 13th Battalion, 'fought well', according to Lieutenant Colonel Marks' after-action report, but he adds that it was 'with a dash that needs to be tempered by experience.'[80] He rated the officers highly but feared that the NCOs lacked the experience to step up effectively once the officers were casualties. They had – as we have already seen – suffered casualties by getting too close to the creeping barrage, and, not unsurprisingly for troops under fire for the first time, tended to bunch up. An American platoon was organised into seven squads, and Marks noted that 'no single American platoon arrived on its objective complete, and… one Platoon commander lost five of his seven squads. Of course, they all turned up eventually, but many of them far away on the final objective of the adjoining battalion [21st Battalion].'[81]

Lieutenant Colonel Marks later recommended two 132nd Regiment men for bravery awards: 1390307 Corporal R. Miller and 1390351 Private Shelley were both commended for their coolness under fire, Miller for good leadership of his squad, and Shelley for helping to mop up enemy posts beyond the final objective line.

Once again, the German regimental history shows how the Germans misinterpreted Australian intentions: 'The line held at this point was approximately 1 km behind the previous

78 Second Lieutenant Arthur James Hall MM is commemorated on the Villers-Bretonneux Memorial.
79 There are 15 different accounts of the incident in Fairbairn's Red Cross file: six adhere to the version in the text above, but five attest that Fairbairn went out to rescue the wounded Cima and was killed in the attempt. Four accounts shed no light on either version. 3759 Corporal Norman Stanley Bathurst Fairbairn, 27 years old, is buried in Villers-Bretonneux Military Cemetery, grave III. D. 10. 2421 Corporal Arthur William Cima MM (awarded for his actions at Zillebeke, Belgium in September 1917) survived the war, but was blinded.
80 AWM: 4 23/30/45 Part 1. War Diary 13th Battalion.
81 AWM: 4 23/30/45 Part 1. War Diary 13th Battalion. Report on Operations.

front line trench. The enemy had envisaged a much more extensive advance. This is evident from the fact that his creeping barrage extended about one and a half kilometres east of Hamel.'[82]

The casualties of 13th Battalion cannot be regarded as heavy, but they were substantial. Two officers and 24 other ranks were killed. Six officers and 93 other ranks were wounded. One other rank was missing. The total number of casualties was 126. With a strength engaged of 22 officers and 488 other ranks,[83] this represents a casualty rate of 24.7 percent (36.3 percent for officers). The Americans suffered seven other ranks killed, four officers and 42 other ranks wounded, and four other ranks missing. A total of 57 casualties. With a strength engaged of five officers and 222 other ranks, this represents a casualty rate of 25.1 percent (80 percent for officers).[84] The German defenders of *IR 13* had suffered 43 fatalities. Gallantry awards to 13th Battalion men for this action totalled one DSO, one MC, three DCMs, two bars to MMs and sixteen MMs.

* * *

On the left brigade frontage, 15th Battalion faced the longest advance to the Blue Line, ranging from 2,000 to 2,500 yards. They would move to the north of the woods, but would initially come up against the strongly garrisoned and daunting 'Pear Trench' redoubt.

D Company of 16th Battalion had executed a raid on Pear Trench on the night of 15/16th June. (14th Battalion were raiding Vaire Wood at the same time). Two parties, each of one officer and thirty other ranks, were to enter the system at the junction of trenches at the north-east corner of the redoubt, gaps having been blown in the wire by Bangalore Torpedoes.[85] Party No.1, under Second Lieutenant Taylor, would then proceed westwards along the front line trench, with Party No.2, under Lieutenant A. Dowling, heading south-west along the support trench line. This second party would cross the road and form a block in the trench running southwards towards Vaire Wood before meeting Party No.1 coming the other way near where the road exits the northern edge of the redoubt.

Each party, advancing in and alongside the trenches, would fire white flares at intervals to signal their progress to the other group. One red flare would be the signal to call off the raid and evacuate the system.

Prisoners and materiel captured would be escorted back to the point of entry and thence back to the Australian trenches. While all this was going on, a third party of two NCOs and 10 men under Sergeant O'Neill were to work their way down the road from P8. b. 15.20, deal with one German machine gun known to be positioned on that road before securing the stretch of road within the redoubt to help with the evacuation plan.

Each man would be armed with a rifle, bayonet and six Mills bombs. Each trench-blocking party would also carry one Lewis gun with eight magazines and 20 extra grenades per man. Trench mortars, 18-pounder guns and Vickers machine guns would supply stationary protective barrages. (See sketch map).

82 Groos & von Rudloff, *Infanterie-Regiment 13*, p.307.
83 The figures are those given by the 13th Bn war diarist. The author is aware that they do not reconcile with those in Table 3.
84 The figure for American fatalities for 4–6 July 1918 was later recorded as 27. See Appendix B.
85 The Imperial War Museum web site (iwm.org.uk) describes a Bangalore Torpedo as follows: an explosive charge fixed on the end of a long tube, to which could be attached additional lengths to extend it, so that it could pushed across the ground to clear obstacles without endangering the operative. In particular they were used to clear paths through barbed wire entanglements.

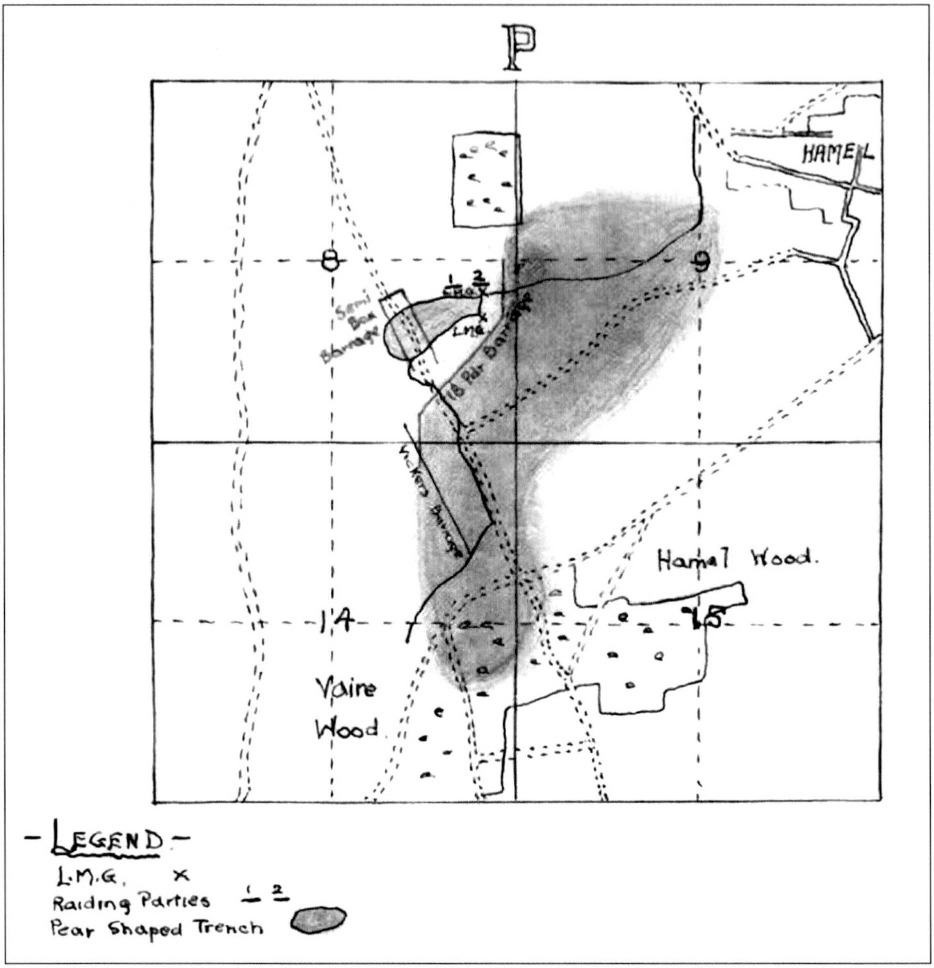

The Pear Trench raid. (AWM)

The whole scheme was scheduled to last a maximum of 10 minutes. That was the plan. The last sentence of the first paragraph of the 'Narrative' of the raid in the 16th Battalion's war diary, is the epitome of understatement: 'Operation took place at ZERO, and an entry was gained in BOSCHE trenches. Unfortunately, the O.C. No. 2 Party and two senior Sergeants were wounded on the BOSCHE parapet *and the show went a bit wrong*.'[86]

No. 1 Party made its way some distance along the German trench, bombing enemy dugouts, but at Zero plus five minutes, some of the 18-pounder shells began to fall short, causing casualties amongst the raiders. German resistance also proved stiffer than anticipated, and with no news of Party No. 2, Taylor decided to send up the red flare at Zero plus 8½ minutes. The after-action report continues the narrative:

86 The German defenders threw grenades at the wire cutting party. AWM: 4 23/33/31 Part 1. War Diary 16th Battalion (author's italics).

> Wounded were evacuated and an orderly retirement took place.... There was a considerable number of prisoners in the line but they could not be persuaded to leave their trenches and left no alternative but to do them in, about 15 were punished in this way. A few Hun prisoners were got back and three light machine guns.[87]

The only brief mention of No. 3 Party in the report states that they 'had a lively time.' Australian casualties were 15 wounded and one missing, with little to show for their efforts.[88]

On the morning of 4 July, 15th Battalion (Lieutenant Colonel Terence Patrick McSharry) formed up – going into the assault with a battalion strength of 21 officers and 615 other ranks (not including the attached American units)[89] – in four waves in column of platoons, 'partly in crop, partly in cleared ground',[90] with A Company on the left flank and B, C and D Companies stretching away to the south in that order up the rising crest of the ridge. Each company was equipped with six Lewis guns with 16 magazines per gun.

A Company (Captain Ernest Kenneth Carter) had the unenviable task of tackling Pear Trench before continuing to the Blue Line with the rest of the battalion. He was to be assisted in this by three tanks of No.1 Section, A Company, 8th

Lieutenant Colonel Terence Patrick McSharry, CO 15th Battalion. (AWM)

Captain Ernest Kenneth Carter, A Company, 15th Battalion. (AWM)

87 AWM: 4 23/33/31 Part 1. War Diary 16th Battalion.
88 The 14th Battalion raid on Vaire Wood, lasting 12 minutes, was described in the after-action report as going 'without a hitch.' Eleven prisoners were brought in, along with one captured machine gun. One dug out was destroyed and a 'number of the enemy killed' at the cost of two Australian other ranks killed and 11 wounded.
89 The attached American contingent from 132nd US Infantry Regiment numbered seven officers and 209 other ranks, making an overall total of 28 officers and 824 other ranks.
90 AWM: 38 3DRL606/190/1. Bean's Notebooks.

Tank Battalion (Captain C.E. Scott). A Company was to be slightly understrength, however, as two sections under Captain Toft were to form their liaison unit with 44th Battalion and move along the inter-brigade boundary.

When the barrage proper came down at 3:10 a.m., according to the war diary, it 'appeared to fall accurately', but the narrative continues:

> a number of the guns were firing short, particularly on the left flank of our battalion, where shells were falling fully 200 yards in rear of the main barrage. This short shooting continued right up to the final objective and was responsible for a large number of casualties – we had 12 killed and about 30 wounded whilst lying up at the tape.[91]

Among the dead was Lieutenant Spencer of A Company, who 'collected a direct hit and was killed instantly.'[92]

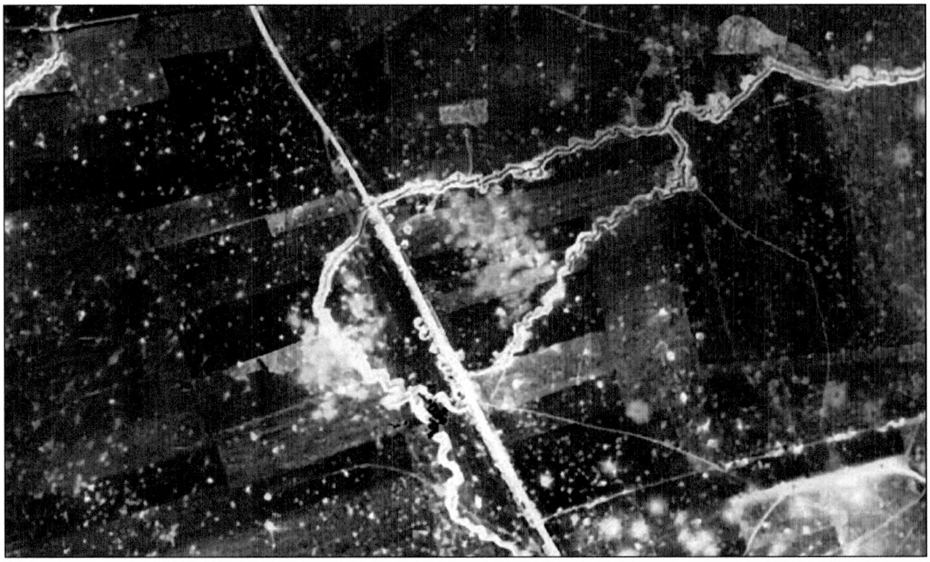

Pear Trench. Aerial reconnaissance photograph taken 30 June 1918. (AWM)

The artillery barrage did little or nothing to help A Company with their assault on Pear Trench. The initial line of the barrage was to the west of the redoubt, and 'the first lift took [it] over the Pear shaped trench.'[93] This meant that the German wire was undamaged, the garrison unharmed, and the 10 machine gun crews had time to set up their weapons before the first wave of Australian infantry arrived.

91 AWM: 4 23/32/40. War Diary 15th Battalion.
92 Lt. T.P. Chataway, *History of the 15th Battalion Australian Imperial Forces War 1914-1918* revised and edited by Lt Col. Paul Goldenstedt (Brisbane: William Brooks & Co Ltd, 1948), p.213. Lieutenant William James Spencer, age 30, is buried in Villers-Bretonneux Military Cemetery, grave II. C. 8.
93 Chataway, *History of the 15th Battalion.* The heavy artillery barrage started to the east of the redoubt.

Lieutenant William James Spencer (centre), 15th Battalion. (AWM)

Spencer's headstone. (Author)

Captain Scott's tanks were also noticeable by their absence: with the darkness of the early morning, the smoke produced by the barrage, and the fact that Pear Trench was situated just over a rise on a reverse slope, 'some tanks found it impossible at the outset to be sure of their proper direction.'[94] None of No. 1 Section found the redoubt, and the three tanks were nowhere to be seen when their help was needed.[95] This is confirmed by Lieutenant Colonel McSharry's after-action report, in which he states, bluntly: 'I saw no tanks tackle Pear Trench and none of my officers saw them.'[96]

In this sector, the meticulous planning was of no avail: a planned 'all-arms' attack devolved into an infantry versus infantry scrap, and the inevitable heavy casualties ensued.

On A Company's left wing, Captain Toft's party, according to his after-action report, written on 7 July, also suffered casualties from their own barrage:

94 Bean, *The Official History*, vol.VI, p.287.
95 Remarkably, in the 8th Tank Battalion's 'War Experiences' document (TNA: WO95/112-5, p.33), the author claims that 'The capture of PEAR-SHAPED REDOUBT in the HAMEL battle was successfully carried out by one Section, one tank making a direct frontal attack and the remaining two flank attacks.' This is pure invention.
96 AWM: 4 23/4/34. War Diary 4th Australian Brigade. Part 2. Appendix 107.

> About ¼ of our guns on this Sector were firing in amongst us while the remainder was 100 yds ahead. We lost some casualties by this fire and had to stop until the 4 minutes were up & the barrage lifted. The next bound brought us to near the Pear Shaped Trench on our left Boundary. Here we came under Machine Gun fire from 2 Guns but which did not cause any casualties.[97]

Toft's unit 'rushed Pear Shaped Trench' and were met by machine gun fire, rifle fire and a shower of grenades. 'The enemy made a good fight',[98] but the Australians were able to push on through sally ports and over sections where the wire was thinnest.[99] As the artillery barrage made its first lift, Captain Carter, with the rest of A Company, was able to see that some of the Germans were 'standing up in the mist ahead throwing bombs.'[100]

Almost immediately, machine gun fire opened up on the advancing Australians causing a considerable number of casualties. Undaunted, A Company pressed on, coming up against rolls of concertina wire with a belt of barbed wire behind them. Some of the men managed to scramble through the entanglements, whilst others tried to climb over. It was at this point that Captain Carter was hit, both legs being broken.[101] The forward momentum was lost. Many of the men, wounded or not, made the sensible decision to go to ground in the face of such intense fire. Two of the many men killed at this point were Private 'Curly' Worthington and Private 'Jack' Gnatz. Worthington got as far as the enemy wire, but as he was struggling to get through, a machine gun bullet caught him in the neck. Gnatz was hit in the stomach.[102]

The company's Lewis gunners, some firing from the hip, began to return fire, and the men, as instructed when held up, awaited the arrival of the tanks. They managed to silence two of the German machine guns, and as it became clear that the tanks were not coming to the rescue, the men were obliged to rush these positions unsupported, 'dash[ing] in with the bayonet.'[103] It was here that a Lewis gunner, Private Henry Dalziel, won a Victoria Cross: acting as No.2 in the Lewis gun section, he and his No. 1, the only two unwounded men left in the team, had helped with the neutralisation of the first two German machine gun positions, but almost immediately, a third gun opened up from the front line trench a short distance to the left, just where it crossed the road. (See map above). Dalziel fitted a fresh magazine to his mate's Lewis gun, drew his revolver, rushed the German position, killed the crew and captured the gun,[104] losing his trigger finger to a bullet wound in the process. Dalziel refused to go back to have his wound treated and

97 AWM: 4 23/32/40. War Diary 15th Battalion. Report by Captain Toft, A Coy.
98 AWM: 4 23/32/40. War Diary 15th Battalion. Report by Captain Toft, A Coy.
99 A sally port is a passage used by troops to make a sortie out of a fortified position. In this instance, it probably refers simply to lanes through the German wire.
100 Bean, *The Official History*, vol.VI, p.287.
101 Carter survived but lost a leg.
102 7832 Pte George Herbert 'Curly' Worthington is buried in Crucifix Corner Cemetery, grave IX.B.14. 2314 Pte John Henry 'Jack' Gnatz, a runner in IV Platoon, A Coy, was evacuated by stretcher bearers to the dressing station, from where he was sent to No.5 Casualty Clearing Station at Crouy. He died from his wounds on 6 July. He is buried in Crouy British Cemetery, grave III.D.25. His brother, William Hermann Gnatz, served in 31st Battalion and survived the war.
103 AWM: 4 23/32/40. War Diary 15th Battalion. 'Narrative.'
104 Bean's *Official History* states that Dalziel killed two machine gunners. The recommendation for the gallantry award says 'the entire crew.' Pedersen also says two, but Dalziel's own version, written in 1942, claims 'seven.'

The grave of Private George Herbert Worthington, 15th Battalion. (Author)

The grave of Private John Henry Gnatz, 15th Battalion. (Author)

took part in the subsequent advance to the final objective. He was later badly wounded in the head whilst collecting ammunition boxes dropped from 9 Squadron aircraft.[105]

The attackers were now able to push into the redoubt, along its rear wings and down the sunken road that ran through it, where 'every dug out had a bomb thrown into it.'[106]

Private Henry Dalziel VC, 15th Battalion. (AWM)

105 The 25-year-old 1936 Pte Henry 'Harry' Dalziel survived. He died on 24 July 1965. During the preparations for the battle, Dalziel had been with the Transport Section, hauling supplies forward. Following the withdrawal of the American troops, volunteers had been called for to boost 15th Battalion's numbers in the attack. Harry was one of those volunteers.

106 AWM: 4 23/32/40. War Diary 15th Battalion. Report by Captain Toft, A Coy.

Thirty or so Germans made an attempt to run off in the direction of Hamel village, but 'machine gun and rifle fire accounted for most of them.'[107] As the Australians reached the rear trench of the redoubt, some of the enemy surrendered, raising their hands. Others, behind, however, continued to throw grenades. '[I]n the heat of the moment, this action appeared to be rank treachery, and the Queenslanders, whose own losses had been heavy, killed right and left in both the trench and the sunken road.'[108]

By the time A Company had made it through the redoubt, the creeping barrage was some 300 yards ahead of them, but the 10-minute pause in the barrage allowed them to catch up and reorganise. Even so, persistent 'shorts' in the barrage required them to halt some distance short of the planned line.

The defence of Pear Trench redoubt by *IR 55* had inflicted most of 15th Battalion's 242 casualties: they were easily the heaviest of any of the assaulting battalions that day and accounted for almost half of the battalion's strength. Pedersen summarises the Pear Trench struggle:

> Two hundred yards across and one hundred deep, strongly-garrisoned, bristling with well-sited machine guns manned by skilful gunners and with several trench mortars providing extra punch, the redoubt resembled the positions encountered during the offensives on the Somme or Ypres, where unit casualties on this scale were routine. When the tanks did not arrive, the infantry had to advance without any protection from mechanical resources; in other words, to expend itself on heroic physical effort in the old way. It was the very antithesis of Monash's philosophy and the losses were not surprising.[109]

Men of 15th Battalion asleep in Pear Trench. (AWM)

107 AWM: 4 23/32/40. War Diary 15th Battalion. Report by Captain Toft, A Coy.
108 Bean, *The Official History*, vol.VI, p.290.
109 Pedersen, *Battleground Europe: Hamel, Somme*, p.77.

Private Darcy Page, 15th Battalion, in Pear Trench. (AWM)

German losses in Pear Trench were also heavy. Lieutenant Colonel McSharry's report recounts that: 'Fritz fought fairly well in the Pear Trench but our fellows crawled all over him. There are about 50 Dead huns in the Pear.'[110] With the one company of *III. Bataillon* in the front line positions overrun and suffering heavy casualties, *IR 55*'s forward commander, *Hauptmann* von Busse, ordered the remaining two companies forward in an attempt to regain ground. *Leutnant* Ball, light machine gun in his hand, led this counterattack forward. The writer of *IR 55*'s regimental history claims that the enemy's advance 'was brought to a standstill',[111] but the Australians were already on the Blue Line, with no intention of attempting any further advances. The 'counter attack' cost *Leutnant* Ball his life, and *III. Bataillon* had been so drastically weakened that it was replaced in the battle zone by two companies of *I. Bataillon*, with *Hauptmann* Schröter taking command. Units of *II. Bataillon*, initially in reserve in Morcourt, were also ordered forward, but by the time they arrived on the battlefield, 'the fight was already over.'[112]

Two vital components of Monash's plan to minimise casualties had failed: the artillery barrage had almost completely missed the redoubt, and the tanks specifically tasked with its suppression had managed to bypass it. The question has to be asked as to whether it might have been wiser to avoid a frontal attack on Pear Trench. The position, given a good pounding by heavy artillery, could have been outflanked and isolated, rendering the German garrison redundant and forcing its surrender later that morning. Indeed, the regimental history of *IR 55* relates how the officers feared that exact manoeuvre: 'Through the outflanking and gassing of the '*Nebelmulde*' [Pear Trench] position, the front line garrison would be in danger of being completely cut off. The chances of timely support being sent forward were as good as nil.'[113]

Fortunately, the second stage of A Company's advance after the artillery pause, now with Lieutenant Jack Hynes in command, was much easier. The tanks had appeared and were advancing ahead of the infantry, and no real opposition was encountered as they moved onto the Blue Line. The tanks continued beyond the final objective and were harassing and mopping up

110 AWM: 4 23/4/34. War Diary 4th Australian Brigade. Part 2. Appendix 107.
111 Walter Schultz, *Infanterie-Regiment Graf Bülow von Dennewitz (6. Westfälisches) Nr. 55 im Weltkriege* (Detmold: Verlag der Meyerschen Hofbuchhandlung [Max Staercke], 1928), p. 231.
112 Schultz, *Infanterie-Regiment Graf Bülow von Dennewitz*, p.231
113 Schultz, *Infanterie-Regiment Graf Bülow von Dennewitz*, p.230.

isolated enemy posts. Vickers and Lewis guns were set up to cover the consolidation of the new positions against the threat of counterattack. None materialised.[114]

Captain Simon Fahey Porter, B Company, 15th Battalion. (AWM)

B Company (Captain Porter), advancing to the south of A Company, encountered their first opposition in the southern part of Pear Trench, where they captured two large trench mortars and their crews before setting up a regimental aid post. A short hand-to-hand struggle had overcome the German resistance, and the men, under a 'very erratic' artillery barrage,[115] continued their advance 'down into the Hollow and up onto the next ridge' where 'little opposition was met.'[116] After a pause on the 10-minute halt line, the advance continued, crossing the road running up to Hamel village from the woods with no trouble; the next opposition was not encountered until they approached the next road (running south from Hamel through map squares 16 a & b). There, the Germans had positioned several machine-gun emplacements. These, with the help of the tanks, were quickly overcome and bypassed, and the Blue Line was reached with relative ease. With Lewis guns positioned out ahead, digging in commenced.

At some point during the attack (no clues as to exact timing are evident in the battalion papers), Captain Porter, commanding the company, was wounded. Lieutenant Jack Rae took over command, but he, too, was wounded on the final objective.[117]

Next in line to the south was C Company (Captain R. Glasgow): they too complained of the artillery firing short, and as a result, the first wave was unable to move forward until three minutes after Zero, being forced to wait for the barrage to lift. Even so, moving behind the curtain of shells, their own shrapnel still inflicted casualties.

As they approached their first obstacle, Vaire Trench, adjacent to the road, they came under fire from the left, from German machine guns in Pear Trench, which had not yet been captured. The German garrison in Vaire Trench, many of them wearing gas masks, was overrun rapidly and effectively, dugouts were cleared, and opposition 'did not in any way interfere with the

114 According to the Australian narrative but see the *IR 55* version of events above.
115 AWM: 4 23/32/40. War Diary 15th Battalion. B Coy's After Action Report.
116 AWM: 4 23/32/40. War Diary 15th Battalion. B Coy's After Action Report.
117 Captain Simon Fahey Porter MC, age 31, was evacuated, but died of his wounds in hospital in London on 25 November 1918. He had gained his Military Cross at Zonnebeke, Belgium, on 26 September 1917. He is buried in Brookwood Military Cemetery, grave IV. J. 22. Lieutenant John McIntyre Rae was so severely wounded that he was never able to rejoin the battalion.

advance.'[118] Indeed, the speed of their advance meant that for a while after crossing this trench, they were out of touch with B and D Companies on their flanks. The three companies were able to join up again in the valley running north from Hamel Wood. Glasgow reported that he first saw and heard the tanks here. After the 10-minute pause, the advance continued to schedule. German strongpoints along the road in map square 16 a. did little to delay the company's advance, the tanks here finally proving their worth by being 'of great assistance in clearing up the German positions.'[119]

Lieutenant George Edward Fewster, 15th Battalion. (Author)

C Company arrived on the Blue Line at Zero plus 90 minutes, exactly on time, and began the process of consolidation. Glasgow's report claims, perhaps erroneously, that C Company only suffered 'two men wounded after we reached the objective.' Chataway's battalion history states that Lieutenant Fewster, embarking on a 'minor operation after C Coy obtained its objective',[120] was killed, curtailing the mission. Red Cross Reports offer confusing evidence, however, with some testimonies locating Fewster's death at Pear Trench. Others suggest that Sergeant Hollamby was killed at the same time, whilst trying to push the line forward.[121]

With the tanks pushing out as far as Accroche Wood to cover the consolidation, it is interesting to note that the other German history of *IR 55* also claims that although the Australians 'broke through' the 'first line positions', the insertion of their *III. Bataillon* into the line successfully halted any further advances at the '*Schwerinerwald*', and that further attempts to push forward were repulsed. '*Schwerinerwald*' was what the Germans called the northern part of Accroche Wood. The author, Poetter, keen to promote the battalion's achievements, was clearly ignorant of the fact that the Australians had no designs on Accroche Wood that day.[122]

On the battalion right wing stood D Company (Captain E.M. Bradley), ready to skirt the northern edge of Vaire Wood. Yet again, at Zero hour, their own artillery became a serious threat as they began moving forward. Lieutenant Farrelly, in charge of the rear platoon of D

118 AWM: 4 23/32/40. War Diary 15th Battalion. After Action Report by Capt. Glasgow.
119 AWM: 4 23/32/40. War Diary 15th Battalion. After Action Report by Capt. Glasgow.
120 Chataway, *History of the Fifteenth Battalion*, p.216.
121 Lt George Edward Fewster, age 25, is buried in Crucifix Corner Cemetery, grave X.C.13. 1706 Sergeant Charles Hollamby is commemorated on the Villers-Bretonneux Memorial.
122 *Hauptmann* Poetter, *Infanterie-Regiment Nr 55* (Oldenburg/Berlin: Druck und Verlag von Gerhard Stalling, 1922), p.53. Compare Schultz's account above, which shares this misconception.

Company, wrote that: 'two or three guns opened short on our sector and fired right into the left of 'D' Company, and were responsible for about 20 casualties in the first 30 yards.'[123]

On the right, the advance was 'in perfect order', but some of the men on the left, perhaps not surprisingly under a 'friendly' shrapnel barrage, 'were a little… inclined to bunch.'[124] Lieutenant Sloan (No. 15 Platoon) paints a similar picture in his report, adding that 'a few guns were very slow in lifting.'[125]

Despite this obvious and frustrating difficulty, Farrelly noted that: 'The point that I noticed most was the splendid fire discipline of the men, at all times they looked to officers and NCOs for instructions and all orders were promptly obeyed.'[126]

D Company's first wave made short work of the German garrison in their front line trench, where most of the defenders were found to be wearing 'thin' gas masks.[127] Captain Bradley, in his report, makes a telling comment on the relative attitudes of attackers and defenders: 'The enemy did not seem to like the idea of coming to close quarters, but when our chaps did meet opposition they did not hesitate but got straight to work.'[128]

D Company's most serious opposition came from a machine gun post with a system of dugouts, 'the wire of which seemed intact',[129] on the road at the furthest northern tip of Vaire/Hamel Wood (See map). One tank was on hand when requested, 'keeping down fire'[130] from the German machine gun as the infantry stormed the position. Reports on the number of prisoners taken here and sent to the rear range from six, including one officer, to 30. A sizeable group attempted to escape into the wood, but No. 15 platoon opened fire, killing many before they had gone too far.

After reorganising on the 10-minute halt line, where Farrelly noticed that the men on the left were still 'uncomfortably close to the barrage',[131] the advance was largely unopposed until the sunken road south of Hamel was reached. By this point, the fight had gone out of the defenders, and as the tanks pushed through, most of the German garrison tried to escape along Hun's Walk in the direction of Accroche Wood. The Blue Line was therefore soon reached, and No.16 Platoon moved across to the right to fill in a gap and establish touch with 13th Battalion, only to move back up to the left when more 13th Battalion men arrived on the scene.

By 8:00 a.m., a complete line had been formed, with all companies in touch right and left, and with consolidation well in hand, a double apron belt of wire was in place in front of their 'new' front line trench, this materiel having been brought forward by a supply tank. Again, no German counterattack materialised, but even here, Lieutenant Sloan had to report that 'the only casualties inflicted on platoon after reaching objective were caused through a heavy battery of ours falling short.'[132]

123 AWM: 4 23/32/40. War Diary 15th Battalion. 'Report on stunt near Hamel Wood on 4/7/18. Lt Edward Farrelly, 16 Platoon', written 7 July.
124 AWM: 4 23/32/40. War Diary 15th Battalion. Farrelly.
125 AWM: 4 23/32/40. War Diary 15th Battalion. Report written by Lt. B.T. Sloan, 15 Platoon.
126 AWM: 4 23/32/40. War Diary 15th Battalion. Farrelly.
127 AWM: 4 23/32/40. War Diary 15th Battalion.
128 AWM: 4 23/32/40. War Diary 15th Battalion. 'Hamel Stunt.' Report by Captain E.M. Bradley, O/C D Coy.
129 AWM: 4 23/32/40. War Diary 15th Battalion. Sloan.
130 AWM: 4 23/32/40. War Diary 15th Battalion.
131 AWM: 4 23/32/40. War Diary 15th Battalion. Farrelly.
132 AWM: 4 23/32/40. War Diary 15th Battalion. Sloan.

The Lewis gun screen pushed out in front of the Blue Line was busy during the morning as they inflicted casualties on groups of Germans who were trying to establish their own new front line. Once the protective barrage ceased 30 minutes after the objective was reached,

> our planes came over in large formations and held command of the air up till midday when their control was disrupted for about an hour by a flight of up to 35 enemy planes which brought two of our own down. About 25,000 rounds of S.A.A. were dropped by parachutes in and in rear of our lines by our planes.[133]

At least two German aircraft were brought down during the aerial confrontation, both accounted for by the same RE8 (A3662) of 3 Squadron AFC, crewed by Lieutenant A.E. Grigson (pilot) and Lieutenant B.H. James (observer), which was attacked whilst flying a contact patrol at around 9:00 a.m. by two enemy planes, and then again by three more 20 minutes later.

It is probable that a third German aircraft was shot down by RE8 C2347 of 9 Squadron RAF, with Lieutenant H.E. Pryce and Lieutenant J.G. Sanders on board. They reported having dropped ammunition at P.15. d. 2.2. and were then attacked at 10:00 a.m. by three Pfalz scouts at 1,500 feet over Hamel Wood. Sanders fired 120 rounds from his Lewis gun into the enemy aircraft, and one was seen to fall out of control. Pryce was wounded in the dog fight, but landed safely back at the aerodrome. This 'kill' seems to be corroborated by RE8 E21, (Lieutenants Newton and Reynolds) who reported an enemy aircraft seen crashed in square P.15.d. at around 11:00 a.m.

Casualties for 15th Battalion, as reported in McSharry's after-action report, amounted to three officers and 32 other ranks killed,[134] with nine dying of wounds; eight officers and 190 other ranks wounded. The American contingent suffered 13 other ranks killed, with two officers and 44 other ranks wounded. Twelve other ranks were missing. A very uncomfortable proportion of those casualties must have been caused by 'shorts' from their own artillery, although the unsupported assault on Pear Trench is likely to have accounted for the majority. McSharry was clear on the reasons for the success of his battalion's attack:

> The success of the… operation was due to the fine leadership of platoon commanders and the superb dash and daring of the men themselves who dealt with any situation that presented itself on their own initiative. The gallantry displayed both individually and collectively was quite up to the Australian standard.[135]

* * *

The task of 14th Battalion was succinctly summed up in the narrative of operations in the battalion war diary: 'The role of the 14th Battalion was to jump off as reserve and carrying Battalion, establish forward dumps, and on completion of these dumps become support Battalion until the final objective was established.' To accomplish this last task, they would be

133 AWM: 4 23/32/40. War Diary 15th Battalion. 'Narrative' by Lt Col. McSharry.
134 Commonwealth War Graves Commission records put the final fatality count for 4–6 July 1918 for 15th Battalion at 49.
135 AWM: 4 23/32/40 War Diary 15th Battalion, July 1918, Appendix 3.

required to dig a support line in the rear of the Blue Line. On 3 July, the Americans (two officers and 240 other ranks of F Company, 131st Regiment) who had been attached for the upcoming operation, were ordered to withdraw, leaving 14th Battalion's numbers drastically depleted.

The jumping off positions of 14th Battalion were spread across the entire brigade frontage: moving south to north were C Company (Captain W.R. Wadsworth MC), then A Company (Captain N. Wilson) in support of 13th Battalion, with B Company next (Lieutenant William Jacka),[136] supporting the left wing of 16th Battalion and finally D Company (Captain W.R.M. Beamond MC) supporting the right of 15th Battalion.

One platoon (No. 2) of A Company under Lieutenant T.H. Griffith would act independently in the rear of 13th Battalion, tasked with establishing a strongpoint at P.15. d. 2.5. Attached were engineers, two Vickers machine guns and a light trench mortar. The position of this strongpoint would determine the alignment of the new support line. It would also serve as a liaison point for the companies completing their moves north and south of the woods.

Table 4. 14th Battalion 'over-the-top strength'.[137]

	Officers	Other Ranks
HQ	5	42
A Coy	4	95
B Coy	5	86
C Coy	5	102
D Coy	4	84
Total	**23**	**409**

On the right, Wadsworth's C Company moved off at Zero in artillery formation, hurrying, fully laden as they were, in order to clear the front line jumping off positions as quickly as possible so as to avoid the expected retaliation from German artillery. Yet again, however, it was their own guns firing short that inflicted the company's first casualties of the day. They reached their first objective, the site where they were to deposit the materiel they were carrying (at approximately P.20. b. 9.5), without encountering any serious opposition. This task completed, they pushed on and began to dig the new support line with their right wing at P.21. a. 0.3. As day broke, finding that there was an enemy garrison still active in a communication trench ahead of them, at a spot where the assault battalions had left a small gap, one platoon was sent forward to deal with it. As the Australians approached the position, the Germans raised the white flag.[138]

136 Brother of Albert Jacka VC, MC & Bar.

137 AWM: 4 23/31/45 War Diary 14th Battalion. The battalion had tragically suffered 86 casualties, including 18 killed, on the night of 31 May/1 June while the men were sleeping in barns near the village of Allonville, after having watched a show put on by the 4th Division's Concert Party. Two shells – each weighing 254 pounds – from a German naval railway gun some 14 miles away scored direct hits on the barns occupied by the men of A and C Companies. See FitzSimons, *Monash's Masterpiece*, pp.45–50.

138 As recounted in Newton Wanliss, *The History of the Fourteenth Battalion AIF* (Melbourne: The Arrow Printery, 1929), p.306.

> Lts Rule and Wood, with five others, thereupon advanced to take them prisoners, and were not far distant from them when they opened fire again. Pte Dave Floyd was here mortally wounded by one of our 'shorts' and Cpl Stan Cochrane fell dead with a bullet in his brain a moment later. The white flag reprobates fled up the trench when our men got near them, and then Ramsay Wood fell dead with a bullet through the temple. Only three of the little party were now left, so Rule went back and sent forward Sgt 'Red' Campbell and six men with rifle bombs, which enabled the post to be held…. Unwittingly, the little party had now cut off no fewer than forty Germans who finally surrendered.[139]

Rule then sent up two Vickers machine guns, which were positioned so as to be able to sweep the company's unprotected left flank. The position was subsequently taken over by 13th Battalion, and C Company went on to dig 'a continuous line from approx. P.21.a.3.1 to P.21. a. 7.7 with an average depth of 5' 6" & linked up with company on left.'[140] (See Map 5).

The company to the left was A Company. Lieutenant Griffith's No. 2 Platoon was quick off the mark at Zero, close on the heels of the 13th Battalion men. The idea was to skirt the southern edge of Vaire Wood and then turn to the north-east. Before they reached the wood, however, they ran into a row of German dugouts with two machine guns in position (at P.20. a. 7.7.). Captain Wilson's report glosses over the capture of this emplacement, but implies a certain ruthlessness: 'two prisoners were taken and the rest (6) [who refused to come out of the dugout] were dealt with.'[141] The platoon then made it to the artillery halt line with no further trouble and waited for the barrage to restart its forward movement.

The other two platoons, Nos. 1 and 3 (Lieutenants Garton and Davies), halted on the terraced downslope before Vaire Wood (at around P.14. a. 7.2.) until Zero plus 35 minutes. After the artillery halt, No. 1 Platoon moved quickly around the southern edge of the wood and established a dump at its south-eastern corner.

By 4:00 a.m., No. 2 Platoon had moved forward and was constructing the new strongpoint slightly east of the original planned location, and the two other platoons arrived, spread out, and began digging the new support line. Captain Wilson noticed, ahead of them, that there was a gap of about 500 yards in the new front line positions. He sent one and a half platoons forward to fill this gap, and they discovered a number of camouflaged dugouts, which 'had to be mopped up. Four of the enemy were killed and eleven prisoners were taken.'[142] Lieutenants Garton and Davies had captured three trench mortars between them, and, finding that there was plenty of

139 The 'white flag reprobates' incident is not mentioned in the 14th Battalion narrative of events, nor in Wadsworth's after-action report. 317 Private David William Floyd, who enlisted in September 1914, is buried in Daours Communal Cemetery Extension, grave III.D.27. 5762 Corporal Harry Stanley Cochrane, is buried in Crucifix Corner Cemetery, grave V.E.18. One of the Red Cross reports describing his death was written by his brother, 5761 Pte William David Cochrane, No. 10 Platoon, C Coy, who was about 100 yards away. William survived the war. Lieutenant Ramsay Wood, age 30, native of Heaton, Newcastle-upon-Tyne, England, is buried in Crucifix Corner Cemetery, grave X.C.5. Before the battle, Wood could not be persuaded to 'dress down', insisting on going over the top in his best dress uniform. See FitzSimons, *Monash's Masterpiece*, p.204.

140 AWM: 4 23/31/45 War Diary 14th Battalion. After-action report written by Captain Wadsworth, OC, C Coy.

141 AWM: 4 23/31/45 War Diary 14th Battalion. After-action report of Captain Wilson, OC, A Coy.

142 AWM: 4 23/31/45 War Diary 14th Battalion. After-action report of Captain Wilson, OC, A Coy. This section of line was later taken over by 13th Battalion.

The grave of Private David William Floyd, 14th Battalion. (Author)

The grave of Corporal Harry Stanley Cochrane, 14th Battalion. (Author)

The grave of Lieutenant Ramsay Wood, 14th Battalion. (Author)

The grave of Sergeant William Thomas Fisher, 14th Battalion. (Author)

ammunition available, redeployed them and began firing into Accroche Wood. An inspection of these dugouts had revealed cigars and hot coffee: both were 'soon sampled.'[143]

By this point, A Company had only suffered two casualties. One of those had occurred just as they left their original jumping off positions: Sergeant Fisher was killed, probably by shell fire, but whether from friend or foe is uncertain.[144]

B Company's task was to support the left wing of 16th Battalion in its advance through the northern sector of Vaire Wood. As they advanced in the rear of 16th Battalion through Vaire and Hamel Woods with their right flank on Hun's Walk, their main task appeared to be that of encouraging the stream of German prisoners in their movement to the rear. The after-action report also remarks on finding 'many German dead lying on the ground with their gas helmets on.'[145] No. 7 Platoon then helped to clear a dugout of some 15 Germans. 'These prisoners also had their gas helmets on and looked very young and were men of very small physique.'[146]

At the artillery halt, Jacka allowed his men to drop their loads, rest, and smoke. As they resumed their advance, No. 5 Platoon continued following the left wing of 16th Battalion until Hamel Wood had been cleared, before rejoining the rest of the company at the designated dump site. Unencumbered by their loads, they now pushed on and established a link with No. 2 Platoon of A Company as the latter were busy completing the construction of the strong point. B Company promptly 'shook out into line and commenced to dig and consolidate our position. The Officers then moved forward and to the flanks for the purpose of discovering the dispositions of neighbouring units.'[147]

By 10:00 a.m., the new line had been dug to an average depth of four feet six inches and a company HQ had been established about 30 yards behind it. As German aircraft appeared overhead at 10:15 a.m., 'these planes were engaged by us with Lewis guns & in many instances were temporarily driven off.'[148]

Jacka reports only five casualties in his company. One was particularly unfortunate: at around 7:30 p.m. on 5 July, Private Thomas of No. 7 Platoon was standing in the newly dug support line when the Germans sent over a number of shrapnel shells. A piece of shrapnel glanced off the parapet and hit Thomas' cartridge pouch, which exploded and 'blew a hole right through him.'[149]

On the extreme left, D Company (Captain Beamond) set off behind 15th Battalion, and, making a detour to the right to avoid any enemy fire from Pear Trench, did not come under fire until just before the 10-minute halt, when No. 13 Platoon got too far ahead and 'had a few casualties from some of our own 18 Pdr shorts.'[150] According to Lieutenant Colonel Crowther's 'Narrative of Operations', one shell 'wiped out an entire Lewis gun team.'

143 Wanliss, *History of the Fourteenth Battalion*, p.307.
144 1709 Sergeant William Thomas Fisher, age 29 and father of three, is buried in Crucifix Corner Cemetery, grave V.E.4.
145 AWM: 4 23/31/45 War Diary 14th Battalion. After-action report of Lieutenant Jacka, OC, B Coy.
146 AWM: 4 23/31/45 War Diary 14th Battalion. After-action report of Lieutenant Jacka, OC, B Coy.
147 AWM: 4 23/31/45 War Diary 14th Battalion. After-action report of Lieutenant Jacka, OC, B Coy.
148 AWM: 4 23/31/45 War Diary 14th Battalion. After-action report of Lieutenant Jacka, OC, B Coy.
149 Red Cross Report. 12626 Private Claude Edison Thomas, 27 years old, transferred from 14th Coy Australian Army Service Corps in May, is buried in Villers-Bretonneux Military Cemetery, grave III.C.7. His brother, 2433 Pte Rupert Clemence Thomas, age 25, also a member of B Coy, 14th Battalion, was killed in action by shell fire on 8 August 1918.
150 AWM: 4 23/31/45 War Diary 14th Battalion. After-action report of Captain Beamond, OC D Coy.

Once their loads had been deposited at the allocated dump site, they formed up once more and moved on about 150 yards behind 15th Battalion. They witnessed the tanks taking out the German machine gun positions in the sunken road south of Hamel, and then, on reaching their objective, began to dig in. At 4:10 a.m., Beamond sent a 'message rocket' reporting their arrival on the objective.

Following close on the heels of the centre companies of 16th Battalion were a number of 14th Battalion medical personnel, led by the RMO Captain H.C. Trumble. By 3:20 a.m., before the assault troops had dealt with the German front line trenches, they had established a regimental aid post 'on the ledges' on the downslope to Vaire Wood.[151]

The grave of Private Claude Edison Thomas, 14th Battalion. (Author)

> This R.A.P. administered to a great proportion of the wounded of the Brigade, and carried on in fine fashion till relieved on the evening of the 6th instant. With this party went the Battalion Padre (Major F.W. Rolland MC) and through his personal ministrations, hot drinks were available for wounded and stretcher bearers from the moment of the establishment of the R.A.P.[152]

Crowther's 'Narrative of Operations' closes with his estimation of casualty figures for the day. He records one officer killed and one wounded.[153] Other ranks casualties amount to four killed and 49 wounded.[154]

The 4th Brigade's 'Notes on Hamel Offensive', written on 12 July 1918,[155] gives an overall impression of a very well organised and planned attack in which all ranks were well-briefed on what they were expected to do. Following the series of conferences, during which information was disseminated in stages from Monash himself down to the platoon commander, maps and aerial photographs were distributed: message maps and oblique photographs down to every NCO; artillery barrage maps and enlarged oblique photographs down to company

151 AWM: 4 23/31/45 War Diary 14th Battalion. 'Narrative of Operations.'
152 AWM: 4 23/31/45 War Diary 14th Battalion. 'Narrative of Operations.'
153 This officer is Lieutenant Stanley Booley of No. 12 Platoon, D Coy.
154 Commonwealth War Graves Commission records show seven other ranks fatalities for 4–5 July 1918. The author has been unable to establish the exact circumstances surrounding the deaths of two of them. 6859 Pte Leonard Howard Hawksbee is buried in Villers-Bretonneux Military Cemetery, grave XII.C.5. 5394 Pte William Leslie Hughes, D Coy, is buried in Crucifix Corner Cemetery, grave X.C.10. Hughes died at the Dressing Station after sustaining shell splinter wounds to the abdomen.
155 AWM: 4 23/4/34 War Diary 4th Infantry Brigade Part 2.

commanders, with platoon commanders receiving large-scale maps, vertical aerial photographs and maps showing enemy dispositions.

It goes on to describe the artillery barrage as 'excellent', but accepts that some guns did fire short and that it missed the Pear Trench system. It dismisses the enemy retaliatory artillery action in two lines, stating that it 'did not come down until ZERO plus 5½ minutes by which time the whole of the attacking troops were clear', later describing it as 'thin and scattered.'[156] Enemy defensive positions are criticised:

> Very little defensive work appears to have been done in this area. The wire in many places was non-existent and where it did exist it did not prove a very serious obstacle. The trenches were roughtly [sic] dug and badly undercut. Apparently no arrangements for sanitation had been made. Dugout accommodation was ver[y] limited and of a poor type.[157]

Tanks, aircraft and American troops receive fulsome praise.

The tone of the report is rightly positive, with overall casualty figures reaching a total of 32 officers and 579 other ranks.[158] These can probably be categorised as 'acceptable' for an operation where all objectives were gained, consolidated, and held, all within the proposed timetable. The casualty figures should, however, have been lower. Despite the overall success, every battalion suffered unacceptable losses from artillery 'shorts', and 15th Battalion paid a high price for both the failure of the artillery barrage and the non-appearance of tanks at Pear Trench.

156 AWM: 4 23/4/34 War Diary 4th Infantry Brigade Part 2.
157 AWM: 4 23/4/34 War Diary 4th Infantry Brigade Part 2.
158 Killed and wounded. Calculated, with the usual caveats, from battalion war diaries and including American figures.

4

The Attack of 11th Brigade

The battalions of 11th Brigade formed the left – or northern – wing of the main attack on a frontage of approximately 2,000 yards. The brigade war diary sums up the task before it:

> a) The 43rd Battalion will… capture and mop up HAMEL. After clearing the town all troops will be withdrawn from it.
> b) The 44th Battalion will, avoiding the Town of HAMEL, 'leap-frog' through 43rd Battalion and capture and consolidate the BLUE line in the South Battalion area.
> c) The 42nd Battalion will capture and consolidate the BLUE Line within the Northern Battalion area.
> d) The 41st Battalion will be Brigade Reserve…[1]

The accompanying artillery barrage would advance at a rate of 100 yards every three minutes from the start line up to the halt line. Ten minutes later, the barrage would lift 100 yards and then continue its forward movement at 100 yards every four minutes, halting once more 400 yards east of the Blue Line, thence forming a protective barrage lasting until Zero plus 123 minutes.

Almost half of all the tanks deployed for this battle would support the troops in this brigade sector: one section (three tanks) of C Company, 13th Tank Battalion was allocated to 42nd Battalion for the capture of the Blue Line; two sections (six tanks) of C Company 8th Tank Battalion would help 43rd Battalion capture Hamel village; two sections (six tanks) also of C Company, 8th Tank Battalion would accompany 44th Battalion in their assault on the Wolfsberg position, one moving north of Hamel village, the other to the south; two sections (six tanks) of A Company, 8th Tank Battalion were to act as liaison with 4th and 11th Brigades as they advanced to the Blue Line. Six tanks of B Company, 13th Tank Battalion, would form a reserve force, and, finally, two supply tanks would bring essential materiel forward. This brings the total to 29 tanks.

No less than 44 Vickers medium machine guns would add their weight to the assault, 14 of them providing enfilade fire from the northern flank.

1 AWM: 4 23/11/20. War Diary 11th Infantry Brigade. The battalion dispositions can be seen on Map 6.

Pershing's order, however, on 3 July for the withdrawal of attached American units meant that only 42nd Battalion, with three platoons (170–180 men) of C Company, 1st Battalion, 131st Regiment, and 43rd Battalion with E Company (260–270 men) of 2nd Battalion, 131st Regiment, took Americans with them into the attack. The brigade was therefore reduced at a stroke from 3,000 to 2,200 men.

The defence of Hamel and the elevated Wolfsberg position was the responsibility of the under-strength *Reserve-Infanterie-Regiment 202* (*RIR 202*). The regimental history paints a retrospectively gloomy and pessimistic image of the positions they had occupied since 16 June:

> The position was still under construction. The front-line was not yet fully linked-up. This was particularly so in the right sub-sector, where there were wide gaps. There were no communication trenches. Movement from Forward HQ to the front was not possible during daylight hours. The front-line garrison had no reinforced dugouts. The support companies were on the Wolfsberg in old enemy trenches, where they had good shelter in places. The communications system – telephone, lamp signalling and power buzzer – was unsatisfactory and actually unreliable, it being a rather makeshift installation. The construction of the trench positions and the communications system took up all of the regiment's time and efforts. The weak fighting strength of the unit was markedly felt here, as each company was allotted around 700 metres of frontage and with their offensive activities curtailed by the poor observation in No Man's Land due to high crop, and the alertness of the enemy, a state of permanent vigilance was called for, along with constant raiding. As a result of the gloomy weather, the enemy artillery fire was initially only sporadic, but this intensified in the evening and later in the night with heavy bombardments with large calibre weapons on our trenches, on Hamel, the Wolfsberg and the Wuthenau Ravine. During the nights, enemy aircraft appeared, strafing and dropping bombs on our trenches….. At the end of June, Spanish flu, which was rampant along the entire Western Front, took hold in our regiment. At times, each battalion had 60–80 men affected. Even though the illness was not particularly nasty and the high fever usually subsided after four days or so, the resulting weakening of work details had a negative effect on their output.[2]

* * *

The men of 42nd Battalion, lining up on the northern brigade flank, were to move to the north of Hamel, with their right flank on the road running through squares P.3 c & d and P.4 c & d (See Map 6), their ultimate objective being the old British front line system to the north-east of the village, which had been evacuated on 4 April 1918, now designated the Blue Line.

They positioned themselves with A and C Companies in front, left to right, (Captains Warry and Jack)[3] with D and B Companies (Captain O'Bryen and Lieutenant Lewis) close behind them in support.[4]

2 Fritz Bergeder, *Das Reserve-Infanterie-Regiment Nr. 202 auf den Schlachtfeldern des Weltkrieges 1914-1918.* (Berlin & Wilmersdorf: Verlag Tradition, 1927), pp.143–144.

3 Captain Thomas Jack assumed command of C Coy on 3 July 1918 following the death of its previous OC, Captain W.H.A. McDonnell, the day before the Hamel attack.

4 American Officers from C Coy, 131st Infantry Regiment attached to 42nd Battalion were Captain Carroll M. Gale, Lieutenants Charles M. Porter, Albert Jefferson and Fred Rinkliff, and Second

Accounts of 42nd Battalion's attack are short on detail: the battalion war diarist describes the action as follows: '... our men proceeded towards their objective which was taken with very little difficulty and few casualties. All companies were consolidated by 8 a.m. Hun completely surprised gave little resistance.'[5]

No Man's Land in front of 42nd Battalion was very wide and very flat, and the first German trench system was 800 yards away near the road running north from Hamel in squares P. 4 a & c (see map). They were able to follow what appears to have been a very accurate creeping barrage. An American officer attached to 42nd Battalion, Captain Gale, later wrote:

Captain Carroll M. Gale, 131st Regiment. (Public Domain)

> The barrage ... was most wonderful; it surpassed even the great barrage of September 26th,[6] ... the falling shells of the 18-pounders exploding as they hit the ground, formed an almost straight line from the north edge of the action at the Somme to as far south as we could see.[7]

Isolated machine gun posts had been overrun, and the tanks, by now just ahead of the infantry, having caught up with them when the barrage made its second lift, made short work of these enemy positions. After the 10-minute artillery pause, the advance was able to continue up the slope to the Blue Line on the ridge. A hand-written message timed at 4:18 a.m. confirmed that 'British Tanks moving all over Hun system P.4 d. P.4 b.' Another at 4:27 a.m. simply states: 'Have reached objective.'[8]

Casualties were extremely light and only two specific events merit a mention in the after-action report. One German machine gun 'caused trouble' and inflicted casualties on a Lewis gun team, but 'one of the remainder of the crew, L/Cpl. Daley outflanked the Bosche and with the aid of Mills Bombs and the bayonet, got the whole crew.'[9] Another party was going forward led by Lieutenant Sessarago (D Company), when this officer was killed by shellfire. One of his party, Private Lovering, though wounded in the leg by the same shell, 'rushed the gun and just lasted long enough to bayonet the gunner when he fell unconscious without extracting his bayonet.'[10]

Lieutenant John C. Heyl.

5 AWM: 4 23/59/21 War Diary 42nd Battalion.

6 This refers to the American action on that day by the 33rd Division in the Meuse-Argonne offensive.

7 Quoted in Bean, *The Official History*, vol.VI, p.284.

8 Bean, *The Official History*, vol.VI, p.284.

9 Bean, *The Official History*, vol.VI, p.284. 2020 Lance Corporal Michael John Daley MM and his commanding officer, Captain Jack, were killed in the same incident during an action near Proyart on 12 August 1918. Both are commemorated on the Villers-Bretonneux Memorial.

10 Bean, *The Official History*, vol.VI, p.284. 2673 Pte W.F. Lovering survived this action and the war. Lieutenant Frederick Harold Sessarago 'Sessy', aged 21, was hit in the throat by splinters from

As the men consolidated their newly-won positions on the ridge, the tanks pushed forward to harass any German positions in the vicinity and discourage any thoughts of counterattack. The 42nd Battalion's after action report relates a strange episode at this point:

> While this was going on an enemy Tank appeared on the horizon making for one of our Tanks which was partly disabled. When quite close the Hun brought his gun into action but missed our tank turning just in time to avoid trouble. One of our other Tanks came to the rescue and bumped the Hun badly setting fire to him. He then off [sic] in a hurry in a burning condition to the rear of Accroche Wood. The antics of the Tanks rounding up small parties of Huns in shell holes and sending them back was extremely amusing.[11]

The grave of Lieutenant Frederick Harold Sessarago, 42nd Battalion. (Author)

The 42nd Battalion ended the day with A, B and C Companies, north to south, occupying the Blue Line positions to the north-east of Hamel, with D Company some 500 yards further back in support. Casualties were reported as one officer killed, with two wounded. Three other ranks were killed, and 45 were wounded.[12]

* * *

one of our own shells. His batman, 7631 Private John Reed Jones, witnessed his officer's fate and wrote afterwards to Sessarago's mother, but did not tell her that it was a 'friendly fire' incident. 'I wrote to her but I did not mention that it was one of our own shells as I thought it would hurt her' – from Jones' testimony dated 19 August 1918, Australian Red Cross Society Wounded and Missing Enquiry Bureau files, 1914-18 War. 1DRL/0428. Lieutenant Sessarago is buried in Villers-Bretonneux Military Cemetery, grave VIII.B.9.

11 AWM: 4 23/59/21 War Diary 42nd Battalion. This account is prompted by a hand-written message sent to Battalion HQ, timed at 5:32 a.m. This is backed up by a similar message, timed at 5:35 a.m., sent to 11th Brigade HQ, placing the incident in square P.11 a., and another sent to 41st Battalion HQ, timing the encounter at 5:20 a.m. Tellingly, there is no mention of a German tank in the *Official History*, and, more importantly, no mention in any of the 5th Tank Brigade, 8th Tank Battalion or 13th Tank Battalion accounts or diaries. What is reported, in TNA: WO95/114-3, the 8th Tank Battalion War Diary Appendices, p.116, under 'Lessons & Suggestions' is that 'too many Tanks were employed on so small a front, with the result that they masked one another's fire, and in one case *two of them collided*.' It is the author's contention that the infantry 'witnesses' mistook this accident for enemy action.

12 3281 Sergeant Harold Reginald Cocks is buried in Crouy British Cemetery, grave III.B.19. 1138 Corporal John Thomas Holley, C Coy, killed by a machine gun wound to the abdomen, is buried in Daours Communal Cemetery Extension, grave III.D.40. 2003 Private Claverhouse Young, aged 21, died of his wounds on 5 July 1918 and is buried in Villers-Bretonneux Military Cemetery grave III.B.5. Records indicate that C Coy, 131st American Infantry Regiment, suffered no fatalities.

The grave of Sergeant Harold Reginald Cocks, 42nd Battalion. (Author)

The grave of Corporal John Thomas Holley, 42nd Battalion. (Author)

The grave of Private Claverhouse Young, 42nd Battalion. (Author)

It was not until the morning of 2 July that the men of 43rd Battalion (Lieutenant Colonel J. Farrell) were informed of their objective for the coming assault, namely the capture of the village of Hamel. Eleven days earlier, on 21 June, two specialist patrol groups, each led by an officer, and containing men from all four companies, were sent forward. They,

> …lived in the [front] line for two days and did patrol work. As a result of this reconnaissance, it was found the enemy were comparatively close (250 yds) on our right flank near the PEAR TRENCH, and he was also very active

> with Machine guns from this quarter. On the left flank of the battalion attack he was 700 yards away and was not very active. There was very high crop in NO MAN'S LAND which promised good cover, but which made the going much heavier. The enemy had a trench system on the west side of HAMEL which ran through NOTAMEL WOOD and swung S.W. along the high ground… towards PEAR TRENCH. It was anticipated that he had fairly strong garrisons in HAMEL itself in deep dugouts, which surmise proved to be correct.[13]

Lieutenant Colonel John Farrell, CO 43rd Battalion. (AWM)

Brigade conferences 'were held almost daily',[14] and once all the intricacies of the assault had been thoroughly discussed and settled, the battalion officers were informed of the details on 30 June.

At Zero, they would line up on a 1,000-yard frontage, with A Company (Captain J.T. Moran) on the left, B Company (Captain H.S. Cope) in the centre and C Company (Captain R.C. Sexton) on the right. D Company (Major A.W. Lott) would be in support. The four American platoons from E Company, 131st Regiment, (Captain Luke), each composed of seven squads of one NCO and seven men, were spread equally amongst the Australian companies.[15]

The first task was to assault and then bypass the German front line trenches to the west of Hamel before entering the western part of the village. After a pause on the artillery halt line – approximately 1,300 yards from the jumping off positions – during which 44th Battalion would leapfrog to the north and south of the village – the rest of Hamel would be mopped up.

First Lieutenant Alfred N. Clissold, 131st Regiment. (Public Domain)

13 AWM: 4 23/60/23. War diary 43rd Battalion. 'Report on Operations of 4th July 1918.' The names of the two officers are not mentioned.

14 AWM: 4 23/60/23. War diary 43rd Battalion. 'Report on Operations of 4th July 1918.'

15 The two platoons of D Coy, 131st Regiment which had been attached on 1 July were withdrawn the evening before the attack. Some of the Americans in E Coy were deployed as stretcher bearers, runners, intelligence personnel and medical units. The officers from E Coy who were attached to 43rd Battalion were: Lieutenants A.N. Clissold and S.C. Davis, and Second Lieutenants R.L. Lee and E.R. Plummer.

B Company would move straight ahead from the west, whilst A Company would swing south through Notamel Wood, as far as the main east-west road on which the village church was situated, with C Company performing a mirror-image manoeuvre from the south. Six tanks would assist.

Once Hamel had been cleared, 43rd Battalion would withdraw completely to the west of the village, where A and C Companies would dig a line of strongpoints, these to be joined up to form a continuous defensive trench line as soon as it was practicable. With 44th Battalion by then established (it was presumed!) on the ridge to the east of Hamel, its continued occupation would serve no useful purpose, and the withdrawal would mean that any German artillery retaliation could fall harmlessly on an empty village.

On the night of 2/3 July, the line of assembly was marked out by stakes driven far enough into the ground to be hidden by the crops. The following night, just prior to the assault, Lieutenants Tucker and Borthwick superintended the connecting of these stakes by white tape, working with Lieutenant Rhodes and his engineers. Tapes were then also led back to the front line trench, marking the left flank position of each company. Gaps were cut in the wire at these points: at 12:30 a.m. on the morning of the attack, the men were able to file through the gaps, follow the tape in single file as far as the jumping-off line, turn and extend to the right. C Company on the right flank were instructed to move back '50 yards behind the tape in case of shorts from our own artillery on PEAR TRENCH.'[16]

The men were in position ready for the attack by 2:30 a.m., and it was at this point that officers were able to issue a tot of rum to their men. Each man (other than specialists) carried, in addition to his rifle and bayonet, 200 rounds of ammunition, two grenades, 48 hours' rations, two filled water bottles, three sandbags and either a pick or a shovel. Each Lewis gun section carried 18 magazines. Each assaulting company had two platoons extended in line across the front as 'skirmishers or "followers of the barrage"',[17] with the other two platoons behind in artillery formation (sections in single file). D Company, in the rear, adopted this latter formation with all its platoons.

The diary of 165 Private Eric Giles Miller describes the build-up to Zero hour:

> The time was immediately before dawn after a perfect night of early summer – a fresh, calm soft aired night such as would turn men's thoughts to anything but war. What moon there was vanished early and shooting was only spasmodic by the guns of either side. Now and again an aeroplane of ours – no Hun machines were to be heard – droned overhead like a mammoth mosquito, passed on towards Germany, and in the distance delivered a little cargo of bombs. But on the whole the night was strangely still and pleasant as summer nights go behind the fighting lines in France.
>
> During the last few minutes prior to the attack, a thicker humming droned in the air – a string of our aeroplanes flying low to drown with their noise the rattle of the tanks over their last half-mile to the front line.[18]

16 AWM: 4 23/60/23. War diary 43rd Battalion. 'Report on Operations of 4th July 1918.'
17 AWM: 4 23/60/23. War diary 43rd Battalion. 'Report on Operations of 4th July 1918.'
18 AWM: 2018.19.36. Diary of 165 Private Eric Giles Miller, 43rd Battalion. Miller took part in the 4 July 1918 attack and suffered gunshot wounds to the shoulder, back, thigh and neck. He survived the war.

At 3:02 a.m., the artillery commenced their 'usual' morning harassing fire on the German lines, including smoke shells, but this time no gas. The German garrison seemed unaware of the impending assault:

> Here and there a brilliant rocket soared up from the doomed lines, yet seemed to convey no serious note of alarm, merely warning perhaps of the supposed usual gas strafe. To the last moment the little corner of country there among the broad sloping valleys, and its population, the semi-somnolent battalions which the imagination could picture easily enough in their holes, seemed unaware of the mighty pole-axe poised to strike.[19]

The artillery barrage proper began on time at 3:10 a.m.

> There was a big boom from the first counter-battery gun, a 12 inch monster behind the ordered array of the smaller artillery, and the still morning air was henceforth torn and racked with noise. The previous slow succession of bursts along the German line, irregular and rather careless,… now quickened and multiplied like electric sparks over the whole front. Vast billows of smoke rolled about with them, smoke so thick that it was impossible to say for ten minutes or so whether or not the barrage advanced. Gradually the morning light improved and the smoke cleared, and Hamel village began dimly to stand out.[20]

Unfortunately, the fear of artillery 'shorts' falling near Pear Trench was proved right: two guns on that flank 'shot short right through the operation.'[21] Two sections of C Company, positioned in the right rear, one Australian and one American, suffered casualties even before they had moved, including one American officer, Second Lieutenant Plummer, who was wounded. Ironically, the 50-yard safety buffer had actually put them in danger.

Second Lieutenant E.R. Plummer, 131st Regiment. (Public Domain)

The artillery barrage 'played on the Zero line'[22] for four minutes before making its first 100 yard lift. During this time the men moved forward to within 80 yards of the barrage – as close as they dared. Smoke and dust 'formed so dense a screen as to block completely the view of the bursting shells. Overhead shrapnel [bursts were] the best guiding mark of the position of the barrage.'[23]

On the left flank, ahead of A Company, the barrage was 'superb & undoubtedly achieved its object

19 AWM: 2018.19.36. Diary of 165 Private Eric Giles Miller, 43rd Battalion.
20 AWM: 2018.19.36. Diary of 165 Private Eric Giles Miller, 43rd Battalion.
21 AWM: 4 23/60/23. War Diary 43rd Battalion. 'Report on Operations of 4th July 1918.'
22 AWM: 4 23/60/23. War Diary 43rd Battalion. 'Report by Intelligence Officer.' (Lieutenant Richardson). Lt Brian Harold Richardson survived the war and lived to the age of 97.
23 AWM: 4 23/60/23. War Diary 43rd Battalion. 'Report by Intelligence Officer.'

of thoroughly sweeping the ground & forming a fine screen of fire for us to work behind.'[24] Sergeant Ayliffe of No.1 Platoon described the initial advance behind this creeping barrage as 'little more than an early morning promenade.'[25] Captain Moran, OC A Company, submitted his report on the attack on 13 July: his company assembled with Nos 1 and 3 platoons in front as skirmishers, with Nos 2 and 4 behind, designated as 'moppers-up.' As his men pressed forward after the second artillery lift,

> ...some pressure from the left flank caused the Coy to incline slightly towards the right. It was not yet daylight and the darkness was so intensified by the smoke barrage and the dust caused by bursting shell that the stars as well as all landmarks were completely obscured from view.
>
> A blazing building South of Hamel may have been the cause of this edging to the right, furthermore there may have been an inclination to follow a metalled road and telegraph line which there ran obliquely across towards our right front.[26]
>
> However the line responded to an order passed along by the Coy Cdr to 'Left Incline', followed later by 'Right Incline' which regained the original line of advance.[27]

They were heading for Notamel Wood to the north of the village, but it was not until they got quite close to it that a few tall trees became visible, lit up briefly by the flash of bursting shells. 'The advance almost to the wood lay through wheat fields – mostly very high and in ear. Numerous small cleared or cut patches of crop were passed, these had probably been used as listening posts by the enemy and were connected in places by either cords or trip wires.'[28]

Due to the layout of the German trench system in front of the wood, it was the men on A Company's right flank who first encountered enemy positions. Just as they approached this trench, they were overtaken by two tanks. The tanks crossed the trench, crushing two strong-points as they went, with one turning north-east to follow the trench line into the wood, whilst the other headed the opposite way along the trench to the south. The men following encountered an undamaged enemy machine gun post directly in front of them at approximately P 3 d.60.15.[29] Text-book tactics by men of No.1 Platoon under Lieutenant L.S. Watts, (covering fire from the flank and a bombing attack) quickly neutralised the threat: 'the fire from this post was quickly replied to by a L.G. on the left whilst we on the right rushed forward & threw bombs & then rushed in. Some were killed and wounded in the post & three or four taken prisoners & sent back.'[30]

24 AWM: 4 23/60/23. War Diary 43rd Battalion. Report by Sergeant Major Jerome, A Coy. 97 Sgt Robert Henry Jerome, originally from Reading, England, was killed in action, age 33, by shell fire on 30 September 1918 during an attack on the Hindenburg Line. He is commemorated on the Villers-Bretonneux Memorial.
25 AWM: 4 23/60/23. War Diary 43rd Battalion. Report by Sgt G.W. Ayliffe, No.1 Platoon. 'July 4th Operations.'
26 Presumably the road running NW–SE through square P 3.d. See map.
27 AWM: 4 23/60/23. War Diary 43rd Battalion. 'A Coy, 43rd Bn AIF Narrative of events July 2–6 1918.'
28 AWM: 4 23/60/23. War Diary 43rd Battalion. 'A Coy, 43rd Bn AIF Narrative of events July 2–6 1918.'
29 In the trench on the western edge of Notamel Wood. See map.
30 AWM: 4 23/60/23. War Diary 43rd Battalion. 'Report on Operations July 4th 1918 by Lt L.S. Watts, No.1 Platoon.'

Watts and his men were then able to follow the tank, which had turned northwards along the German trench line:

> I and a party passed over the trench & working along the rear of it in conjunction with a party working along the front we cleaned up the whole length of it towards and through Notamel Wood mostly by bombing & rushing forward, encountering five posts in this way. The enemy did not show much fight, in one case he fired to his front, but finding himself attacked in rear as well as the front, quickly surrendered. Some casualties were inflicted and 1 Off. and about 20 men were sent back under escort.'[31]

They continued through the wood, mopping up as they went, and 'very little difficulty was experienced in negotiating the enemy obstacles which were mainly concertina of plain French wire.'[32] Lieutenant Reynolds of No.3 Platoon was suitably impressed by the tanks: 'This was the first time I had seen a tank in action and I think they did wonderfully well, for on passing over the ground in daylight it was noticeable that almost every dugout both large and small had been rolled over by a tank.'[33] Lieutenant A.H. Dalziel of No. 2 Platoon was only slightly less complimentary: 'The tanks worked wonderfully well and undoubtedly prevented casualties in our ranks by their prompt action in dealing with M. Guns. One tank lost favor [sic] for a time though, its insisting on dragging about 2 miles of barbed wire behind it and upsetting all and sundry that fell foul of its track.'[34]

The infantry were able to work in conjunction with the tanks – Lieutenant Coats of No. 4 Platoon described one incident where he was able to direct one tank onto an enemy position in Notamel Wood that was causing trouble

> ...by pulling the bell rope @ the rear of the tank & then communicating with the officer inside. The tank fired on the post with its guns & silenced it, & finished the job by wobbling over the top of the post. This little incident gave us six prisoners & a M.G.'[35]

Captain Moran, A Company, decided, as his men entered Notamel Wood, to position the company HQ and a nucleus garrison including four machine guns 'just clear of the western edge of the wood whilst the remainder of the Coy pushed rapidly onward to mop up the wood and the eastern edge of the village.'[36] The halt line was reached with little delay or enemy interference, and at the appropriate time, two companies of 44th Battalion 'swung outwards skirting the North edge of the village & pushed on to the high ground beyond.'[37]

31 AWM: 4 23/60/23. War Diary 43rd Battalion. 'Report on Operations July 4th 1918 by Lt L.S. Watts, No.1 Platoon.'
32 AWM: 4 23/60/23. War Diary 43rd Battalion. 'A Coy, 43rd Bn AIF Narrative of events July 2 – 6th 1918.'
33 AWM: 4 23/60/23. War Diary 43rd Battalion. 'Battle of Hamel. Report by Lieutenant C.H. Reynolds, OC No. 3 Platoon, A Coy, 43rd Btn.'
34 AWM: 4 23/60/23. War Diary 43rd Battalion. 'The Battle of Hamel, July 4th 1918. Report by Lt. A.H. Dalziel, No. 2 Coy.' Lieutenant Allan Henry Dalziel was awarded the Military Cross for his actions on 4 July 1918. He led his platoon in attacks on several machine gun posts, capturing two guns and a number of prisoners.
35 AWM: 4 23/60/23. War Diary 43rd Battalion. Report by Lieutenant Watts, No. 1 Platoon., A Coy.
36 AWM: 4 23/60/23. War Diary 43rd Battalion. Moran's report.
37 AWM: 4 23/60/23. War Diary 43rd Battalion. Moran's report.

The German account of this part of the assault is very brief: 'At 4:30 a.m.[38] the enemy infantry attacked. Supported by tanks, whose advance was helped by the dense mist, the enemy overran the front line trenches.'[39]

As the artillery barrage and the main thrust of the battle moved onwards after the 10-minute pause, A Company set about their next task: the clearing of Hamel village itself. The descriptions of this task in the various after-action reports are mostly very brief and matter-of-fact. Lieutenant Watts' account of the action – the most detailed – is typical. He and his batman took charge of a group of Americans and

> ... went into Hamel. On entering the village we saw a party of about ten of the enemy in a street to our right [. W]e fired on these and they immediately turned off and ran towards the centre of the village over the ruins, we ran down a side street, intercepted them, fired on them again, whereupon they surrendered, one of these was killed and three wounded, including an Officer.... The Americans were fighting very keenly & were very eager, and we then proceeded [and] searched several buildings for dugouts etc but did not find any. When we arrived in the centre of the village we met Lt Lock, B Coy, and party in the main street & we then proceeded eastwards along the main street and then again northwards up a side street looking into buildings as we went, in this street we passed two tanks going southwards & then met Mr Coates [sic] and party, A Coy, and then Mr Reynolds and party, A Coy, who assured me that their area was well and truly mopped up & also that Mr Dalziel's party had mopped up their area so we then proceeded back to the line of consolidation,... met Capt Moran and, deciding on our posts, started to dig in.[40]

Although not mentioned in his own report, Captain Moran, just as the task of clearing the village was coming to an end, 'placed a 'tri-colour' on the roof of the highest building in Hamel & this was still fluttering gaily when we were relieved.'[41]

Lieutenant L.B. Coats of No. 4 Platoon in his report describes a very thorough process: 'The mopping up of the wood and village was now being carried out in earnest, & any piece of trench, dugout, or ruined building was searched, any doubts as to the contents of a dugout were set @ rest by the use of a bomb.'[42]

For his actions in Hamel that morning, 190 Private Edric Neill Toope received the Military Medal. He and a few other men were separated from their platoons by the artillery barrage, so Toope gathered them together and took them into the village as a mopping-up party, capturing several dugouts, one officer and twenty other ranks.

With the mopping up completed by 5:00 a.m., the men withdrew to the pre-arranged consolidation line, and a series of six posts were established, running north-south through squares P 3 b and d. (see Map 7), with a machine gun section placed on the right flank of each company sector. Around that time, German 15 cm shells began falling in and around these positions,

38 'German time' was one hour ahead of 'Allied time.'
39 Bergeder, *Reserve-Infanterie-Regiment Nr. 202*, p.144. The regimental history does not mention the fight for Hamel village.
40 AWM: 4 23/60/23. War Diary 43rd Battalion. Watts' report.
41 AWM: 4 23/60/23. War Diary 43rd Battalion. Coats' report.
42 AWM: 4 23/60/23. War Diary 43rd Battalion. Coats' report.

Tricolour raised by Captain J.T. Moran, 43rd Battalion. (AWM)

two falling simultaneously on a 'double section post',[43] killing one Private and wounding a further nine other ranks. Although the shelling continued intermittently for the rest of the day, no more casualties were suffered once the posts were 'well dug in.'[44]

The ammunition drops by the RAF began at 9:00 a.m., and Moran witnessed the unfortunate fate of one of the aircraft: 'One parachute appeared to foul a plane which tilted and had the fabric torn away from its right lower wing. A spiral descent was attempted but the plane could not be righted and eventually nose-dived and crashed on the Hill just E of Hamel, about P 10 b. 20.90.'[45]

No. 9 Squadron RAF dropped around 112,000 rounds of small arms ammunition along the front, although two drops drifted over into Accroche Wood and were recovered by the Germans. Two allied aircraft from No. 9 Squadron crashed whilst engaged in the ammunition dropping missions. Both RE8s, numbers C4580 and B5073, crewed by Lieutenant Harris with Lieutenant Bell, and Lieutenant Riekie with Lieutenant Knowles, respectively, failed to return to base. It is unclear how these aircraft were brought down: it may have been artillery shells, but for one, its fate seems to match the story told by Captain Moran. The dramatic photograph below shows the final moments of the episode, but it is not certain which aircraft is in which image.[46]

43 AWM: 4 23/60/23. War Diary 43rd Battalion. Moran's report.
44 AWM: 4 23/60/23. War Diary 43rd Battalion. Moran's report.
45 AWM: 4 23/60/23. War Diary 43rd Battalion. Moran's report.
46 Lt. Harris and Lt. Knowles are buried in Villers-Bretonneux Military Cemetery, graves XV.A.5 and XVII.B.8. Lt. Riekie is commemorated on the Arras Flying Services Memorial. Lt. Bell appears to have been injured, but survived. In the *Official History*, Bean indicates (in footnote 99 on p.309 of

A RE8 falling to earth. (AWM)

Wreckage of RE8 B5073. (AWM)

B Company, under the command of Captain Cope, tasked with capturing the village of Hamel as far east as the artillery pause line, was in position on the jumping-off tape by 1:00 a.m. on the 4th. Their first wave was composed of Lieutenant Olsson's No. 5 Platoon on the left, with the Americans of No. 6 Platoon under Lieutenant Lee on the right. In support on the left was the other American platoon, No. 7, led by Lieutenant Symons, a former schoolteacher from South Australia, and on the right was No. 8 Platoon commanded by Lieutenant Lock. Company HQ was placed centrally within this formation. Cope worked his way around both flanks, ensuring that 'we were satisfactorily in touch'[47] with the other three companies.

When the barrage performed its first lift, the four platoons moved off, those in front in extended order, the supports in artillery formation. The line of the barrage was clearly defined, and the men had no problems in following it very closely as far as the enemy front line. Even so, it was always a risk following the barrage too closely, and Private Lawlor of No. 7 Platoon was very badly wounded by a 'short' soon after Zero and died back at the dressing station.[48] A similar fate befell Lance Corporal Bowes, No. 5 Platoon. Bowes, a veteran of numerous 'stunts', had told his mates just before the attack that he did not think he would make it through this one.[49]

As they ran into the German front line, the major source of resistance and danger was, as ever, the German machine gunners. It often took personal and individual bravery to overcome the strong points: 2657 Private Joseph Gallagher was awarded the DCM for one such episode:

> On the 4th July, 1918, at Hamel near Corbie, this man showed conspicuous gallantry and devotion to duty.
>
> He acted as No. 1 of the Lewis gun team and his Section encountered an enemy strong-point with two Machine Guns and 30 men. The enemy opened with fire and bombs and

vol.VI) that both crew of the aircraft in the photographs died. This would therefore suggest that it is B5073.

47 AWM: 4 23/60/23. War Diary 43rd Battalion. Cope's Report.

48 2594 Private Alfred John 'Ginger' Lawlor, age 24, is buried in Crucifix Corner Cemetery, grave IX.D.20, with the inscription: 'He hath fought the good fight. Now is the victor's triumph won.'

49 2288 Lance Corporal Joseph Bowes, aged 29, is buried in Villers-Bretonneux Military Cemetery, grave XII.B.5.

The grave of Private Alfred John Lawlor, 43rd Battalion. (Author)

Lance Corporal Joseph Bowes, 43rd Battalion. (Author)

> killed all the Section except GALLAGHER, who immediately got his Lewis gun into action firing from the hip. He was carrying two spare magazines on his shoulder strap. After using these, he with two men from another section, rushed the post and captured two guns and 7 prisoners, the only ones left alive.[50]

Another example is that of 351 Private William O'Brien, who received a Military Medal after capturing a machine gun, which was holding up his platoon, by coolly leading the bombing section around the flank of the enemy position and killing the garrison. It was with a frontal attack using grenades that 250 Corporal Norman Barber succeeded in putting another machine gun out of action. His commander and sergeant had been wounded, and Barber had taken charge of the platoon.[51]

Some of the German front line garrison could be seen running back into the village at the sight of the approaching Australians, but it was just to the rear of this line that, after advancing for the best part of a quarter of an hour, they encountered their first real opposition in the form of a strongpoint centred on a heap of mangelwurzels, a root vegetable. With the tanks not yet up with the infantry, and with the artillery barrage having moved past it, it came down to an

50 AWM: Personal file of Private Gallagher, Recommendation for Award.
51 Barber was awarded the Military Medal.

infantry fight. The leading platoons went to ground, and with the German machine gunners silhouetted 'against the glare of the burning village',[52] began returning fire and throwing grenades, 'most of which… rolled down the front of the mound and exploded harmlessly.'[53]

Cope found Lieutenant Symons, who was nearby, and told him to take his platoon of Americans, move down the road and outflank the machine-gun post to the left. This he managed to do, and with No. 5 Platoon rushing the position from the front, the fight was over in five minutes. Fifteen Germans were killed and around 40 prisoners taken, most of the latter emerging from a dugout behind the mound. The tactics had proved successful, but it was here that B Company suffered most of its casualties that day. Lieutenants Olsson and Symons were wounded, and with No. 5 Platoon now leaderless, it fell to Private D.J. Anderson, Symons' runner, to take charge and lead the men through the rest of the action.[54] One of those killed during the attack on the machine gun post was Corporal Eschner, a Lewis gunner of No. 6 Platoon, who was wounded in the abdomen and thigh by the explosion from a stick grenade, and who died at around 10:00 a.m. at No. 5 Casualty Clearing Station.[55]

The company was then able to push on quickly into Hamel, each platoon having been designated a particular sector of the village to clear. This task was completed with seemingly little difficulty within half an hour. The responsibility for signalling that the entire village was clear fell to B Company. After A and C Companies reported their sectors clear at 4:31 and 4:54 a.m., respectively, three green rockets were launched into the air at five minutes to five to announce that 'the town was ours.'[56] During the search, Private Schulz, part of the depleted battalion HQ unit, along with two German-speaking Americans, had found a dugout that was full of the enemy. He went into the dugout alone and ordered its garrison to come out. Four officers and 23 men – an entire battalion HQ – were taken prisoner.[57]

With B Company's part in the attack over, they withdrew from the village and began to dig a communication trench from the original jumping-off line forward some 1,200 yards to A Company's newly-dug positions to the north-west of Hamel. This onerous task carried on until they were relieved at 11:30 p.m. on 5 July by units of 41st Battalion.

On the right flank of the battalion frontage, C Company began deployment on the jumping-off tape at around midnight. As they stood, crouched, or lay in their allotted positions, their right flank perilously close to Pear Trench, the barrage came down at 3:10 a.m., and as mentioned above, a number of shells, falling short at approximately P.8.b.2.4., inflicted casualties even before they had a chance to move. Lieutenant Canaway describes the incident: 'The Coy suffered heavily from short shooting before we moved. I have since found out that all our Company HQ was wiped out except Capt. Sexton & 4 Runners – also the American platoon suffered heavily.'[58]

Not surprisingly, as the men of C Company were called forward, those on the right flank who had suffered most from the short shooting were slow to move. Lieutenant Canaway sent his batman to hurry them on, 'they then all advanced and the whole line appeared to be coming

52 Bean, *The Official History*, vol.VI, p.295.
53 Bean, *The Official History*, vol.VI, p.295.
54 227 Private David John Anderson was awarded the Military Medal.
55 4783 Corporal Lawrence Eschner, is buried in Crouy British Cemetery, grave III.B.22.
56 AWM: 4 23/60/23. War Diary 43rd Battalion. Cope's Report.
57 1105 Private (Temporary Corporal) Boyce Vincent Schulz was awarded the Distinguished Conduct Medal.
58 AWM: 4 23/60/23. War Diary 43rd Battalion. Canaway's report.

along in perfect order.'[59] No. 9 Platoon, on this right flank, soon came under machine gun fire from the direction of Pear Trench (located according to the battalion CO's report at P.8.d.9.9. – see map), killing the platoon commander, Lieutenant Brook.[60]

At this point, Corporal Shaw, a Lewis gunner in No.9 Platoon, and an American, Corporal H.G. Zyburt, made straight for the machine gun post. Shaw fired several bursts from the hip at the enemy position, his bullets hitting the machine gun and destroying its firing mechanism. This enabled Zyburt to rush the position and bayonet three of the crew.[61] An American officer, Captain Gale, witnessed this event and later wrote that Corporal Shaw had 'prove[n] the value of a Lewis gun in the hands of a brave and determined man.'[62] Shortly afterwards, a section under Corporal Krantz ran into another machine gun post. Krantz got a Lewis gunner from the neighbouring 15th Battalion to fire at it as he and an American rushed in and bayonetted the crew;[63] 2281 Lance Corporal S.H. Krantz received the Military Medal.

The grave of Lieutenant Frank Richmond Brook, 43rd Battalion. (Author)

Lieutenant Canaway was still acutely aware of 'friendly' shells falling short and urged his men to follow the creeping barrage even more closely, meaning that the shorts 'exploded well behind them, the platoon thus making its advance between the two sets of shell-bursts.'[64] As they neared the German front line, Canaway, aware of the topography of the enemy trench system, sent a message to his right flank section asking them to let him know immediately they encountered wire obstacles. The reply came back almost immediately, and Canaway ordered his men to rush the trench. He continues the narrative:

> I entered the enemy F.L. [Front Line] about P.9.c.40.95. Immediately we got to the trench – the light not being at all good – I found the enemy trying to get a light M.G. going – there were also a fair number of the enemy there which was evidently a platoon post. I called on the men to rush & jumped across the trench. The men closed round the position & several jumped in the trench. As I jumped across, one of the enemy jumped out of the trench &

59 AWM: 4 23/60/23. War Diary 43rd Battalion. Canaway's report.
60 Lieutenant Frank Richmond Brook, aged 35, is buried in Villers-Bretonneux Military Cemetery, grave III.C.3.
61 Bean, *The Official History*, vol.VI, p. 289. Zyburt, wounded on 4 July, was awarded the Military Medal.
62 Sanborn, *131st US Infantry in the World War*, p.52.
63 The American is unnamed in the account.
64 Bean, *The Official History*, vol.VI, p.285.

> rushed me. A revolver bullet in the stomach stopped him. He was wearing a peaked cap but I did not know whether he was an Officer or an NCO. Meantime the men were carrying on. The enemy did not appear to be fighting at all but did not throw their hands up & seemed surprised to see us. We cleaned up the crowd & bombed a dugout & then left the remainder to be mopped up by the rear platoons. I have been told since that on the Coy's front 4 light M.G's were found with their covers on.[65]

The men pushed on, crossing a support line (or perhaps, according to Canaway, a communication trench) with no opposition. The artillery barrage halted, pausing on its appointed line for 10 minutes, and Canaway reorganised his men near a heap of mangelwurzels at P.9.d.80.95,[66] getting them ready to advance into the village and begin their task of mopping up. The odd German machine gun post had been missed by the barrage, and the previously mentioned Corporal Shaw of No. 9 Platoon saw one open fire from behind a bank some 200 yards away to his right.

> He made for it and, when 100 yards distant, began hosing it with his [Lewis] gun at the hip as he went. When he was thirty yards from it a German officer bravely rushed towards him firing a revolver, but was killed by his fire. As Shaw reached the post, the last survivor of the crew came at him. Shaw, whose magazine was now empty, hit him on the head with his revolver and then shot him. Eight Germans lay dead in the post and the casing of the gun was pierced with Shaw's bullets.'[67]

Corporal Francis Middleton Shaw DCM, 43rd Battalion. (AWM)

Shaw was awarded the DCM.[68]

It was only at this stage of the advance that the tanks caught up with C Company. One of them proved useful as the eastern outskirts of Hamel were reached. C Company came up against a strong point containing three machine guns. Private Stanton, although wounded in the neck, went over to the tank and directed it onto

65 AWM: 4 23/60/23. War Diary 43rd Battalion. Canaway's report.
66 This is a second heap, not the one referred to earlier in the narrative!
67 Bean, *The Official History*, vol.VI, p.300.
68 577 Corporal Francis Middleton Shaw, age 23, born in Tasmania, was killed by German shell fire on 12 August 1918 near the village of Proyart. He is buried in Heath Cemetery, Harbonnières, grave VII.D.10.

the enemy position.[69] Unfortunately, another tank, probably from C Company, 8th Tank Battalion, operating on the right flank of 43rd Battalion, 'caused casualties by firing into our men.'[70] It fired into a 'platoon of Australians and one of Americans, scattering them so that it was long before their leaders could collect their men.'[71] One of those 'leaders', Lieutenant Canaway, downplayed the incident in his report, stating merely that 'an incident happened which scattered my men. I eventually got them together again.'[72] After speaking briefly with Captain Sexton,[73] he began to move his men forward into the village after the artillery pause, stopping a tank that was emerging from it and speaking to its commander, who reported that he had passed through part of the village without meeting any opposition. Leaving one Lewis gun section outside the village as support, Canaway and his men proceeded to mop up their designated section of the village:

> We moved rapidly from house to house & on encountering any small dugouts called out to inmates to emerge. If no reply was given, the place was bombed. Three big dugouts were encountered – The inmates came up immediately when called upon but did not show any fight. Each man was searched – also souvenired. In each case I found one of the enemy who could speak English & on his assurance of all being out a bomb was thrown down & I then made the enemy NCO in charge go down into the dugout & I followed. All papers were collected. 2 NCO's and about 40 men were got out of the first dugout. The second I got an officer & 9 men. I had to threaten to shoot the officer for speaking to the men & he immediately became mute. The 3rd big dugout was an R.A.P. [Regimental Aid Post]. There I found a doctor & about 20 S.B.'s [stretcher bearers] & A.M.C. [Army Medical Corps] details also 4 wounded men. The wounded were carried out by their SB's. A few more strays were picked up & I then moved back to the position I had to take up & reported to Capt Cope that my part was all clear when he fired his three greens. I then heard that Capt Sexton had been wounded so took charge of the remainder of the Coy which had been rather badly cut up.[74]

Canaway reorganised his men into four sections, distributing his six Lewis guns between them. He promoted his one remaining Sergeant to CSM on the spot and, after sending reports back to battalion HQ, withdrew from the village and began digging a series of posts between P 9.d.50.50 and P 9 b.10.80. (see Map 7). Leaving Lieutenant Roberts, commander of No. 12 Platoon, in charge of the digging, he established his company HQ at P 9 a.35.40, and after sending a request back to battalion HQ, he was joined by some signallers who brought up a signalling lamp, enabling communication to be established with the rear. He returned to see that the digging was well under way, but he was forced to vacate his left-hand post as it suddenly came under heavy enemy artillery fire. Moving the men from there right across onto his right

69 2924 Private Horace Tennyson Stanton was awarded the Military Medal.
70 AWM: 4 23/60/23. War Diary 43rd Battalion. Appendix ii.
71 Bean, *The Official History*, vol.VI, p.300.
72 AWM: 4 23/60/23. War Diary 43rd Battalion. Canaway's report.
73 Some accounts state that Sexton was wounded early in the attack. Canaway insists that he was 'quite all right then.' The exact timing of Sexton's wounding must remain uncertain, but it seems likely that it was after the artillery pause.
74 AWM: 4 23/60/23. War Diary 43rd Battalion. Canaway's report.

flank, he established a fire bay on what was now his left flank, placing a Lewis gun there which could fire right across A Company's front. By 2:00 p.m., the posts were almost finished and well camouflaged, so the men were given a short rest before the task of connecting the posts – thus forming a continuous trench line – commenced.

Earlier, at some point during the morning, Corporal Ryan reported to Canaway that he had seen a large quantity of small arms ammunition in a burning house in the village and asked permission to go back and retrieve it. Permission was granted, and Ryan and a small party brought in 73 boxes 'in good order' and some boxes of grenades, 'so we were made secure as regards ammunition.'[75] With three Vickers machine guns now also deployed along the new defensive line, C Company sat back and awaited developments. Most of the day's casualties had been caused by artillery shorts and by a tank. 'Leaving these two causes out, casualties would have been down to a minimum.'[76]

D Company 'were the reserve company and consequently had no definite task allocated.' Thus ran the after-action report of its OC, Major A.W. Lott.[77] With No. 16 Platoon, made up of American troops, ordered out of the line on 3 July, the company's remaining three platoons were deployed for the attack as follows: No. 14 Platoon formed up on the left behind A Company; No. 15 Platoon – Americans from E Company, 131st Regiment – were in the centre supporting B Company; No. 13 Platoon took up their positions on the right behind C Company. All were in position, in artillery formation, by 2:00 a.m., and lay down to rest in the wheat fields, the crop being four feet high in places. The rum ration arrived 30 minutes later.

When the attack went in, D Company's task was to follow the assaulting companies until the latter reached and then crossed the German front line. After the artillery pause, as soon as the mopping up phase began, D Company units moved back 300 yards or so and waited, in case they were needed, 'until the 'all clear' signal was given by the Companies in front. During this time we were employed in searching and escorting prisoners, and giving assistance to wounded men.'[78]

At around 5:30 a.m., D Company was ordered to fall back to their old front line, occupying the sector from P 8.b.40.60 to P 2. D.75.15. (see Map 7). They then began work on a new communication trench running from this old front line forward to C Company's series of new posts just to the west of Hamel, with parties alternating three hours' digging with three hours' rest. In the evening, a party from No. 13 Platoon 'was detailed to assist the 44th Batt'n, which had leapfrogged through our Bn by carrying up a supply of bombs.'[79]

Casualties in D Company were light, with four killed and seven wounded: eight of the eleven were American. The after-action report written at the end of July by the 43rd Battalion's intelligence officer, Lieutenant Richardson, gives the following battalion casualty figures: two officers and 17 other ranks were killed, four officers and 74 other ranks were wounded (one each of which remained on duty), making a total of 97 casualties. Commonwealth War Graves Commission records show a final total of 26 fatalities for 4–5 July 1918.[80] American fatalities from 131st

75 AWM: 4 23/60/23. War Diary 43rd Battalion. Canaway's report.
76 AWM: 4 23/60/23. War Diary 43rd Battalion. Roberts' report.
77 AWM: 4 23/60/23. War Diary 43rd Battalion. Lott's Report.
78 AWM: 4 23/60/23. War Diary 43rd Battalion. Report by Lieutenant Polden, commanding No. 13 Platoon, D Coy.
79 AWM: 4 23/60/23. War Diary 43rd Battalion. Report by Major Lott, OC D Coy.
80 The second officer killed was Second Lieutenant Edgar Robert Davidson. He is buried in Villers-Bretonneux Military Cemetery, grave XII.D.10. His death is reported in the Battalion War Diary,

Regiment attached to both 42nd and 43rd Battalions numbered 12, none of them officers. These are mostly members of E Company, but include one each from D, K and M Companies.[81]

The report also estimates that 100 enemy were killed and 450–500 prisoners taken, these belonging to the *RIR 202, 43. Reservedivision* and the *IR 13, 13. Division.* Aside from a substantial number of papers and maps, 25 machine guns, five *Minenwerfer* and one range finder were captured. It is assumed that the 75,000 rounds of British small arms ammunition salvaged from the burning house by Corporal Ryan had been left there by British troops when Hamel was evacuated during the German attack on 4 April.

Bravery awards were distributed as follows:

Military Cross: Lieutenants R.A. Canaway (C Coy) and A.H. Dalziel (A Coy)
Distinguished Conduct Medal: 1105 Temp. Corporal B.V. Schulz (HQ), 577 Corporal F.M. Shaw (C Coy), 2657 Private J. Gallagher (B Coy)
Military Medal: 2924 Private H.T. Stanton (C Coy), 250 Corporal N. Barber (B Coy), 351 Private W. O'Brien (B Coy), 227 Private D.J. Anderson (B Coy), 2281 Lance Corporal S.H. Krantz (C Coy), 1031 Private F. Angus (A Coy) and 190 Private E.N. Toope (A Coy).

Lieutenant Colonel Farrell's 'Report on Operations' concluded with paragraph 17, 'General Remarks', in which he made several observations on how the attack procedures might be improved in the future. He suggests that Zero Hour was too early, with smoke and dust combined with the darkness, making it difficult for the infantry to see where they were going. With the tanks only catching up to the infantry at the 10-minute pause line, he recommends that they start closer to the front line. In his opinion, the creeping barrage was too slow at the start of the attack: 100-yard lifts every two minutes for the first 300 yards would have been better. His final 'remark' is not a suggestion for improvement, but a comment on the method of combat utilised by his men: 'The number of bayonet wounds was remarkable. Most of the enemy were wounded with the bayonet. One man had the bayonet driven through from chest to back. Two dead Boche in HAMEL had been stuck through the throat.'[82]

This final point was corroborated by the Regimental Medical Officer in his report, in which he states: 'A feature of the German wounded was the large percentage of bayonet wounds, mostly in abdominal & thoracic regions.'[83] He added that wounds to Australians were mostly caused by grenades or shells. Most of the latter were sadly caused by shells fired from Australian guns.

* * *

The Blue Line, the final objective for the day lay, of course, along the 260 feet-high ridge to the east of Hamel, and included the strongly garrisoned 'Wolfsberg' redoubt. The task of capturing

but there is no indication of how or where he was killed. This final total does not include Lieutenant Leslie Waterhouse, who was wounded in the back on 4 July, but died of complications including pneumonia in the 3rd London General Hospital on 23 July. He is buried in Brookwood Cemetery, London, grave IV.B.1.

81 See Appendix II and Sanborn, *The 131st*.

82 AWM: 4 23/60/23. War Diary 43rd Battalion. 'Report on Operations of 4th July 1918.'

83 AWM: 4 23/60/23. War Diary 43rd Battalion. 'Report by R.M.O. for July 1918'

it was entrusted to 44th Battalion. Their instructions in the orders sent down on 2 July, expressed in the simplest of terms, were as follows:

> The 44th Battalion will, avoiding the town of HAMEL, leap frog through the 43rd Battalion and capture and consolidate the BLUE LINE from P.10.d.66.35. to P.4.d.50.15.... Two sections (SIX TANKS) of 'C' Coy 8th TANK Battalion are allotted to 44th Battalion for capture of BLUE LINE. One section moving NORTH and one section SOUTH of the village of HAMEL.[84]

The four companies were to assemble, with A and B Companies on the left, and C and D Companies on the right, behind 43rd Battalion, but 'well forward and clear of our own front line',[85] this to avoid being caught under any German retaliatory shelling. If all went to plan, units would leapfrog 43rd Battalion positions during the artillery pause (between Zero plus 31 and Zero plus 41), ready to advance as the creeping barrage resumed its forward movement. Officers participating in the attack were listed as follows:

Commanding Officer: Lt Col. J.P. Clark DSO.
Adjutant: Capt. C.L. Biles MC
Signals Officer: Lt. H.R. Hughan
Intelligence Officer: Lt. G.B. Kilgour
Liaison with 15th Bn: Lt. C.R. Davies MM
Liaison with 42nd Bn: Lt. R.B. O'Carroll MM
Liaison with 4th Bde: Capt. C. Longmore.
Supervising the Assembly: Capt. M. Lewis & Lt. E.C. Rogers.
Medical Officer: Capt. R.L. Kenihan MC.
A Coy: Capt. W.J. Stables, Lt. A.J. Munro, Lt. C.J. Piper, Lt. E.E. McGrath, 2/Lt. W. Stewart.
B Coy: Lt. J.S. Everett, Lt. F.A. Leeds, Lt. C.R. Cornish, Lt. K. Sheridan.
C Coy: Capt. H.L. Fowler, Lt. A.L. Smith, Lt. C.H.S. Pole, Lt. J. Paton.
D Coy: Capt. E.C. Adams, Lt. F.O. Gaze, Lt. W.G. Faulkner, Lt. H. Scarr, Lt. R.G.D. Andrews.

The American troops attached to 44th Battalion on 1 July were withdrawn from the line two days later. The battalion history claims that 'a good number heard the order with deaf ears and took part as originally arranged. Some of their officers shed their American uniforms and entered the scrap as Diggers.'[86]

Assembly was completed by 2:50 a.m. on the 4th.[87] At 3:10 a.m., the artillery barrage came down on the German front line and 'pounded, battered, and chopped it to pieces with shells of

84 AWM: 4 23/61/22. War Diary 44th Battalion. Hamel Offensive Instruction No.1. 2.7.18.
85 AWM: 4 23/61/22. War Diary 44th Battalion. Hamel Offensive Instruction No.1. 2.7.18.
86 Captain C. Longmore, *Eggs-A-Cook! The Story of the Forty-Fourth. War – as the Digger Saw it* (Perth: The Colortype Press Ltd, 1921), p.147.
87 A Coy by 2:50 a.m., B Coy by 2:30 a.m., C Coy by 2:44 a.m. and D Coy by 2:15 a.m.

every calibre – light, medium, heavy, gas, shrapnel, high explosive, and phosphorous shells. The Boche here suffered four minutes' hell before the barrage began to lift.'[88]

Following closely on the heels of 43rd Battalion, A Company, on the left flank of the battalion frontage, moved off with all four platoons in line, No. 2 Platoon on the left (Lieutenant McGrath and 33 OR), then No. 1 Platoon (Lieutenant Piper and 33 OR), No. 4 platoon (Lieutenant Munro and 26 OR) and finally on the right, No. 3 Platoon (Lieutenant Stewart and 33 OR). With Captain Stables and 19 OR forming company HQ, this gave a total of five officers and 144 other ranks. Any opposition was dealt with by 43rd Battalion, and during the artillery pause, A Company leapfrogged their compatriots and deployed into line, ready to advance up the slope of the ridge towards the Wolfsberg. The tanks were by this time 'well in front of us, moving forward toward the final objective.'[89]

B Company were held up slightly as they passed through Notamel Wood, 'when some confusion arose due to the fact that enemy prisoners started to pass through our lines, and apparently thinking that resistance was at hand, the men showed an inclination to crowd.'[90] Section commanders soon rectified the situation, however, and by the time they emerged from the wood, order had been restored. They then deployed, linking up with A Company on the left and D Company on the right.

D Company had also been delayed: they came under fire from the Pear Trench position and had to deal with several machine-gun posts, meaning they fell well behind the creeping barrage. The artillery pause allowed them to catch up, however, and they were ready to advance as the second phase of the battle commenced.

C Company, after a seemingly incident-free passage south of Hamel village, lined up in support behind the other three companies. As 44th Battalion had advanced, it was noticed that

> … the enemy followed his usual procedure by filling the air with Very lights and rockets – white, red, green, golden and showers – but whatever their significance, his barrage remained particularly feeble, and our boys advanced with practically no resistance from artillery, the machine guns giving the most trouble. A kind spurt from the uncanny 'tank', however, soon disposed of the defending 'gallants'.[91]

At Zero plus 41, the barrage began its relentless creep forward once more at the rate of 100 yards every four minutes. The tanks followed it, and in their wake came the infantry, their advance shielded by a smoke barrage on either flank.

None of the five accounts in the 44th Battalion war diary has much to say about the capture of the Wolfsberg position on the crest of the ridge. The men moved up the slopes 'as darkness gave place to day',[92] where 'little opposition was encountered except in isolated posts, but these were quickly and systematically mopped up by the advancing sections.'[93] It would appear that by the time the infantry crested the slope and reached the enemy trench system, the tanks had

88 AWM: 4 23/61/22. War Diary 44th Battalion. Appendix 2. 'Narrative of Hamel Offensive.' The writer is mistaken here: smoke was used, but no gas.
89 AWM: 4 23/61/22. War Diary 44th Battalion. Appendix 3. 'Narrative of Hamel Operation. A Coy.'
90 AWM: 4 23/61/22. War Diary 44th Battalion. Appendix 4. 'Narrative of Hamel Operation. B Coy.'
91 AWM: 4 23/61/22. War Diary 44th Battalion. Appendix 2. 'Narrative of Hamel Offensive.'
92 AWM: 4 23/61/22. War Diary 44th Battalion. Appendix 2. 'Narrative of Hamel Offensive.'
93 AWM: 4 23/61/22. War Diary 44th Battalion. Appendix 3. A Coy.

already wreaked havoc. 'Eight tanks wobbled here and there over the slopes and summit of the ridge, clearing the Boche out of his strong defences.'[94] Charles Bean, writing for the *Newcastle Morning Herald,* described the scene thus:

> There was moving along the top of [the Wolfsberg] a low, grey monster… It moved slowly along the crest sideways, like some legless insect – perhaps a wood-louse would be the most resembling. There was another and another to right and left of it, and crowds of infantry between them. They moved up to that skyline along its whole length.[95]

Only D Company appears to have met active machine gun nests in any number on top of the ridge, but these were 'rushed' with 'great assistance' from the tanks, and captured 'what proved to be a Battalion headquarters, sending back an estimated number of 100 prisoners including a Colonel and 5 other officers.'[96] Captain Adams reported that he

> … found the trenches to be very badly knocked about, and a system of deep dug-outs, entrances to which were immediately covered, poured forth their enemy occupants…. Many enemy were seen to be on the retreat down the hollow ground and fire was brought to bear on them. Consolidation was at once carried on with, the trench being improved for our own defence and for the improvement of our field of fire. In addition to our own Lewis guns we were able to mount 4 captured enemy machine guns which added greatly to our defence as well as preserving our own Lewis gun ammunition.'[97]

The A Company account tells a similar story:

> At 4:45 a.m. our objective was reached and consolidation was immediately begun, here the Company lost 2 Officers and 15 O/ranks wounded…. No. 1 Platoon dug in on the right of the Company front and connected up with B Coy on the right. The position they consolidated contained two large German Dugouts… (at approx.. P.10.b.99.70). In these two dugouts, Mr. Piper and his platoon took 2 Officers and 35 O/ranks prisoners, captured 2 machine guns & a new German anti-tank gun with 43 rounds of ammunition, this being a unique capture inasmuch as the 'tank' people reported a new German anti-tank gun being used against them.[98]

As the remaining platoons dug in and established platoon posts to the left of No.1, joining up with 42nd Battalion units, a strongpoint still held by the enemy at P.11.a.20.60 was proving troublesome. 'Energetic bombing' soon neutralised the threat.[99]

94 AWM: 4 23/61/22. War Diary 44th Battalion. Appendix 2. 'Narrative of Hamel Offensive.'
95 *Newcastle Morning Herald*, 31 August 1918.
96 AWM: 4 23/61/22. War Diary 44th Battalion. Appendix 6. D Coy Account.
97 AWM: 4 23/61/22. War Diary 44th Battalion. Appendix 6. D Coy Account.
98 AWM: 4 23/61/22. War Diary 44th Battalion. Appendix 3, A Coy. The gun was a Mauser 'Tankgewehr' M1918, almost 1.7 metres in length, and weighing 18.5 kg, using 13.2 mm ammunition.
99 AWM: 4 23/61/22. War Diary 44th Battalion. Appendix 3, A Coy.

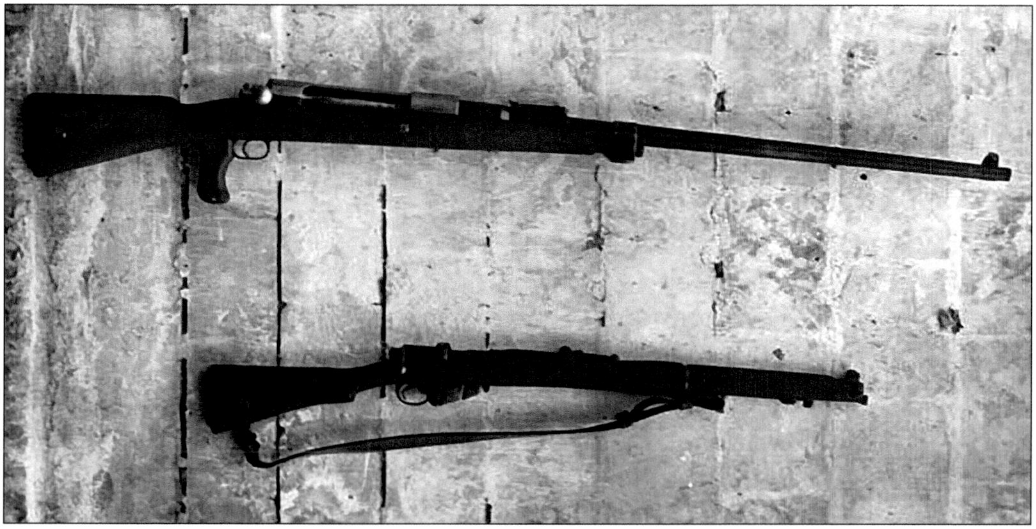

A German anti-tank rifle, Mauser 'Tankgewehr' M1918 and a British Lee Enfield rifle. (AWM)

B Company had suffered casualties on the slopes of the Wolfsberg: Lieutenant Leeds and Sergeant Campbell of No. 6 Platoon, along with Lieutenant Sheridan of No.7, were wounded, 'and it was here that Sgts Dorizzi and Ingvarsen [sic] displayed their initiative and grip of the situation by immediately assuming command of the platoons.'[100] They led their platoons onto the ridge, made sure that contact was made with neighbouring units and organised the digging of new positions. One of them pushed forward about 100 yards ahead of the main defensive line.

With A Company established on the left, B Company in the centre, and D Company covering the right flank of what was in effect a small salient on the crest of the ridge, C Company settled into positions in support. Battalion reports recount how,

> ...batches of prisoners belonging to the 202nd R.I.R. came streaming in from all directions' during the morning, a sizeable proportion of them 'being very young perhaps between sixteen and twenty years of age. Up went their hands at sight of a khaki figure and a look of terror gripped these youngsters, all of whom seemed quite broken in spirit and perfectly docile, when any of our boys advanced towards them.[101]

100 AWM: 4 23/61/22. War Diary 44th Battalion. Appendix 4. B Coy. 2271 T/Sgt Edgar Joseph Dorizzi was awarded the Military Medal, and 1661 Sergeant Jens Eduard Valdemar Karl Ingvarson, age 23, born in Denmark, was awarded the Distinguished Conduct Medal for his leadership of his platoon and for his actions during the German counter attack (see below). He received a Bar to his DCM for capturing a German machine gun nest in the Hindenburg Line on 29 September 1918. Ingvarson survived the war, returning to Australia in June 1919. During the Second World War he was attached to the 2nd Australian Training Corps, but did not serve overseas. He died in 1993 at the age of 99.

101 AWM: 4 23/61/22. War Diary 44th Battalion. Appendix 2. 'Narrative of Hamel Offensive.' The regimental history of *RIR 202* insists on a far more active defence of the ridge, stating that *Leutnant* Paulsen and parties of *12. Kompanie* 'managed successfully to halt the enemy advance on the Wolfsberg.' Bergeder, *RIR Nr. 202*, p.144.

Tank H52 (9001) stranded outside Hamel village. (AWM)

The only threat that the German forces were able to summon up during the morning was aerial: at about 11:00 a.m., a large formation of over 30 enemy planes appeared, 'and for an hour or two the air was dominated by the enemy as it had previously been by the British, more than thirty German machines being overhead at once, diving at the newly-formed posts, dropping bombs and machine-gunning the troops there.'[102]

Aircraft of No. 3 Australian Squadron were able to re-establish their dominance by midday, and thereafter, 'a lull in the battle' ensued.[103] The tanks had all withdrawn by this point, except for the two damaged and stranded on the battlefield, one near Hamel, the other on the slope of the ridge. Of the 60 tanks that went into action, only seven were damaged or disabled: one hit by enemy shelling south of Vaire Wood; three broke tracks, two were damaged as a result of shell strikes (one hostile and one friendly), and one damaged descending a steep bank in No Man's Land; the seventh suffered a mechanical failure on its way back to the rallying point.

Casualties amongst the tank crews during the battle had been light: 8th Battalion suffered 11 wounded, one of them, Sergeant Norman, who subsequently succumbed to wounds,[104] and 13th Battalion came out with eight other ranks and four officers wounded. The battalion's ordeal was not over, however:

> On the evening of the battle about 10:30 p.m. an enemy aeroplane dropped three bombs into the gully in which both Companies had raillied [sic], inflicting losses on these sections which had fought on the right flank. The two Section Commanders, Capt. WALKER and Capt. LARKINS were killed, as were Lieut. BERRY and 2/Lt. ATACK with 3 other ranks. 2/Lt. HULTON and 3 other ranks were wounded and this Officer and two of the men died on the following day. It is probable that the real objective of the attacking plane was certain gun emplacements hard by, but it must be admitted that these Officers, worn out by their exceptional exertions, had taken insufficient care to protect themselves on their return. The lesson was not lost by the Battalion.[105]

102 Bean, *The Official History*, vol.VI, p.309.
103 AWM: 4 23/61/22. War Diary 44th Battalion. Appendix 2. 'Narrative of Hamel Offensive.'
104 91731 Sgt William Norman is buried in Crouy British Cemetery, grave III.D.4.
105 TNA: WO95/115/2. History of the 13th Tank Battalion. Second Lieutenant Percy Atack is buried in Villers-Bretonneux Military Cemetery, grave XIX.B.8, as are Lieutenant John Leslie Berry, grave XIX.E.5; Captain Lockhart Henry Larkins, XIX.D.8; Captain Thomas Percival Patterson Walker, XIX.E.7; 304427 Pte A.V. Billington, XIX.E.9; 301630 Pte F. Gannon, XIX.A.8; 300450 Cpl

The grave of Sergeant William Norman, 8th Tank Battalion. (Author)

The grave of Second Lieutenant Percy Atack, 13th Tank Battalion. (Author)

The grave of Lieutenant John Leslie Berry, 13th Tank Battalion. (Author)

The grave of Captain Lockhart Henry Larkins, 13th Tank Battalion. (Author)

The grave of Captain Thomas Walker, 13th Tank Battalion. (Author)

The grave of Private A.V. Billington, 13th Tank Battalion. (Author)

Awards to the Tank Corps were, of course, forthcoming: one DSO, nine MCs, and 10 MMs.[106]

The regained aerial superiority allowed ammunition drops from the air to resume, but, presumably as a result of the earlier German aerial observation, 'the Boche gunners engaged in a lively sniping with their 10.5 cm shells, thinking to cause casualties as our men endeavoured to get the welcome ammunition. His admirable scheme failed entirely.'[107]

The lull in enemy activity lasted into the evening, but B Company became increasingly aware of a German strongpoint 'operating half left' of their position.[108] It was hoped that the 11th Light Trench Mortar Battery could be enlisted to help clear this annoyance, but with its commander,

T.J. Sullivan, XIV.E.10. The three men who died of wounds on 5 July are buried in Crouy British Cemetery: Second Lieutenant Benjamin Wright Hulton, grave III.D.11; 301626 Pte William Allison, grave III.D.13; 300208 Pte E. Haydock, grave III.D.17.

106 8th Battalion: D.S.O.to Lt-Col. J.D.Y. Bingham. M.C. to Lt R.O.G. Jefferies, Lt J. McCaffery and 2/Lt F.W. Prentice. (The 8th Battalion War History does not record any award of the MM). 13th Battalion: M.C. to 2/Lt G.A. Edward, 2/Lt H. Mayo, 2/Lt J. Rawlinson, 2/Lt T. Dower, 2/Lt R.B. Kay, 2/Lt R. Anderson. Bar to MM to Cpl A.A. Watson. MM to Sgt R.M. Green, Sgt C. Lynn, Pte J. Benns, Pte W.T. Waite, Pte T. Roberts, Cpl J. Ryan, Cpl E.A. Mettam, Pte F.H. Hurst, A/Sgt A.C. Scrivenor.

107 AWM: 4 23/61/22. War Diary 44th Battalion. Appendix 2. 'Narrative of Hamel Offensive.' Two parachutes were carried by the wind into German territory and fell into Accroche Wood.

108 AWM: 4 23/61/22. War Diary 44th Battalion. Appendix 4. B Coy Report.

Lieutenant Adams, having been evacuated wounded, there was a delay, and it was eventually decided that a fighting patrol from A Company would be sent out to storm the redoubt. They were to go in at 10:30 p.m. At 9:45, however, the Germans launched a counterattack on the Wolfsberg position.

It was at 10:00 a.m. on the 4th, that *1. Bataillon*, *RIR 202* (*Major* von Zingler), stationed in reserve at Chemnitz Camp, received orders 'to launch an immediate counter-attack to regain possession of the Wolfsberg.'[109] Three companies were to move forward, but

Lieutenant Colonel John Denis Yelverton Bingham DSO, CO 13th Tank Battalion. (ukphotoarchive.org)

> The whole morning, enemy barrage fire of the heaviest calibre pounded the battlefield, particularly the approach routes through the Somme valley and the Buchhain Hollow. Squadrons of up to eighty enemy aircraft circled continuously over our positions at low altitude, making any attempt to move impossible. Even individual soldiers were machine-gunned and bombed. At around 12 o'clock, a large formation of German aircraft appeared and forced the enemy aircraft back. Once this formation of ours pulled back after an hour or so, the enemy flyers returned in great numbers and soon regained total air superiority.
>
> Under these circumstances, the advance of the *1. Bataillon* proved time-consuming and they suffered heavy losses. The attack could not be carried out until the evening.[110]

With support from their artillery, and by moving along a communication trench, at around 10:00 p.m., the three companies managed to force their way, led by a squad of bombers, into the most easterly trenches of the Wolfsberg redoubt. Seven Australians and a machine gun were captured.[111] The weakened German units could not hold on, however. At 10:10 p.m., as reported in the 44th Battalion 'Narrative of Hamel Offensive',

> … our S.O.S. signal (3 green lights) shot up into the darkness from three different points in the front line and immediately our machine guns from every part of the countryside spat out a murderous belt of fire on to No Man's Land and the enemy's defences. Our artillery were soon in action too and placed a wall of steel [of] bursting shells between our men and the enemy.[112]

With a party of Germans estimated at 200–300 strong having recaptured a 200-yard-long stretch of the new Australian front line trench straddling A and B Companies' positions, the artillery's 'wall of steel' was falling behind the attacking enemy force.

109 Bergeder, *Das Reserve-Infanterie-Regiment Nr. 202*, p.145.
110 Bergeder, *Das Reserve-Infanterie-Regiment Nr. 202*, p.145.
111 Various accounts put the haul of prisoners from B Company at seven, 10, 11 or 12.
112 AWM: 4 23/61/22. War Diary 44th Battalion. Appendix 2. 'Narrative of Hamel Offensive.'

Whilst an Australian counterstroke was being planned, the Stokes mortars of the 11th Light Trench Mortar Battery, now under the command of Sergeant J. Distant, and 'well supplied with bombs from a carrier tank',[113] was throwing shells into the German positions and onto the communication trench.

Captain Adams (D Company) sent a request back to Captain Fowler (C Company, in support) asking him to send a platoon forward to reinforce the front line. From this, and other units, including a section of Americans under Corporal Powell (131st Regiment), and the men of the trench mortar battery who had by then fired off all of their ammunition, bombing parties were organised under Lieutenant Gaze of D Company and Lieutenant Cornish of B Company. These would attack up the front line trench from the south. A party under Captain Stables of A Company would simultaneously assault the German position from the north. 'So, the plan is the two bombing parties start 200+ yards apart, and work their way towards each other till fritz is squeezed out.'[114] This coordinated pincer attack went in at 2:45 a.m.,[115] the Australians going 'bald-headed at the Huns from both flanks.'[116] Stables' party on the northern flank, meeting strong resistance, was held up. The southern party, however, including Sergeants Padgett and Ingvarson, and Privates Tierney, Lynch and Angus, drove the Germans back, one bay at a time, forcing a number of them down into dugouts and pushing the rest out of the front line and back down the communication trench. Under heavy fire, and trying to rush along a communication trench that was becoming gradually more and more shallow, 'the enemy fled helter-skelter over the open with the Western Australians after them bombing, snapshooting and firing Lewis guns from the hip.'[117] Those who had been driven into the dugouts, numbering six officers and 50 other ranks, were captured, along with 10 machine guns. The Australians captured earlier by the enemy were freed. Sadly, just at the point when the German resistance began to disintegrate, Private Lynch was killed, shot through the head.[118]

The success was 'overwhelming.'[119] By 3:00 a.m., it was reported that the front line was cleared of the enemy, and C Company units moved up to occupy the newly recaptured section of the line.[120] During the night of 4/5 July, and for most of the following day, German machine guns and artillery 'gave much trouble,... especially to parties working forward to our front line', the machine gun bullets 'just skimming the convex slope of the hill.'[121] No further German counterattacks followed, however.

113 Bean, *The Official History*, vol.VI, p.315.
114 Longmore, *Eggs-a-Cook!*, p.149.
115 This is according to D Coy's report. A Coy's report gives the time as 3:00 a.m. Bean, in the *Official History*, times it at 2:00 a.m. The narrative of 44th Battalion states merely that the attack took place 'during the small hours.'
116 Longmore, *Eggs-A-Cook!*, p.148.
117 Bean, *The Official History*, vol.VI, pp.316–317.
118 638A Private James Joseph Lynch, C Coy 44th Battalion, age 24, is buried in Villers-Bretonneux Military Cemetery, grave I.F.7.
119 Bean, *The Official History*, vol.VI, p.317.
120 For their actions during this attack, the following received gallantry awards: Lieutenant Cyril Richard Cornish received the DSO. Lieutenant Frederick Owen Gaze was awarded a Bar to his MC. Sergeant Ingvarson received the D.C.M. 2767 Private C.P. Tierney earned an M.M., as did 1031 Private F. Angus (43rd Battalion). Two Americans were also honoured: Corporal R.H. Powell received the M.M., and Corporal T.A. Pope, who rushed and captured a machine gun single-handed, was awarded the D.C.M., as well as the American Medal of Honour.
121 AWM: 4 23/61/22. War Diary 44th Battalion. Appendix 2. 'Narrative of Hamel Offensive.'

Private Jens Ingvarson DCM & Bar, 44th Battalion. (AWM)

Private James Joseph Lynch, 44th Battalion. (AWM)

Corporal Thomas A. Pope, DCM, Medal of Honor, 131st Regiment. (Public Domain)

Lynch's Headstone (Author)

Casualties for the 44th Battalion for the period 4–6 July were listed by the adjutant, Captain Biles, as follows: four officers wounded, 25 other ranks killed,[122] 153 wounded, and 13 missing. A total of 195.

The war diary of 41st Battalion (Lieutenant Colonel A.R. Heron) contains reports from each company relating to the events of July 1918. All four have very little to say concerning the battalion's involvement on the day of the assault on Hamel. B Company's report states simply that the attack 'was so successful that the 41st Bn was not required.'[123] Infantry Brigade Order No. 128, issued on 2 July, was also short on detail: '41st Battalion will be Brigade Reserve'.[124]

Lieutenant Colonel Alexander Robert Heron, CO 41st Battalion. (AWM)

Toward the end of June, 41st Battalion was operating with three companies of four platoons each, as a consequence of the gassing and evacuation of all but four members of A Company at Villers-Bretonneux on 25 May. It was hoped that A Company could be reformed early in July as gas casualties gradually returned to duty, but in the end, X Company was formed as a composite unit, bolstered briefly before their untimely departure by one platoon of American troops.

The approach march began at 9:30 p.m. on 3 July. B and X Companies (Captains W. Uren and G. Thomas) skirted the town of Corbie from the north, and were led across the Somme by means of 'barrel bridges' by their guide, Lieutenant Freeman, before taking up positions respectively in squares J.32 and J.31 (just off Map 6). C and D Companies (Temporary Captain R.R. Wood and Lieutenant J.J. Hanley) passed through the eastern edge of La Neuville and moved along the northern Somme towpath before crossing near Hamelet, where they took up positions in the Reserve Line. All four companies were in position by 1:00 a.m. C and D Companies crossed paths with tanks that were making their way forward, and 'cheerful remarks were passed between the different arms.'[125]

As the attack developed, the men of 41st Battalion were initially reduced to the role of spectators, the intelligence officer, Lieutenant F.W. MacGibbon, noting that through his binoculars at around 4:30 a.m., he was able to watch seven tanks on the ridge nearing the final objective. It was at about that time that the first German prisoners began to stream back through their lines.

122 Commonwealth War Graves Commission records show 30 fatalities for this period.
123 AWM: 4 23/58/21. War Diary 41st Battalion. B Coy Report.
124 AWM: 4 23/58/21. War Diary 41st Battalion.
125 AWM: 4 23/58/21. War Diary 41st Battalion.

Captain William Uren, 41st Battalion. (AWM)

Lieutenant R.R. Wood, C Company, 41st Battalion. (AWM)

B Company moved up during the evening and helped consolidate the newly won positions by digging trenches in and to the north of Notamel Wood. As the German counterattack on the Wolfsberg developed, word was sent back from 44th Battalion that they required more grenades: a carrying party from C Company, 41st Battalion, who had meanwhile taken up positions to the south of Hamel, was sent forward with the requisite items. The battalion held their positions for the next 72 hours, undisturbed by the German artillery shoot on the morning of the 5th, which fell largely on the by then empty village. The whole enterprise had cost the battalion one dead and eight wounded.[126]

The grave of Private William David Pickering, 41st Battalion. (Author)

126 The one immediate fatality was 256 Private William David 'Pick' Pickering, aged 23, who is buried in Villers-Bretonneux Military Cemetery, grave VIII.B.10. He was in B Coy and was acting as batman to Lieutenant Thomas Wright. The 15 written reports in the Australian Red Cross Society Wounded and Missing Enquiry Bureau Files are wildly

Table 5. Total casualties recorded in 11th Brigade war diary

Unit	Officers	Other Ranks
41st Bn	-	7
42nd Bn	3	48
43rd Bn	7	90
44th Bn	5	149
11th TM Bty	1	2
USA	3	45
Total	**19**	**341**

Table 6. Estimated German losses in 11th Brigade war diary

	Officers	Other Ranks
Prisoners taken	16	430
Wounded prisoners	3	90
Killed during attack	8	350
Killed by artillery and during counterattack	4	300
Total:	**31**	**1,170**

These figures are inevitably inaccurate. In the *Official History*, Bean offers the exact same numbers for 11th Brigade. Commonwealth War Graves Commission records give the following totals for fatalities suffered between 4–6 July: two in the 41st Battalion, four in the 42nd Battalion, 26 in the 43rd Battalion, 30 in the 44th Battalion, and one in the 11th Trench Mortar Battery, making a total of 63. The Americans of 131st Regiment, 33rd American Division, attached to 43rd & 44th Battalions, suffered 12 fatalities. It is probable that a large proportion of these losses were sustained during the attack, unsupported by tanks, on Pear Trench, and through short shooting by the Australian artillery, and must therefore be classified as 'avoidable.'

Allied dead in front of Pear Trench. (AWM)

inconsistent regarding the time and location of his death, but all agree that he was killed by an enemy shell landing in the trench he was occupying. 2893 Private Thomas Warren died of his wounds on 6 July and is buried in Crouy British Cemetery, grave III.E.6.

5

The Diversionary Attacks

The 5th Australian Division (Major General Sir Joseph John Talbot Hobbs), deployed to the north of Hamel between the Somme and the Ancre rivers, also had a role to play on 4 July. They were to initiate a series of limited actions which would serve to divert German attention away from the main attack: whether they achieved this goal or not is debatable, but these operations were to cost over 60 Australian lives.

Orders for the operations were delivered in person by the divisional commander on 30 June as he visited the headquarters of both 14th and 15th Brigades.[1] The former, under Brigadier General J.C. Stewart, occupying the line just to the north of Sailly-Laurette was to organise a 'Chinese' attack and a raid on the German lines.[2] The latter was to attack, capture and hold a stretch of the German front line just to the south of the Ancre.

The commander of 15th Brigade, Brigadier General Harold 'Pompey' Elliott, was very unhappy with this arrangement. He had been pushing for a similar operation to the east of Ville-sur-Ancre for some time, and had 'desired to attack in the dark so as

Major General Sir Joseph John Talbot Hobbs, GOC 5th Australian Division. (AWM)

1 See AWM: 4 23/14/27 War Diary 14th Brigade June 1918 and AWM: 4 23/15/28 War Diary 15th Brigade June 1918.
2 'Chinese' attack: a fake or 'dummy' attack.

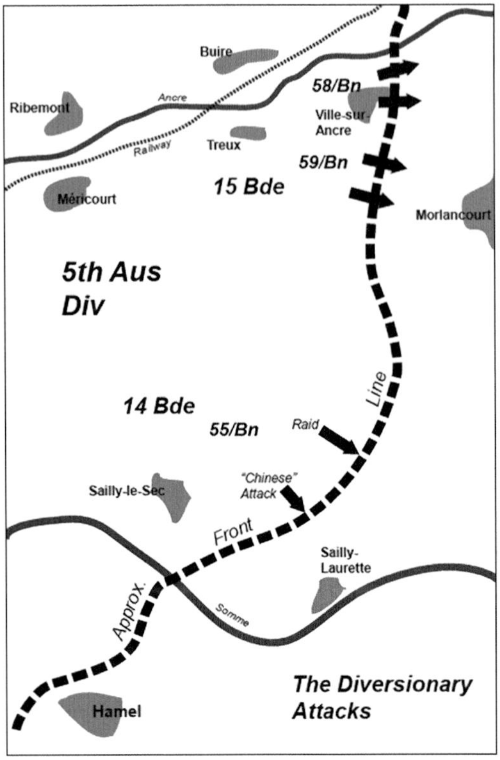

The Diversionary Attacks.

Brigadier General Harold 'Pompey' Elliott, commanding 15th Brigade. (AWM)

to have the line consolidated before morning, when he expected it to be severely shelled from Morlancourt heights.'[3]

Hobbs insisted that it should be simultaneous with the attack on Hamel, but Elliott feared that his men would suffer heavy casualties if they were forced to dig in by daylight. There followed a discussion as to whether the operation should be downgraded to a raid, but in the end, the decision was to hold any ground won. Elliott's operation thus became a diversion by default. His mood did not lighten in the following days, and it would appear he made sure that his views were committed to paper: part of the entry in the brigade diary for 3 July reads:

> The Brigadier is very much opposed to the operation of advancing the line taking place at dawn. He considers it should have been a night operation to allow of our men digging in during the hours of darkness. However we have orders to attack at 3:10 a.m. and arrangements have been made accordingly.[4]

The purpose of these operations north of the Somme was detailed in the brigade diaries. Brigade Order No.149 in the 14th Brigade diary states:

3 Bean, *The Official History*, vol.VI, p.319.
4 AWM: 4 23/15/29 War Diary 15th Brigade July 1918.

OBJECT OF OPERATION
2. i) To capture or kill as many of the enemy as possible.
ii) To destroy enemy defences.
(iii) To obtain identifications and other information.
(iv) To create a diversion to operations being carried out elsewhere.[5]

This operation, carried out by 55th Battalion, was classified as a 'raid': once the objectives had been achieved, the men would return to their own lines. There was to be no attempt to capture enemy trenches or to push forward their own front line.

The 15th Brigade diarist lists the objects in retrospect in the 'Report on Operation Carried out East of VILLE-sur-ANCRE, July, 5th [sic] 1918', written on the 6th:

a) In conjunction with other minor operations along the Divisional front to create a diversion for the operation taking place South of the RIVER SOMME.
b) To improve our observation along the MORLANCOURT VALLEY.
c) To improve our position respecting the initial stages of any future operations.
d) To kill or capture as many of the enemy as possible.[6]

The 'Chinese' attack was the responsibility of 55th Battalion (Lieutenant Colonel Percy William Woods). In charge of the operation was Lieutenant William E. Campbell, who would be assisted by five other ranks from C Company. Fifteen groups of dummy *papier-mâché* figures made by 8th Field Company Australian Engineers were to be placed in No Man's Land an hour before Zero. From Zero to Zero plus 35 minutes, the figures would be raised and lowered by means of long control wires to give the impression that an infantry assault was taking place, even though the operation would be 'carried out without artillery co-operation.'[7]

The diary of engineers details their role:

> The supply of, and arrangements for getting 'Chinamen' into the 'lie' position was the job of this unit. Fifteen – 3 men groups of 'Chinamen' were constructed at Coy Dump, 10 of these being sent forward to a forward dump two nights before operation, as Battalion Commander stated he only required 6 groups, giving a total of 18 figures. At midnight 3/4th July these groups were successfully got into the 'lie' position by 2nd Lt Brain and 6 sappers. This was approximately 40 to 30 yds out from our front line and about the same from enemy line. Groups were arranged slightly in echelon, control wires were about 250 yds long.[8]

Perhaps rather surprisingly, the ruse proved successful, 'drawing considerable machine gun and Minenwerfer fire. Some of the figures were practically smashed to pieces by Machine Gun fire.'[9]

5 AWM: 4 23/14/28 War Diary 14th Brigade July 1918.
6 AWM: 4 23/15/29 War Diary 15th Brigade July 1918.
7 AWM: 4 14/27/35 War Diary 8th Field Company Australian Engineers July 1918. 14th Australian Infantry Brigade Operation Memorandum No. 1, 2 July 1918, received 11:15 a.m.
8 AWM: 4 14/27/35 War Diary 8th Field Company Australian Engineers July 1918.
9 AWM: 4 23/72/29 War Diary 55th Battalion. Appendix 8. 'Report on Minor Operations carried out by 55th Battalion, on 4th July 1918.'

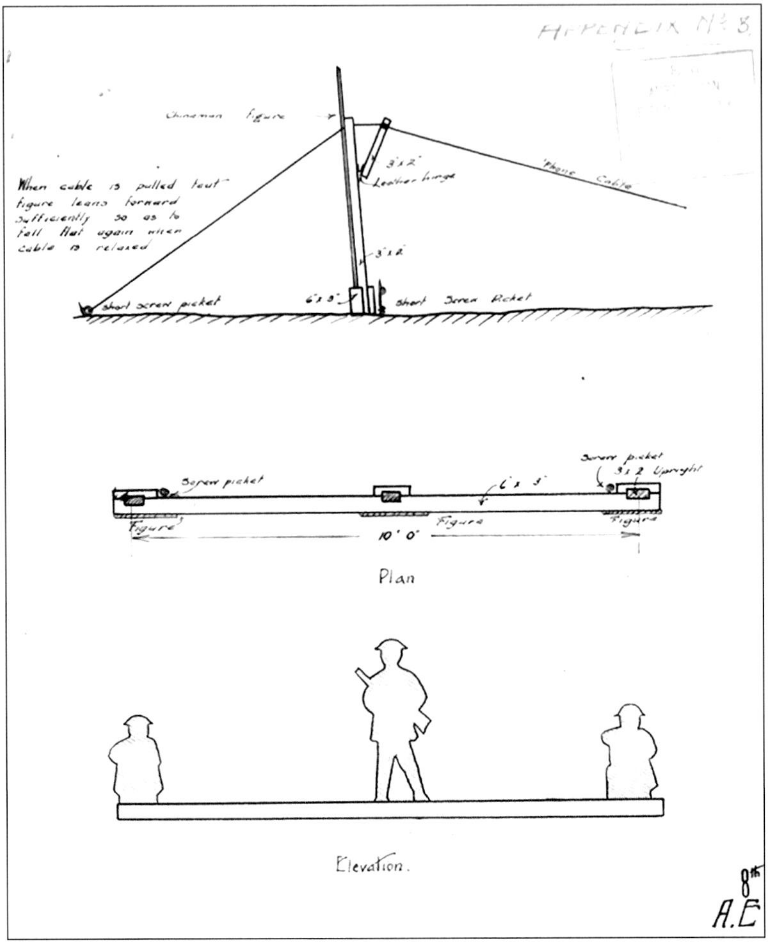

Diagram of 'Chinese' Attack figures made by 8th Field Company Australian Engineers. (AWM)

The Engineers recovered the figures during the night 4/5 July, and reported that four out of the six groups 'were found to be pretty well shot up.'[10]

* * *

The section of enemy trench to be raided by men from three companies of 55th Battalion was several hundred yards to the north. The raiding party was to consist of six officers and 200 men: one officer and 90 other ranks from A Company; two officers and 80 other ranks from B Company, and two officers and a platoon – 30 other ranks – from C Company. Captain K.R. Wyllie would be the officer in overall command.

The first objective, some 220 yards from the 'Hopping Off' tapes, was the German front line trench between K.19.d.77.25 and K.19.d.92.60. The second, another 220 yards further on, was the support trench between K.20.c.10.15 and K.20.c.16.54. (see map).

10 AWM: 4 14/27/35 War Diary 8th Field Company Australian Engineers July 1918.

Artillery support would come from four batteries of 18-pounders: they would shell the German second line from Zero to Zero plus 3 and then lift beyond it and form a 'box barrage' to hem the German defenders in and prevent reinforcement either from the rear or from the flanks. Smoke shells would make up 10 percent of all shells fired. Six light trench mortars would bombard the German front line trench during the three minutes following Zero before moving to targets beyond the second line. Two trench mortars would add their weight to the bombardment of the wire in front of the German second line before concentrating on the trench junction at K.20.a.2.1.

Eighteen Vickers machine guns of the 5th Australian Machine Gun Battalion would be firing on targets beyond the German support line – targeting in particular known machine gun posts – and to the flanks for the duration of the raid. What was left of 55th Battalion – those garrisoning the front line – were to pour rifle and Lewis gun fire into the German positions on either flank of the targeted sector.

The raiding party would advance in two waves, each divided into two groups, right and left, each under one officer. The first wave, tasked with taking the first objective, consisted of two officers and 80 other ranks, split into 10 sections numbered 1 to 10 from right to left. Sections 1 and 10 (on each flank) were bombing parties. Numbers 2, 3, 8 and 9 were Lewis gun sections. The left group was commanded by Lieutenant Bill Piddington, the right by Lieutenant George Donaldson. (See diagram below).

The second wave, 20 yards behind, split into 16 sections, also with similarly-tasked bombing parties on each flank, would advance in file under the command of Lieutenants Louis Stafford and Luther Chadwick – left and right respectively – leapfrog the first wave and take the second objective. Five pairs of stretcher bearers would bring up the rear.

Each man, in addition to his rifle, would carry two grenades, his haversack on his side and his entrenching tool in front of his body. A number (unspecified) would also carry wire cutters and hedging gloves.

Instructions for each wave were quite specific. The 'Addenda to Battalion Order No. 116' states:

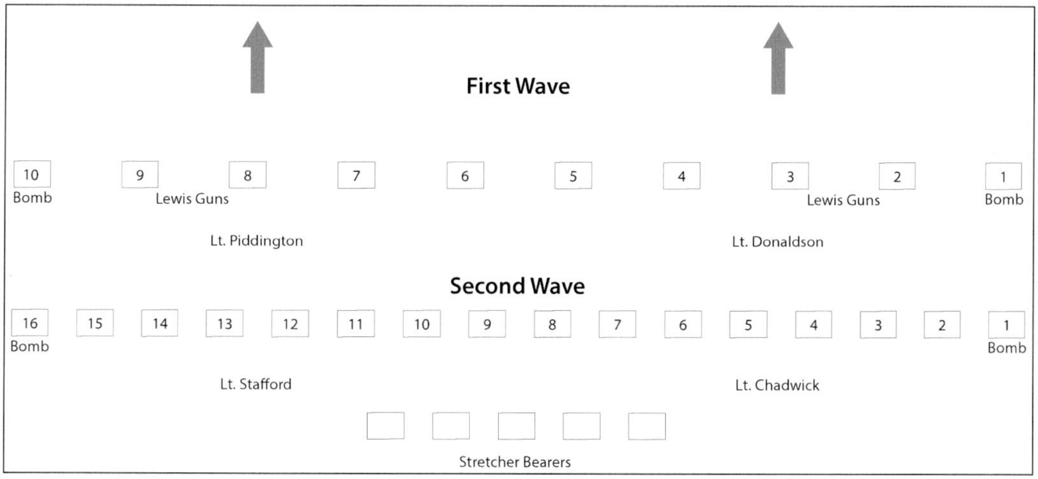

The formation of 55th Battalion raiding party, 4 July 1918.

a) Action of first wave. – First wave will take the first objective at the point of the bayonet and kill or capture the occupants of the trench. Sections 1 and 10 will immediately proceed to clear traverses to the flanks to a distance of 30 yards. Lewis gun sections will take up positions on the flanks and engage any retreating enemy or hostile machine guns firing from flanks of first or second objective. No man of first wave will attempt to return to our lines, whether wounded or with a prisoner, until the second wave and Stretcher bearers have passed over. Immediately this has happened any prisoners and wounded men will be rushed back to our lines. Remaining sections will destroy any guns or material that cannot be removed and search all dug-outs and dead in their sector of the trench. The first wave, with the exception of the Officers in charge and the flanking, bombing an[d] Lewis gun sections, will withdraw on the completion of their task. The sections remaining will withdraw on the orders of the party leaders when the withdrawal of the second wave has taken place.

b) Action of second wave. – second wave will leap across first objective and proceed to second objective. Leaders must locate gaps in wire and rush sections through, immediately opening out for assault on second objective. No's 1 and 16 sections will form bombing blocks on flanks and the remainder of the party will kill or capture the garrison and destroy or remove machine guns or material with the utmost despatch. Before giving the signal to withdraw the party leaders must satisfy themselves that the task has been completed and that no members of the party, dead or alive, are left in the trench. In the withdrawal the second wave must be on the lookout to carry back or assist any wounded en route.

c) Action of Stretcher bearers. – Stretcher bearers will follow second wave across the first objective to second objective and immediately proceed to work back to 'Hopping Off' line.'[11]

The whole operation was to last no more than 30 minutes.[12]

The day before the raid, 3 July, was fine, bright and sunny, and was devoted to making final preparations. The men earmarked to take part were rested as much as possible, and during the afternoon the officers explained the scheme to them, making sure that everyone was 'thoroughly conversant' with the details of the plan and with their role within it.[13] The men were given a hot meal at 10:00 p.m., and by midnight, they were ready to move forward. Having removed all other means of identification, each man was given new identity discs: rather like the system of numbered brass 'tags' or 'checks' used in the coal mining industry to make sure that everyone had returned safely to the surface after their shift, the disc would be handed in as the soldier made it back to his original front line trench after the raid.

Meanwhile, parties from C Company under Captain F.J. Cotterell had been working on improving the jumping-off positions. Unfortunately, they were seen by the Germans and had to complete their work under persistent bursts of machine gun fire, suffering two casualties in the process. Also out in advance of the Australian front line, under cover of darkness, was a party led by Lieutenant Norman Lewis Wilson, busy laying the tapes on which the raiders would form up. These were all in place, pegged down, with the exact positions of each section clearly

11 AWM: 4 23/72/29 War Diary 55th Battalion. July 1918. Appendix 5.
12 Supporting artillery fire was scheduled to cease at Zero plus 30 mins.
13 AWM: 4 23/72/29 War Diary 55th Battalion. July 1918.

marked, by 1:30 a.m. The medical officer, Captain Norman John Mackay, had established an advanced dressing station in a front line dugout on the right flank of the assembly position.

All working parties were clear of the front line by 2:00 a.m., and were making their way back to the support trenches using a different route to that being used by the raiders, going in the opposite direction along Cootamundra Sap. Captain Wyllie's men, at his signal, 'hopped the bags and moved silently across no man's land to the tapes',[14] and by 2:50 a.m. Wyllie was able to report to battalion HQ that everything was ready. 'Judging by the 'normal' levels of enemy machine gun fire and the absence of artillery and *Minenwerfer* fire, the assembly had been completed without being observed by the Germans.'[15] The after-action report in the 55th Battalion war diary states that 'Every man knew his position and every man was on it.'[16]

The artillery and trench mortar barrage came down on time at 3:10 a.m., synchronising exactly with the barrage for the 4th Division attack south of the Somme. The aforementioned report states that the barrage was 'excellent.' Evidence might suggest otherwise.

An account from Private Bert Bishop, not taking part in the operation himself, but watching events, states:

> The air filled with screeching shells and whistling bullets, the swish of mortars and bombs. A horror filled us as we saw what was happening. The barrage, instead of falling on the German lines, was falling anywhere at all. It fell on our own trench, some of it even behind us, while the poor wretches in no-man's-land caught the worst of it.[17]

Brigadier General Stewart (14th Brigade) wrote in his diary: 'The 55th Coy Commander who carried out the raid [Wyllie] is very cut up at his casualties and blames our trench mortars.'[18] On the other hand, in his after-action report, Lieutenant Colonel Woods remarked that: 'At Zero the Barrage fell and one minute later *enemy* trench mortar barrage came down close in front of our trenches. Casualties were caused by this fire all along the 'hopping off' line during the three minutes period of waiting.'[19]

Regardless of where the shells originated, the men out on the tapes waiting for the artillery barrage to commence its first lift had no choice but to endure the hail of fire. According to the Red Cross files, in a report written by Private Lyttle, one shell accounted for both Corporal Hamilton and Lance Corporal Hart, both in B Company:

> We were lying on the tape ready to go over the top, when one of our 6" Stokes mortars burst behind them, and Hamilton was hit in the back and killed outright. Hart died while S/Bs [stretcher bearers] were binding him up. He was wounded in the head.'[20]

14 Timothy J. Cook, *Snowy to the Somme. A Muddy and Bloody Campaign, 1916-1918* (Newport: Big Sky Publishing Ltd, 2014), p.218.
15 Cook, *Snowy to the Somme*, p.218.
16 AWM: 4 23/72/29 War Diary 55th Battalion. July 1918. Appendix 8.
17 Bert Bishop, *The Hell. The Humour, The Heartbreak* (Kenthurst: Kangaroo Press, 1993), pp.181–182, quoted in Cook, *Snowy to the Somme*, p.219.
18 AWM: 315 419/099/002 Papers: James Campbell Stewart.
19 AWM: 4 23/72/29 War Diary 55th Battalion. July 1918. Appendix 8. (Author's italics).
20 AWM: 1DRL/0428. Australian Red Cross Society Wounded and Missing Enquiry Bureau Files, 1914–18 War.

Private Harvey, a stretcher bearer, was also killed by shellfire while returning after carrying a casualty out of the line.[21] Private Joseph Cazenave's report confirms that the same fate befell Private MacDonald, 'killed right at the start by some of our own shells which fell short.'[22] Cazenave helped to carry MacDonald's body back.[23] Cook, in *Snowy to the Somme,* adds Corporal Walter Allen to this growing list: he was 'riddled' by shell fragments, and was 'placed on a stretcher and was on his way rearwards when a shell burst in front of the stretcher party, killing Allen and wounding a stretcher bearer.'[24]

It was surely with some sense of relief that the first wave was finally given the signal to advance, and the men were able to get up and run towards the German lines. The second wave and the stretcher bearers followed immediately. Shells were still falling amongst them, and the German machine gunners also opened fire, the latter claiming three more casualties during the mad dash across No Man's Land. Although smoke shells limited vision to only a few yards, Captain Wyllie somehow managed to keep his men in formation, and the first wave, led by Lieutenant Donaldson, finding little or no German wire to hinder their progress, were soon at the first objective: the German front line trench. The trench turned out to be only lightly manned: two posts were found, one of them containing a machine gun and its crew. Corporal Alec Penny, at the head of his section, rushed the machine gun and

> …it was his own bayonet skilfully thrusted which killed the German gunner in the act of firing. A quick withdrawal, a vigorous thrust, and a second Hun was pinned. Following a third a little way up the trench, he too fell victim to Cpl. Penny's skill with the bayonet. Inspired by their leader's pluck and example, his men worked along either flank accounting for every one of the enemy in that part of the trench.[25]

Penny, who personally carried the German machine gun back to the Australian lines at the end of the raid, was awarded the DCM for his actions. This first trench was searched and found clear to a distance of around 40 yards on either flank. One surviving German soldier was sent back as a prisoner. The first wave had completed its task.

The second wave 'leap-frogged' through the first wave and headed for the next German trench line. Here, the barbed wire entanglements, 10 to 12 feet wide and rather low, appeared largely undisturbed by the artillery bombardment. Cook, in *Snowy to the Somme*, suggests that this was 'possibly because the medium trench mortars and artillery tasked with wire cutting were firing short.'[26] Even so, this, according to Lieutenant Colonel Woods, 'did not prove a very difficult obstacle',[27] and two parties were able to work their way through and rush the trench.

21 2674 Lance Corporal William Barker Hart, 1665 Corporal Ernest Hamilton, and 2684 Private William Raymond Harvey are all buried together in Franvillers Communal Cemetery Extension, graves I.G.8, I.G.7 and I.G.9 respectively.
22 AWM: 1DRL/0428. Australian Red Cross Society Wounded and Missing Enquiry Bureau Files, 1914–18 War.
23 3186 Private John MacDonald is buried in Franvillers Communal Cemetery Extension, grave I.G.12.
24 Cook, *Snowy to the Somme*, p.219. 1612 Cpl Walter Otto Herbert Allen is commemorated on the Villers-Bretonneux Memorial.
25 Extract from the recommendation for the DCM for 2415 Corporal Alec Penny, 55th Battalion.
26 Cook, *Snowy to the Somme*, p.220.
27 AWM: 4 23/72/29 War Diary 55th Battalion. July 1918. Appendix 8.

The second line German trench was much more strongly manned, and the garrison was prepared to put up something of a fight. On the left flank, Lieutenant Stafford led his party onto the parapet of the trench and encountered a group of 'up to twenty' Germans.[28] Stafford shot the nearest one with his pistol. He managed to kill a second but was then himself shot in the chest by a German officer, a wound that would prove fatal. Stafford's batman, 3219 Private Swift, 'succeeded in killing the Boche',[29] and with two or three of his mates jumped into the trench. They worked their way along it, accounting for nine more Germans.

On the right, Lieutenant Chadwick's party also reached the German second trench, coming directly up against a machine gun post. Chadwick's MC recommendation details his actions: 'The enemy garrison resisted strongly and hand to hand fighting ensued. Lt Chadwick (with his revolver) and the men nearest him (with rifle and bayonet) accounted for the whole of [the] machine gun crew.' When the order to withdraw was given, Chadwick 'lifted the captured gun to his shoulder and withdrew to our lines.'[30]

Also in that sector, Private John Hannah was the first man in his section to reach the German trench. There, he encountered a German bombing party of six men who were lobbing stick grenades at the raiders.

> He [Hannah] approached unnoticed from the flank, and his dash and daring were demonstrated with such suddenness that the Germans were taken completely by surprise. Thrusting with his bayonet he killed the first German just as he had thrown a bomb at one of the raiding sections a little to the flank. He shot a second man with his rifle. Following the retreating Germans a little down the trench, he accounted for two more with the bayonet, and shot a fifth. The last member of the garrison surrendered and was taken prisoner by Pte HANNAH. The way was then cleared for the remainder of the section, who, working to the flanks, dealt further destruction, inspired all the time by their comrade's dash.[31]

Hannah, slightly wounded during the encounter, was awarded the DCM.

Four dugouts were discovered in the second line. They were of a substantial size and depth, being reached, it was estimated, by 12 to 16 steps and were deemed too big to be mopped up using hand grenades; they were destroyed by throwing Stokes Mortar rounds into them. The raiders also found a heavy machine gun embedded in a concrete base: it proved impossible to remove it, so this too was blown up.

As mopping up went on, Lewis gunners were deployed to the flanks of the sector to protect the raiders from counter attack. One of these, Private Farrell, had been seriously burnt about the face, having been injured by a shell that burst near him as he crossed No Man's Land. Despite the painful wounds, he continued to man his post, 'sweeping with fire from his gun the enemy posts to the flank' until ordered to withdraw.[32] His MM was thoroughly deserved.

With all objectives gained and mopping up complete, the order to withdraw was given, and the men made their way back, as best they could, across No Man's Land. Although not

28 Cook, *Snowy to the Somme*, p.220.
29 AWM: 4 23/72/29 War Diary 55th Battalion. July 1918. Appendix 8.
30 Recommendation for the Military Cross for Lieutenant Luther Chadwick, 55th Battalion.
31 Recommendation for the Distinguished Conduct Medal for 2491 Private John Leonard Leslie Hannah, 55th Battalion.
32 Recommendation for the Military Medal for 5076 Private Coulson Montague Farrell, 55th Battalion.

threatened by machine gun fire, the Germans had put down a heavy counter-bombardment on the Australian front lines and on No Man's Land at Zero plus nine minutes. More casualties were inevitable at this point, and several men distinguished themselves by carrying wounded comrades back to safety.[33] Two of their fallen mates were, however, left behind.[34]

As per the plan, the men in the first wave waited in the German front line trench for the second wave to withdraw through them before joining the move on Lieutenant Donaldson's order. It is possible that Lieutenant Piddington was killed at this juncture by an enemy shell.[35] Woods' after-action report classifies Piddington as missing, however, and suggests that he had already crossed back over the Australian front line trench, going 'to the rear over the top' when he disappeared.[36]

Assessment of the raid's efficacy began almost immediately. Lieutenant Colonel Woods' view was that: 'Considering the nature of the operation and the success obtained in drawing enemy fire, I do not consider the casualties excessive.'[37] In the same report, Woods does, however, remark that the casualties were 'very heavy'. In the raid, one officer and six other ranks were killed, and 29 other ranks were wounded. In the trenches, two other ranks were killed, and one officer and 26 other ranks were wounded. One officer and one other rank were posted as missing. This amounts to an overall figure of 67 casualties, though later accounts put it at 83, out of a raiding party of 206 men. The latter figure gives a casualty rate of just over 40 percent.

Cook assesses the raid as follows:

> The raid had been skilfully undertaken and achieved all of its objectives. Despite the travails endured by the attackers, the Australians claimed 45 enemy dead, captured three prisoners (all of whom were wounded)[38] and seized two light machine guns. More importantly, given the tremendous volume of artillery and machine gun fire put down by the Germans in the sector, it is likely that some of the enemy leadership had fallen for the feint and believed the main Australian attack was occurring along Morlancourt Ridge.[39]

He later states, however, that: 'Given the success of the 'Chinese Attack', one cannot help but speculate whether the raid was needed, and whether the more pervasive use of papier-mâché figures, combined with some artillery demonstration, could have achieved the same outcome as flesh and blood.'[40]

Brigadier General Stewart appears not to have been convinced, writing in his diary that: 'People seem to be quite satisfied with our part of the show yesterday, although there is not much

33 In this regard, 3351 Private Frederick William Doherty was Mentioned in Corps Orders: 2646 Private Theodore Ambrose Foret, 4834 Private Michael Kerin and 3254 Private Thomas James were awarded the Military Medal.

34 The aforementioned Lieutenant Stafford and 5182 Private Charles Robert Sinclair. Their bodies were never recovered and they are both commemorated on the Villers-Bretonneux Memorial.

35 Cook, *Snowy to the Somme*, p.221.

36 AWM: 4 23/72/29 War Diary 55th Battalion. July 1918. Appendix 8. Lieutenant William Thomas Piddington's body was later recovered, and he is buried in Franvillers Communal Cemetery Extension, grave I.G.11. The details of his demise must remain uncertain.

37 AWM: 4 23/72/29 War Diary 55th Battalion. July 1918. Appendix 8.

38 Identified as belonging to *3. Kompanie, RIR 232.*

39 Cook, *Snowy to the Somme*, p.222.

40 Cook, *Snowy to the Somme*, p.223.

glowing in it.'[41] Also, questioning the pre-raid security, given the size of the German front line garrison and the rapidity of the artillery response, he added: 'One prisoner states that he knew the attack was coming as they had been told by a deserter on the night 2/3rd. This was the very night the 53rd lost a man on patrol and the circumstances of finding the Bosch quite prepared are very suspicious.'[42]

If the Germans did know of the raid in advance, and of its limited scope, it might be difficult to argue that it constituted a serious diversion from the major attack going on to the south. This is by no means certain, however, and the raid's diversional efficacy must remain moot.

* * *

The attack made by 15th Brigade, to the east of the village of Ville-sur-Ancre, was meant to capture and hold a stretch of German front line trench extending southwards from a ruined house (referred to in some accounts as an 'old mill') on the river bank (E.26.a.25.55) to a point south of the Méaulte road (K.2.a.10.20 – see Map 8). It would be executed by A and B Companies of 59th Battalion and D Company of 58th Battalion. Lieutenant Colonel J.J. Scanlan of 59th Battalion would be in command. One company of 60th Battalion and a further platoon from 58th Battalion were made available 'for repelling counter attack if required.'[43]

Lieutenant Colonel John Joseph Scanlan, CO 59th Battalion. (AWM)

The assault would be supported by a creeping artillery barrage supplied by 18-pounders, with 4.5-inch howitzers and machine guns targeting known enemy strongpoints beyond the final objective line. Trench mortars would also be involved. (See map below).

Phase one of the barrage was very short, from Zero to Zero plus one minute: the 18-pounders would bombard line 'A', and 3-inch Stokes mortars would concentrate on the German front line trench (line 'B'). The 18-pounders would then lift to line 'B', remaining there for two

41 AWM: 315 419/099/002 Papers: James Campbell Stewart.
42 AWM: 315 419/099/002 Papers: James Campbell Stewart.
43 AWM: 4 23/15/29. War Diary 15th Brigade. Appendix 7. '15th Australian Brigade Order No. 172. 2 July 1918.'

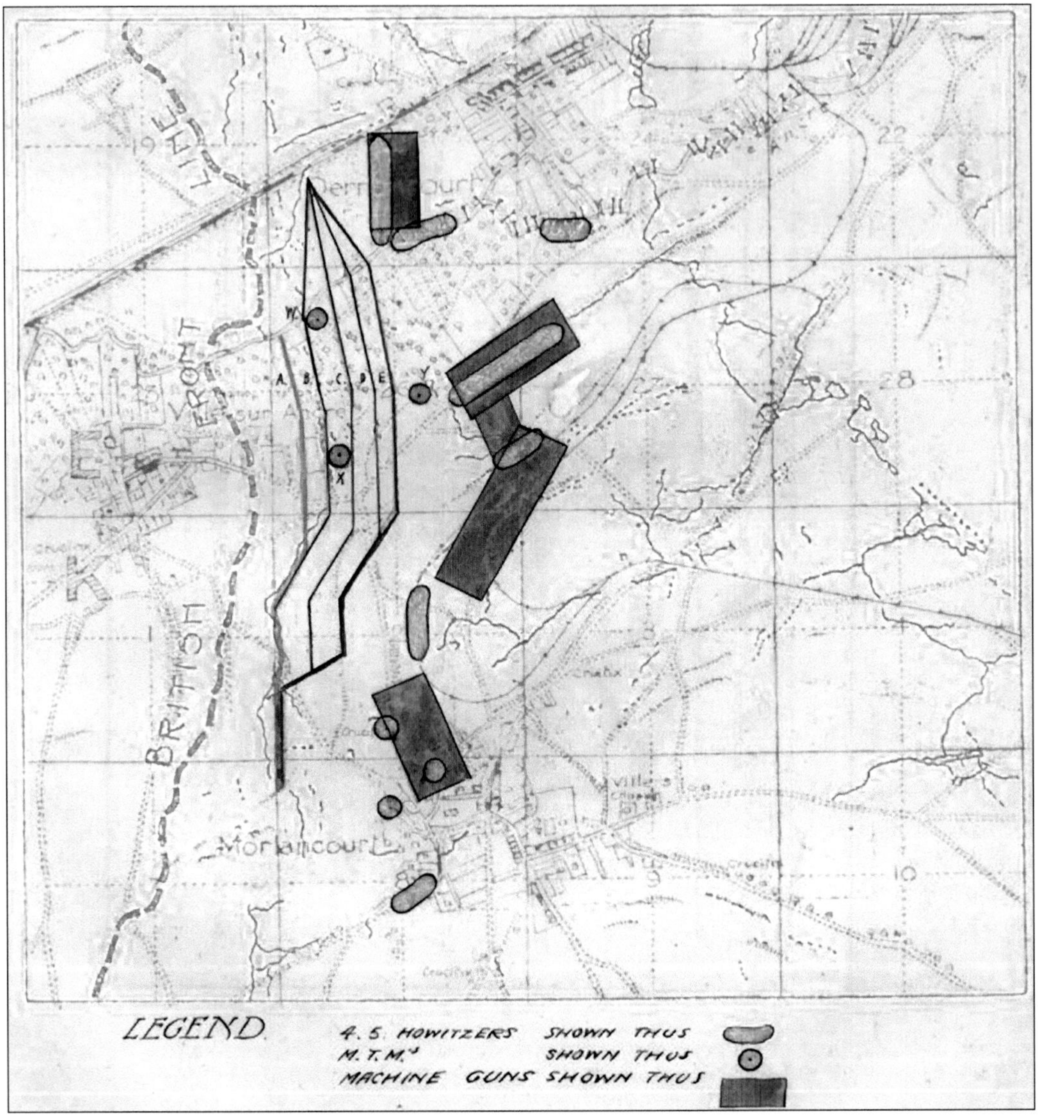

Trench mortar, artillery and machine-gun fire plan. (AWM)

minutes, whilst the Stokes mortars continued as for phase one. At Zero plus three, the 18-pounders were to lift 100 yards onto line 'C', and the mortars would switch to the flanks, remaining there until the cease fire, in particular forming a block at K.2.c.0.9 on the right. At Zero plus four, the creeping barrage would move onto line 'D', followed by a further lift onto line 'E' at Zero plus five, where it would remain until Zero plus 90. Howitzer target areas are shown in light grey shapes on the map, with machine gun targets in darker grey rectangles. The speed of advance of the creeping barrage – in lifts of 50 yards at a rate of 100 yards per minute – is unusually rapid.

With the creeping barrage reaching its final position five minutes after Zero, the infantry would have to move quickly to keep up. To help in this regard, in the southern sector of the attack, two saps, 100 yards in length, were dug towards the German front line and from there onwards as 'Russian' saps, these to be opened up just prior to the assault. The right-hand sap would serve as a 'defensive flank'; the left-hand one, dug towards an enemy sap head, was to serve as 'a main communication sap.'[44]

The deployment of troops along the attack frontage was uneven. In the right sector, the two companies of 59th Battalion covered a front a little in excess of 1,000 yards: the left sector, slightly longer, was to be assaulted by just three platoons of 58th Battalion (with one more platoon in support). Each platoon was divided into two half-platoons of only 10 men each, consisting of one officer or platoon sergeant, two scouts, two bombers, two riflemen, and three Lewis gunners. With a total, therefore, including the support platoon, of only 80 men, Acting Company Sergeant Major McPhee, of D Company, in his written after-action report, estimated that the enemy, 'on this occasion, outnumbered us by at least 5 to 1.'[45]

The attack formation adopted by 59th Battalion was inevitably denser and deeper: each company deployed four platoons, each occupying a frontage of about 70 yards. In front were four pairs of scouts. Ten yards behind these came eight sections of riflemen and bombers, and a further 25 yards back were eight Lewis gun sections, along with stretcher bearers, signallers and the company HQ, the latter positioned in the centre between the two attacking companies. On the extreme right, a party of 12 men under the command of Second Lieutenant Stephen Facey DCM, 'a leader specially trusted for his bravery and capacity',[46] were to construct a pair of trench blocks at K.2.c.1.9. (see Map 8) and defend this flank against any enemy counterattack.

B Company of 59th Battalion, led by Captain K.G. McDonald, on the left battalion frontage, had assembled in their front line trench at 11:30 p.m. An hour later, the jumping-off tapes were in position, and guides led the attackers out, all parties being in position by 3:05 a.m. The artillery barrage came down exactly on time at 3:10, 'very intense with well defined limits.'[47] One minute later, with the order to advance given simultaneously by all platoon commanders, Captain McDonald 'saw the whole company rise and move steadily forward until we had got about 80 yards when I noticed the two centre platoons [Nos. 6 & 7] sagging back, this was caused by their encountering barbed wire in the crop.'[48]

Before McDonald had the chance to rectify the problem, both flanking platoons – No. 5 on the right and No. 8 on the left – had reached the German trench. No. 6 Platoon, on meeting the belt of wire, were greeted, from a range of about 20 yards, by machine gun fire from a post directly ahead of them. Corporal Ibbotson, looking for guidance from his platoon commander,

44 AWM: 4 23/15/29. War Diary 15th Brigade. Appendix 7. 'Report on Operation' by Lieutenant Colonel Scanlan, CO 59th Battalion. A 'Russian Sap' is a tunnel dug at a shallow depth, allowing troops to move forward unobserved and without danger from enemy small arms fire. The subsequent removal of the tunnel roof converts it instantly into a standard trench.

45 AWM: 4 23/75/30 War Diary 58th Battalion, Appendix 7. 'Report on Operation on Night 3/4th July 1918, by No. 4152 Sgt. McPhee A.E. Acting C.S.M. 'D' Company, 58th Battalion AIF'

46 Bean, *The Official History*, vol.VI, p.321.

47 AWM: 4 23/76/30 War Diary 59th Battalion. Appendix 7. 'Narrative by O.C. 'B' Company, 59th Battalion A.I.F'

48 AWM: 4 23/76/30 War Diary 59th Battalion. Appendix 7. 'Narrative by O.C. 'B' Company, 59th Battalion A.I.F'

Lieutenant Rawson, found the latter badly wounded. With No. 7 Platoon on his left also partly held up, Ibbotson went off in search of Captain McDonald.

On the right, No. 5 Platoon 'encountered no opposition or wire going across. We advanced quietly to within a few yards of [the] enemy trench, then yelled and charged.'[49] Once in the trench, with a 'few enemy dead and two live ones who offered no resistance',[50] Lieutenant McPherson noticed the German machine gun, well off to his left, which was causing the problems in the centre. He saw Corporal Rusden throw a Mills bomb and fire at the machine gunner with his rifle, but with no effect. Almost immediately, Rusden was wounded in the thigh by the detonation of a German stick grenade.[51]

On the left flank, the men of No. 8 Platoon were able to reach their objective with little opposition, finding the German trench only very lightly manned. Six of the enemy

The grave of Corporal Arthur Stuart Keylock Rusden, 59th Battalion. (Author)

> …with a machine gun which they were either too frightened to use or else we surprised them as immediately we jumped in three of the[m] 'Kameraded.' Two were a bit late and suffered in consequence…. Two others further up the trench were bombed, one being taken prisoner wounded, and the other killed.'[52]

The sixth was also taken prisoner, and, after a little persuasion, 'set up a captured machine gun so that we could make use of it.'[53]

Just to their right, those on the left flank of No. 7 Platoon who did not encounter any wire in No Man's Land were able to capture two Germans in a listening post before 'hopping into the trench' [54] under enfilade fire from the right.

49 AWM: 4 23/76/30 War Diary 59th Battalion. Appendix 7. 'Narrative by Lieutenant W.J. McPherson, No. 5 Platoon Commander.'
50 AWM: 4 23/76/30 War Diary 59th Battalion. Appendix 7. 'Narrative by Lieutenant W.J. McPherson, No. 5 Platoon Commander.'
51 5215 Corporal Arthur Stuart Keylock 'Rus' Rusden, B Coy, 59th Battalion, was placed on a stretcher, but died of his wounds before he could be evacuated. He is buried in Méricourt-L'Abbé Communal Cemetery Extension, grave III.E.6.
52 AWM: 4 23/76/30 War Diary 59th Battalion. Appendix 7. 'Narrative by Corporal G.A. Abbott, No. 8 Platoon.'
53 AWM: 4 23/76/30 War Diary 59th Battalion. Appendix 7. 'Narrative by Corporal G.A. Abbott, No. 8 Platoon.'
54 AWM: 4 23/76/30 War Diary 59th Battalion. Appendix 7. 'Narrative by L/Cpl R.E. Lyons, No. 1 Gun Team, No. 7 Platoon.'

It became clear, with No. 6 Platoon and part of No. 7 still held up in No Man's Land, that about 200 yards of the German trench in the centre was still firmly in enemy hands. Corporal Ibbotson had, by this time, found Captain McDonald and made him aware of his platoon's plight before going back to try to get his colleagues to move to the right to 'outflank' the obstacle.

The centre platoons, now faced with three German machine guns, had lost most of their officers and platoon sergeants and had suffered around 50 percent casualties. Such a scenario had been discussed in preparation for the attack, however, and a contingency plan had been devised. The men of No. 5 Platoon on the right, and those from the left-hand sections of No. 7 on the left began to bomb their way inwards along the German trench towards the machine gun post in the centre. This 'pincer' movement proved successful, and five of the German machine gunners were killed, the rest either wounded or taken prisoner. As the Australians closed in on him, one of the machine gunners had jumped out of the trench with his gun and began firing at those coming up towards him from the south. Lieutenant McPherson fired three shots 'and silenced him.'[55]

Just as the machine gun post was being overwhelmed, 50 or so Germans appeared about 200 yards away to the rear, running forward to reinforce the line. Corporal Lyons (No. 7 Platoon), making his way southwards along the German trench, noticed the new arrivals and immediately ran back to where he had set up a Lewis gun post and informed his No.1 – who was evidently unsure of the nationality of this group in the half-light and the smoke – that they were, in fact, German. The Lewis guns accordingly opened fire 'in a few seconds and soon dispersed the Huns.'[56]

With the whole length of the enemy trench now captured, the men still stranded out in No Man's Land could finally move forward, and consolidation of the newly won position was able to start. The supervision of this task fell to Lieutenant McPherson, as Captain McDonald had been informed that he would have to take over command of the whole battalion line, as both Captain Akeroyd, A Company, and his second in command, Lieutenant Scattergood, had been wounded.

McPherson first established Lewis gun posts and then got the rest of the men busy digging in. As he moved along the line, he discovered that Lieutenants Rawson, Myers and Campbell had also been wounded.[57] Consolidation proved slow and difficult, the enemy trench being 'very shallow and narrow.'[58]

A Company (Captain Akeroyd) on the right sector of the 59th Battalion attack frontage, watched the artillery barrage fall on the enemy trench, Lieutenant Stavely asserting that it was excellent, 'with the exception of odd shells falling short.'[59] As the barrage lifted, 'the charge was

55 AWM: 4 23/76/30 War Diary 59th Battalion. Appendix 7. 'Narrative by Lieutenant W.J. McPherson, No. 5 Platoon Commander.'

56 AWM: 4 23/76/30 War Diary 59th Battalion. Appendix 7. 'Narrative by L/Cpl R.E. Lyons No. 7 Platoon.'

57 Lieutenant James Gerald Rawson died of his wounds on 5 July. He is buried in Vignacourt British Cemetery, grave II.E.14.

58 AWM: 4 23/76/30 War Diary 59th Battalion. Appendix 7. 'Narrative by Lieutenant W.J. McPherson, No. 5 Platoon Commander.'

59 AWM: 4 23/76/30 War Diary 59th Battalion. Appendix 7. 'Narrative of Operations as seen by Lt. W. Stavely on morning of 4th inst..'

made at once, the usual shouting and cheering from our men could be plainly heard above the din.'[60]

But for a little bunching on the right, the men held their formation well. As the smoke from the barrage cleared from the German front line, Platoon Sergeant Dawson could see a German machine gun dead ahead, and Lieutenant Stavely was heard to shout, 'We'll get that bloke.' As they made for the post, Duncan saw that there was only one German there, and as they jumped into the trench, Stavely shot him dead with his revolver. Working along the trench for about 50 yards, Stavely watched 'our boys dealing with the Hun satisfactorily.'[61]

It would seem that the Australians were not keen on accepting the enemy's surrender. Sergeant Duncan continues the narrative: 'We started to do a bit of mopping up but the Boche won't fight and so we killed some, but had to send a few prisoners back to let the people in rear know that we didn't take an empty trench.'[62]

Lieutenant James Gerald Rawson, 59th Battalion. (Author)

Sergeant Stanford of No. 1 Platoon confirms that at that point, 'the good work of killing commenced.'[63] A good number of the German garrison were able to escape by running back through the ripening crops. Lieutenant Stavely watched them flee, but 'as the light was not good, I got one only.'[64]

At around 4:00 a.m., with the two companies of 59th Battalion rather too thinly stretched, and with a gap between them, No. 10 Platoon of 60th Battalion went forward under Lieutenant M. Gordon to reinforce the right wing of 59th Battalion. Forty minutes later, Lieutenant Ashman led No. 12 Platoon, 60th Battalion, forward to fill the gap between the companies.

There was one more job to do: advanced posts needed to be set up, around 50 yards or so beyond the German trench and this needed to be completed before the standing protective barrage ended. Lieutenant Stavely set about reconnoitring these new positions, beginning on

60 AWM: 4 23/76/30 War Diary 59th Battalion. Appendix 7. 'Narrative of Operations as seen by Lt. W. Stavely on morning of 4th inst..'
61 AWM: 4 23/76/30 War Diary 59th Battalion. Appendix 7. 'Narrative of Operations as seen by Lt. W. Stavely on morning of 4th inst..'
62 AWM: 4 23/76/30 War Diary 59th Battalion. Appendix 7. 'Narrative by Sgt H. Duncan, No. 2 Platoon, 'A' Coy, 59th Battalion AIF'
63 AWM: 4 23/76/30 War Diary 59th Battalion. Appendix 7. 'Narrative by Sgt G.W. Stanford, No. 1 Platoon, 'A' Coy, 59th Battalion AIF'
64 AWM: 4 23/76/30 War Diary 59th Battalion. Appendix 7. 'Narrative of Operations as seen by Lt. W. Stavely on morning of 4th inst..'

the left flank and moving gradually down to his right. As he did so, both he and Sergeant Stanford became aware that 'the right flank was having an exciting time.'[65]

There, the special party under Second Lieutenant Facey – 11 men and a corporal – was tasked with building a double trench block. As they had moved off from the jumping off tape, they had seen that 'a good many shells seemed to fall short',[66] and by the time they reached the enemy trench, two men and the corporal had already been wounded.

The grave of Second Lieutenant Stephen George Facey, 59th Battalion. (Author)

The party worked southwards along the trench for about 120 yards, 'clearing out dug outs and saps',[67] before starting to build the two blocks about 20 yards apart. As Private Maginn and five others worked on the outer barricade, Lieutenant Facey went back to supervise the building of the second one. It was half-finished when Lieutenant Stavely arrived on the scene. Facey advised him that all was in hand and that he had 'a nice Blighty',[68] but would stay and finish the job. Stavely returned to his unit, and it was only minutes later that Private Maginn at the outer block received word that his officer had been killed by a sniper.[69] Two more men were wounded at the block, one by a bullet in the arm, and another receiving a shell splinter in the hand.

Maginn continues his narrative:

> We had our second block nearly finished when we had a sudden surprise, by an enemy bomb bursting near our heads, wounding another man near the eye. Fritz showered his

65 AWM: 4 23/76/30 War Diary 59th Battalion. Appendix 7. 'Narrative by Sgt G.W. Stanford, No. 1 Platoon, 'A' Coy, 59th Battalion AIF'
66 AWM: 4 23/76/30 War Diary 59th Battalion. Appendix 7. 'Narrative by Private E.J. Maginn, 'A' Company.'
67 AWM: 4 23/76/30 War Diary 59th Battalion. Appendix 7. 'Narrative by Private E.J. Maginn, 'A' Company.'
68 AWM: 4 23/76/30 War Diary 59th Battalion. Appendix 7. 'Narrative of Operations as seen by Lt. W. Stavely on morning of 4th inst..'
69 Second Lieutenant Stephen George Facey DCM, C de G. (Belgium), age 31, is buried in Méricourt L'Abbé Communal Cemetery Extension, grave III.E.1. He won his DCM as a Sergeant in Polygon Wood, near Ypres, in September 1917, where he attacked an enemy machine gun post, killing three of the garrison and capturing one officer and 10 other ranks. He later single-handedly captured a German pill box and its entire garrison. A letter to his mother from Major General Talbot Hobbs, (GOC 5th Aus. Division) informs her that he was 'nearly recommended for the VC.' He had been promoted Second Lieutenant on 1 May 1918.

> bombs over rather fast and as we had only a few bombs left we had to go back a little. We sent down to the left for bombs and a few more men.[70]

The remaining men regrouped behind the rear block and were met there by Sergeant P.L. Little, who had heard the fracas and come along to see if he could be of any help. The grenades and reinforcements arrived, courtesy of Lieutenant Stavely, who collected them, and 2182 Sergeant Hutchinson and his party, who did the carrying. This included 14 boxes of No. 36 Rifle Grenades brought forward by Corporal Thomas and four of his mates from No. 10 Platoon, 60th Battalion. Lieutenant Stavely comments on their speedy arrival: 'more bombs were procured and passed along at the "toot."'[71]

Resupplied, Little and his group went forward once more,

> … throwing our bombs as we went, and other men firing rifle grenades from the rear. Fritz still kept up his supply of bombs, but going back at the same time and we kept going until we got back to our first position. We built up our blocks as strong as we could, putting trap bombs in the forward one, and when all was finished everyone came back behind the rear block. We had plenty of bombs now, and were quite sure we could hang on should he make another attempt to push us back.[72]

But for a few enemy shells landing nearby, the party at the block were undisturbed for the rest of the day.

The whole 59th Battalion line was shelled intermittently throughout the day. Also, in the morning, they were briefly strafed by an enemy aircraft flying low over their positions, but the pilot decided upon discretion in favour of valour when the Australians attempted to bring him down with machine gun fire.

At around 8:50 p.m., a heavy enemy artillery barrage fell on the captured line, and Captain McDonald could see troops 'massing in the crop on the hill about K 3.a.3.5'[73] and also further over on the right flank.

McDonald sent up the SOS flares at 8:57 p.m., and got an immediate and very effective reaction: '[Our] barrage was excellent, falling about 60 yards from our trench at the nearest point and swept the whole of the valley in front. The howitzers sweeping the right edge and pounding the top of the hill…. Lewis guns… sweeping valleys to the right and left with a steady and continuous fire.'[74] The enemy barrage persisted, however, for a further 45 minutes, but the Australian guns carried on for another half hour after that: 'We saw no indication of any attempt on the enemy's part to drive the counter attack home.'[75]

70 AWM: 4 23/76/30 War Diary 59th Battalion. Appendix 7. 'Narrative by Private E.J. Maginn, 'A' Company.' The Germans were a party from *2.* and *3. Kompanie* of the left-front battalion of *RIR 52*. Bean, *The Official History*, vol.VI, p.322.

71 AWM: 4 23/76/30 War Diary 59th Battalion. Appendix 7. 'Narrative of Operations as seen by Lt. W. Stavely on morning of 4th inst..' 'Toot' is army slang for the French phrase *'tout de suite'* – 'immediately.'

72 AWM: 4 23/76/30 War Diary 59th Battalion. Appendix 7. 'Narrative by Private E.J. Maginn, 'A' Company.'

73 AWM: 4 23/76/30 War Diary 59th Battalion. Appendix 7. 'Narrative by O.C. 'B' Company, 59th Battalion AIF'

74 AWM: 4 23/76/30 War Diary 59th Battalion. Appendix 7.

75 AWM: 4 23/76/30 War Diary 59th Battalion. Appendix 7.

Sergeant Stanford (No.1 Platoon) ends his report thus: 'They [the Germans] began to settle down again… and thus ended a perfect day and a lively time.'[76] This 'perfect day' – all objectives taken, consolidated, and held – had cost the 59th Battalion, according to a contemporary report, a total of 68 casualties: two officers killed and 15 wounded,[77] and five other ranks killed and 46 wounded.

* * *

The attack made by the three platoons of D Company, 58th Battalion, involved

> …the capture of the new German front line in the marshes and the drier flats below the hills immediately north of the entrance of the Morlancourt pan. The marshes could be held by either side only by scattered posts, and on that front – 750 yards from the Ancre to the Méaulte road… the German posts to be captured lay along a cross-road, one of the few comparatively dry positions on the flats.'[78]

This road, running north-south through squares E 26 a and c (see Map 8), was designated the final objective line. A support platoon would line up behind the others on the extreme left; its deployment was marred by an inauspicious start to proceedings. Lieutenant Tasker had been chosen to command this unit and was instructed to start out early and get his men to dig in just ahead of the Australian front line. As he reached the outpost line in the marshes, Lieutenant Fleming, in charge of the 57th Battalion men temporarily holding the position, told Tasker 'that the ground ahead was too boggy for digging.'[79] Bean relates the incident which followed: 'Fleming went out with [Tasker] to prove it, when a bomb suddenly exploded almost beneath them, wounding both – it had been thrown by an Australian listening post, of whose existence Tasker had been unaware. After endeavouring to carry on, Tasker telephoned for another officer to take charge, and Col. Watson sent Lieut. Flintoft.'[80] Flintoft joined his new command 'just 5 minutes before ZERO.'[81]

At around 11:30 p.m. the previous night, the men involved in the assault had been formed up in the Reserve Line for a final briefing from Captain Dawson MC. Dawson could only reinforce what the men already knew: they had been able to study a relief model of the ground and had practised their tasks on a daily basis. Lieutenant Colonel Watson added a few words of encouragement, including extolling the merits of the Mills Bomb. The men then endured a one-hour wait in the front line, an inevitably anxious period punctuated by an issue of rum brought up by the officers. The jumping-off tape was all in place by 12:30 a.m., and the men followed the guides forward onto it at around 2:55 a.m.

76 AWM: 4 23/76/30 War Diary 59th Battalion. Appendix 7. 'Narrative by Sgt G.W. Stanford, No. 1 Platoon, 'A' Coy, 59th Battalion AIF'
77 Commonwealth War Graves Commission records finalise the fatalities for 4–5 July at two officers and 17 other ranks.
78 Bean, *The Official History*, vol.VI, p.319.
79 Bean, *The Official History*, vol.VI, p.323.
80 Bean, *The Official History*, vol.VI, p.323.
81 AWM: 4 23/75/30 War Diary 58th Battalion Appendix 7. 'Report by Lieut. W. Flintoft, Platoon Commander, Support Platoon, in Operations carried out on night 3rd/4th July 1918.'

On the right flank, No. 15 Platoon under Lieutenant Davies, was greeted, as they got up to move forward, by a German machine gun firing – probably too high – but causing no casualties. The only surviving after-action report for No. 15 Platoon is courtesy of 3021 Private Boyle. He writes:

> The first real resistance we got was when we got to our objective. We came on 5 of his posts within a space of 100 yards – they threw a few bombs, but our chaps were all very eager and used their rifles and bombs freely. We soon cleared them, taking no prisoners, and having no casualties.[82]

They mopped up and then went to the aid of No. 13 Platoon on their left, which they presumed to be embroiled in a bombing duel. When they got there, they found that No. 13 Platoon had subdued the opposition and captured the post, so they returned and began consolidating their own sector of the newly won trench, having gained contact with 59th Battalion on their right. They dug three posts: a machine gun post on each flank and a bombing post in the centre. Private Boyle suggests that they suffered three killed and six wounded. Among the latter was their platoon commander, Lieutenant Davies, but he stayed at duty until relieved 48 hours later.

The barrage 'fell beautifully.'[83] Lieutenant Willis, commanding the centre platoon, remembered the machine gun barrage starting 'just a few seconds ahead of everything else',[84] and yelling 'Get ready to move!' His report goes on:

> This was one of the grandest moments of my life. Every man of my two half platoons raised his head in the dim light just as one man, and I received all the 'buck' I needed. Sergt. Eales was in charge of the left half and I was proud to be with the right half. I might say that each half had its two scouts well out in front. On the word 'Go' we all moved forward.[85]

After 60 yards or so, they 'met a machine gun post, and killed the 4 men occupying it.'[86] Out front, the two scouts, Privates Meadows and Lush, were firing at the crew of a known machine gun post when Lieutenant Willis arrived on the scene. Four more Germans were killed here, Willis managing to 'drop two of them with [his] revolver as they ran away.'[87] One of these turned out to be an officer. The terrain was not favourable to a rapid advance: 'The going at this stage was very bad, the ground being marshy and covered with long, tangled undergrowth, thickly interspersed with deep shell holes.'[88]

82 AWM: 4 23/75/30 War Diary 58th Battalion. Appendix 7. 'Report on Operation on 4th July 1918 by No. 3021 Pte T.S. Boyle, 15th Platoon, 'D' Company.'
83 AWM: 4 23/75/30 War Diary 58th Battalion. Appendix 7. 'Report on Operation on 4th July 1918 by Lieut H.D. Willis, Commanding No. 13 Platoon, 'D' Coy, 58th Battalion.'
84 AWM: 4 23/75/30 War Diary 58th Battalion. Appendix 7. 'Report on Operation on 4th July 1918 by Lieut H.D. Willis, Commanding No. 13 Platoon, 'D' Coy, 58th Battalion.'
85 AWM: 4 23/75/30 War Diary 58th Battalion. Appendix 7. 'Report on Operation on 4th July 1918 by Lieut H.D. Willis, Commanding No. 13 Platoon, 'D' Coy, 58th Battalion.'
86 AWM: 4 23/75/30 War Diary 58th Battalion. Appendix 7. 'Report on Operation on 4th July 1918 by Lieut H.D. Willis, Commanding No. 13 Platoon, 'D' Coy, 58th Battalion.'
87 AWM: 4 23/75/30 War Diary 58th Battalion. Appendix 7. 'Report on Operation on 4th July 1918 by Lieut H.D. Willis, Commanding No. 13 Platoon, 'D' Coy, 58th Battalion.'
88 AWM: 4 23/75/30 War Diary 58th Battalion. Appendix 7. Report by Capt. F.C. Dawson MC on Operation carried out by 'D' Company, 58th Battalion on Night 3rd/4th July 1918, East of Ville-sur-

As the rest of his men struggled on to their objective – the road – Willis became aware of a number of enemy dugouts built along it. Mopping up began, and a number of prisoners soon emerged from their lairs. Sitting them down in the trench, Willis left his batman, Private Harvey, guarding them and went off to get in touch with the platoons on either flank. By the time he returned, a further 11 prisoners had been discovered, and one of his Lewis gun crews, on their own initiative, were digging a post 'well out in front.'[89]

The left half of platoon No.14, under Lieutenant Thompson, encountered serious opposition as soon as they started their advance. The only way forward was 'a narrow strip of marshy ground some 25 yards wide flanked on one side by the River Ancre and on the other by a swamp.'[90] Harassed by machine gun fire from the front and from across the river on the left flank, Thompson and his men gradually worked their way forward, but were halted by a machine gun post straight ahead, about 80 yards from their jumping off line: Thompson led his men in a charge, capturing the post and killing the crew. Other gun crews on the objective were now alerted to the Australian advance and opened fire from their wired-in strongpoint. A text-book assault ensued: covering fire from the front allowed Thompson to lead a party around to the flank and charge successfully from there. Three guns were captured and the Australians made it to the ruined mill on the riverbank. As they began to dig in, another machine gun opened up and the platoon began to take casualties. It was as Thompson was organising another 'rush' that 'their gallant leader… was shot dead…. The gun was at once rushed and the whole of the crew bayonetted, by our men.'[91] One of the other casualties was Corporal Skinner, also killed.[92]

Corporal Edwin Charles Skinner, 58th Battalion. (AWM)

Ancre.
89 AWM: 4 23/75/30 War Diary 58th Battalion. Appendix 7. Willis' report.
90 AWM: 4 23/15/29. War Diary 15 Brigade, Appendix 7. 'Report on Operation Carried out East of VILLE-sur-ANCRE, July 5th [sic] 1918.'
91 AWM: 4 23/15/29. War Diary 15 Brigade, Appendix 7. Lieutenant Ivo Garfield Thompson is buried in Ribemont Communal Cemetery Extension, grave II.AA.2. He was recommended for a posthumous Victoria Cross by his battalion commander, Lieutenant Colonel Watson, this supported by witness statements from Pte Boyle, CSM McPhee and Lt. Willis. He was not awarded the VC, being simply 'Mentioned in Despatches.'
92 4642 Corporal Edwin Charles Skinner is commemorated on the Villers-Bretonneux Memorial. The Commonwealth War Graves Commission give his date of death as 5 July 1918.

The right half of the platoon managed to rush the first line of German outposts, but were then held up by machine gun posts in a clump of trees protected by barbed wire entanglements. A group managed to outflank this position unnoticed by the machine gun crews and attacked and captured it from the rear. This cleared the way to the final objective: the road. 'Here again, for a couple of minutes, the Germans put up a bit of a fight, but those who were not casualties fled for their lives.'[93]

Captain Dawson estimated that about 50 of the enemy had run back to a strongpoint 400 yards behind the road. As digging in commenced and the need to prepare their newly-won position against counter attack was prioritised, it became clear that several Lewis guns 'were temporarily put out of action by stoppages, or by getting choked with mud.'[94] Four days earlier, Lieutenant Hackworthy of 15th Machine Gun Company had instructed Dawson's men on how to operate the enemy's machine guns, and this now proved 'of inestimable value', as a number of captured guns were turned around and brought into action.[95] Company headquarters was quickly moved up to a shallow trench behind No. 13 Platoon, and the signallers followed up 'and established themselves in a shell hole with the phone in working order.'[96]

Dawson had received no word as yet from No. 14 Platoon on the left, so a runner was sent to find out what was going on. After a short while, it became obvious that he had not got through, so Acting CSM McPhee, taking a corporal with him, made his way across and found 'our left established not very strongly at our objective in old ruins on the bank of the River Ancre.'[97]

The much-depleted platoon was in need of urgent support, so a runner was sent back to find Lieutenant Flintoft and request that he bring his platoon forward to reinforce the position. Flintoft was just on the point of moving forward anyway, as his 'position was becoming untenable owing to the heavy enemy shell fire.'[98] The men accordingly advanced in single file across the marsh and reached their compatriots. Flintoft went further ahead to see if it was practicable to establish a post 50 yards ahead of the road: the boggy nature of the ground rendered this impossible, so he gave orders for his men to consolidate where they were, and 'dig in for their lives.'[99] Flintoft then went across to see if he could establish touch with the platoon on the right. He discovered a 300-yard gap and immediately sent word back to Captain Keys, asking for a platoon of 57th Battalion to fill the void.

Keys had already sent No. 5 Platoon forward to reinforce Lieutenant Flintoft, but had withdrawn it – save for one double Lewis gun section – once it was established that the objective had been reached. Flintoft's request for reinforcement reached Keys just before 7:00 a.m., and No. 5 Platoon was dispatched once more: with Corporal Bennett in charge, both Lieutenant Fleming

93 AWM: 4 23/75/30 War Diary 58th Battalion. Appendix 7. 'Report on Operation 4/7/18 – by No. 4732 Pte W.J. Bell.'
94 AWM: 4 23/75/30 War Diary 58th Battalion. Appendix 9. Dawson's report.
95 AWM: 4 23/75/30 War Diary 58th Battalion. Appendix 9. Dawson's report.
96 AWM: 4 23/75/30 War Diary 58th Battalion. Appendix 7. 'Report on Operation on Night 3rd/4th July 1918, by No. 4152 Sgt. McPhee, A.E., Acting C.S.M. 'D' Company, 58th Battalion, AIF.'
97 AWM: 4 23/75/30 War Diary 58th Battalion. Appendix 7. 'Report on Operation on Night 3rd/4th July 1918, by No. 4152 Sgt. McPhee, A.E., Acting C.S.M. 'D' Company, 58th Battalion, AIF.'
98 AWM: 4 23/75/30 War Diary 58th Battalion. Appendix 7. 'Report by Lieut. W. Flintoft, Platoon Commander, Support Platoon, in Operation carried out on night 3rd/4th July 1918.'
99 AWM: 4 23/75/30 War Diary 58th Battalion. Appendix 7. 'Report by Lieut. W. Flintoft, Platoon Commander, Support Platoon, in Operation carried out on night 3rd/4th July 1918.'

and his sergeant, Clifford Angus, having been wounded earlier in the day, they accordingly dug in between the two front platoons.[100]

The left of the line was reinforced one final time just before dark when a party of six men with Corporal F.E. Beard from A Company, 57th Battalion, was sent across the Ancre from the north bank via a bridge 200 yards behind the line to help bolster the situation in the face of a possible enemy counterattack. They dug in just to the right of the ruined mill on the riverbank. The battalion lost five men killed on 4 July. The regimental history of *RIR 52* records a limited counterattack being attempted: a small section of trench near the mill was recaptured, but held only briefly as the Germans ran out of hand grenades and were forced back. The chronicler highlights the fate of *Leutnant* Schulze, *6. Kompanie*, who was killed at this point, having only returned from his honeymoon the previous day.[101]

The men of C and D Companies (Captain Jennings and Lieutenant Knight) of 60th Battalion (Lieutenant Colonel H.T.C. Layh DSO) were stationed 'in reserve in Canberra Trench Left [the Australian front line] with HQ at K.1.b.70.95 to be prepared to support the attack either to North or South of road junction E.26.c.5.1.'[102] Platoons were subsequently fed into the line as needed: at 4:05 a.m., Lieutenant Levy led No.11 Platoon forward to fill a gap between the companies of 58th and 59th Battalions; half an hour later, Lieutenant Ashman reinforced the centre with his platoon (No.12); the right company of 59th Battalion was reinforced at 4:40 a.m. by No. 10 Platoon, led by Lieutenant Gordon. A lull ensued until more reinforcements were called for by Captain Dawson at around 6:00 a.m. Lieutenant Knight took No. 9 Platoon forward to help on the left front.[103]

To the front of 59th Battalion's newly-consolidated position was a section of gently rising ground known to the Australians as the

Knight's Headstone. (Author)

100 Bennett's post was shelled by their own artillery at 10:15 p.m., two of his men being wounded. He withdrew his men to a short distance in the rear before re-occupying the post once the guns lengthened their range.
101 Herbert Ulrich, *Reserve-Infanterie-Regiment 52 im Weltkriege. Zusammengestellt aus Berichten, Tagebüchern und eigenen Erlebnissen.* (Cottbus: Lausitzer Verlagsanstalt, 1925), p.512.
102 AWM: 4 23/77/30. War Diary 60th Battalion.
103 Lieutenant M.D. Knight MC, aged 27, was sadly killed by enemy artillery fire whilst leading his men out of the line at around 2:00 a.m. on 6 July. He is buried in Méricourt-L'Abbé Communal Cemetery Extension, grave III.D.12. He enlisted as a Private in 1914, served at Gallipoli and gained his MC at Polygon Wood in September 1917.

'terrace' at the foot of the hill north of Morlancourt. Plans had been drawn up on 3 July for a raid by 60th Battalion to oust the Germans occupying it. Zero hour was to be 12:15 a.m. on the 5th. During the afternoon of the 4th, however, observation of the terrace suggested that it was not as strongly garrisoned as first thought. A patrol led by Lieutenant Stillman MC was sent out into No Man's Land at around 8:00 p.m. They crawled out 'under cover of the crop',[104] to a position from where they could observe the terrace. No sign of the enemy was to be seen. The heavy enemy artillery bombardment that came down at 8:35 p.m., and lasted about one and a half hours, and the Australian reply, delayed any decision on the proposed raid for some time. It was finally decided at 10:50 p.m. to cancel the raid.

The enemy bombardment had cost 60th Battalion several casualties: Lieutenants Stillman and Ashman were wounded, and Lieutenant Moore, attached to the 15th Australian Light Trench Mortar Battery, was killed.[105] Private Teasdale of No. 10 Platoon was also killed by rifle fire.[106] The engagement had cost 60th Battalion 10 killed and a further 18 wounded.

The grave of Lieutenant John Charles Moore, 60th Battalion. (Author)

The grave of Private Cecil Giles Teasdale, 60th Battalion. (Author)

104 AWM: 4 23/77/30. War Diary 60th Battalion.

105 Lieutenant John Charles Moore, age 29, is buried in Méricourt-L'Abbé Communal Cemetery Extension, grave III.E.3.

106 3605 Private Cecil Giles Teasdale, age 23, is buried in Méricourt-L'Abbé Communal Cemetery Extension, grave III.E.5.

The 58th Battalion war diary only gives casualty figures for the entire month of July: these amount to five officers and 80 other ranks. Commonwealth War Grave Commission records show nine fatalities for 4–5 July. For total casualty figures for 15th Brigade, we must therefore rely on Bean's *Official History*. These are shown in the table below. The Commonwealth War Graves Commission records show a total of 43 fatalities for the brigade between 4 and 6 July.

Table 7. 15th Brigade casualties

	Officers	**Other Ranks**
57th Battalion	1	10
58th Battalion	2	39
59th Battalion	6	58
60th Battalion	3	20
Total	**12**	**127**

The after-action report in the 15th Brigade war diary estimates German casualties at two officers and 120 other ranks killed, with one officer and 63 other ranks taken prisoner. For his actions and leadership during the operation, Captain F.C. Dawson, 58th Battalion, was awarded the DSO.

Conclusion

Pamphlet S.S. 218, *Operations by the Australian Corps against Hamel, Bois de Hamel and Bois de Vaire 4th July 1918*, was produced by the British Army Stationery Services shortly after the battle. Its principal aim was to serve as a guide to the planning of future battles: paragraph five (of 81) is concerned with this very objective and is worth quoting in full:

> 5. In applying the lessons derived from the action of the 4th of July to future and perhaps larger operations, certain factors must be borne in mind, some of them local. These were:–
>   a) The German defences were not strong and there was not much wire.
>   b) The hostile air service was comparatively innocuous, owing to our great successes in the air during the previous fortnight.
>   c) The objective was a strictly limited one, well within the effective fire of our field and heavy artillery, as sited for the attack.
>   d) The moral[e] of the enemy's infantry was fair, whereas that of our own was very high.
>   e) The weather was very fine and the going good, as the ground had nowhere been seriously cut up by shell fire, and the chalk is very near the surface.
>   f) Owing to the dry weather the amount of dust thrown up by bursting shells was very great.
>   g) The observation obtained over the area of attack from the ridge East of Corbie was extremely good.

The lessons regarding the use of tanks appear in paragraphs 65 to 77, and include:

> 65. The operations, so far as tanks were concerned, had to conform to the artillery creeping barrage and the tactics of the Australian troops, with the underlying principle of saving as many casualties to the infantry as possible …
>
> 75. Previous to the 4th of July, a short course of training of tanks and infantry had taken place and proved invaluable…
>
> 76. c) Provided the country is suitable, it will be possible in future to move tanks up to a distance of 6,000 yards before the attack. In this case, tanks can move 4,000 yards at

> full speed, halt and fill up, 1,000 yards on half throttle and then go into action at full speed so as to clear the enemy's barrage line. The above procedure would obviate the necessity of harassing artillery fire or employment of aeroplanes prior to zero hour, to which there are objections, when a surprise attack is contemplated…
>
> 77. f)… a creeping barrage is a great protection to tanks in that it prevents hostile machine gunners from taking aimed fire until too late, and thus gives the tanks an equal chance of gaining superiority of fire.
> g)… tanks, even under a creeping barrage, should precede the infantry so as to subdue machine guns uncovered by the artillery before they inflict casualties on the infantry. Tanks can get closer to the artillery barrage than the infantry, if the barrage is a shrapnel one, as the bullets which drop on the heads of infantry and inflict casualties do not affect the tanks.

The pamphlet also trumpets the absence of a preliminary artillery bombardment, which, allied to strict secrecy, gives the attacker the advantage of surprise. The use of aircraft in bombing the enemy's rear areas and in dropping ammunition for the attacking troops is also praised, along with their prior photographic reconnaissance which allowed the distribution of maps and photographs 'to each N.C.O.' (paragraph 79).

The concluding paragraph puts the success of the operation down to detailed planning, excellent all-arms cooperation, the element of surprise, effective counter-battery work and an accurate artillery barrage, the skill and dash of the tanks, and the fighting spirit of the infantry.

The publication admits of only a few instances where improvements might be made, all of these referring to the artillery: there is an admission that 'owing to a few shells falling short', 'a certain number' of Australian casualties were caused by their own artillery; it is suggested that the rate of advance of the creeping barrage was too slow in its early stages, estimating that 100 yards in two minutes would 'probably have suited the infantry better.' It was also realised that the artillery barrage 'had a tendency to jump or pass over unduly quickly certain strong points or defended localities', adding that some of the heavy howitzers might have been better employed 'exclusively against such [locations].' Maintaining the protective barrage 'over rather a longer period' might also have been advantageous.

Buoyed by his success at Hamel, and sure that he now had the formula for continued success, Monash was soon pressing Rawlinson for a further assault, this time on a much larger scale, and with considerably deeper penetration. The crushing defeat of the German army at Amiens in August was the result. Monash, it seemed, could do no wrong, and he still enjoys an almost untarnished reputation: indeed, near the exit to the exhibition at the Sir John Monash Centre at Villers-Bretonneux, his bust sits proudly on a pedestal. No doubt he deserves the accolade, and this author has no desire to knock him off his elevated position. The pedestal does, however, need shaking – just a little.

In *Australian Victories in France in 1918,* published in 1920, Sir John Monash wrote: 'No battle within my previous experience, not even Messines, passed off so smoothly, so exactly to time-table, or was *so free from any kind of hitch*…. It was the perfection of team work.'[1]

1 Monash, *Australian Victories*, p.56. Author's italics.

A bust of Monash on a pedestal, Sir John Monash Centre, Villers-Bretonneux. (Author)

There is no such thing as the 'perfect' battle. On 4 July 1918, the Battle of Hamel may have come close to that level, demonstrating just how effective the correct application of 'all-arms' co-operation could be, and thereafter serving as a useful template for the execution of future operations during the 'Hundred Days' offensive. Shortages of equipment, deteriorating weather and unfavourable geography did not always allow faithful copying, but the main principles remained sound.

Pedersen, in *Battleground Europe: Hamel, Somme*, concludes that '[a]fter the war, Monash made exaggerated claims for the battle.'[2] Sir John wrote, for example, that the battle was fought 'at a cost to us of less than 800 casualties of all kinds.'[3] This figure is clearly wrong: Bean, in the *Official History*, enumerates the losses as follows: 4th Brigade, 504; 11th Brigade, 312; 6th Brigade, 131; 7th Brigade, 115; US units, 176; and 15th Brigade, 142. This makes a total of 1,380. This figure is accepted in modern historiography.

Famously, and quoted extensively, Monash likened a battle plan to an orchestral score. He, doubtlessly, pictured himself as the composer of said score: it may be nearer the truth to consider him as the conductor, possibly the arranger. Plan 'B' – the one enacted – was neither revolutionary nor visionary; nor was it entirely his own; it was an amalgamation of already-understood principles, and it worked very effectively.

There is much to commend in the conduct of this battle. The planning process was meticulous, and details were worked through and agreed at conferences, 'eliminating confusion and uncertainty.'[4] The opportunity for infantry to train with the tank units with which they were to go into battle did much to expel the distrust of the Australian infantry following the disaster at Bullecourt in April 1917 and meant that cooperation between the two arms was largely effective. The new Mark V tanks proved their worth by eliminating countless German machine-gun posts, thereby easing the advance of the infantry, particularly during the storming of the elevated Wolfsberg position. Supply tanks bringing equipment to the newly-established front line positions also relieved thousands of infantrymen of this arduous and dangerous task.

Counter battery provision proved excellent. The vast majority of German artillery batteries were located and disrupted, and Australian casualties from German shell fire were thus minimised. The protective barrage – in conjunction with aerial bombing and strafing – did much to delay and frustrate German counterattack preparations. The ruse to make the German soldiers don gas masks on the morning of 4 July, when no gas was actually included in the barrage, seems to have worked quite well, too, with numerous accounts in the unit war diaries confirming its success. 'Normal' artillery and aerial activity prior to Z Day, including masking the sound of tanks approaching their jumping-off positions, ensured that surprise was achieved along the whole front – a massive advantage to attacking troops.

The RAF contribution was vital. Successful and extensive photographic reconnaissance prior to the attack ensured that all infantry units, supplied with these photographs, were *au fait* with the terrain over which they were to attack. On the day itself, aircraft bombed and strafed German positions both in the front lines and the rear areas, and the innovative use of dropping small arms ammunition by parachute for the advanced Australian machine gun posts also proved very effective.

2 Pedersen, *Battleground Europe: Hamel, Somme*, p. 111.
3 Monash, *Australian Victories*, p.57.
4 Pedersen, *Battleground Europe: Hamel, Somme*, p.120.

All objectives were captured, consolidated, and held (notwithstanding the temporary setback on the Wolfsberg during the night of 4/5 July), and largely to time. The battle was effectively over in 93 minutes. Casualties were not insignificant, but could probably be described as modest.

As in any battle, however, there were negatives. The planning process and the build-up were not smooth: the first plan was ditched after opposition from Monash's own divisional, brigade, and artillery commanders, and was subsequently drastically reworked. The last-minute withdrawal of American troops threatened the entire enterprise: it was only a disingenuous fabrication of a supposed deadline by Monash and Rawlinson – and the calculated passing of the buck to an incommunicado Commander-in-Chief – that partly resolved the situation.

Unfortunately, a significant number of Australian and American casualties were caused by the short firing of their own artillery. Such episodes are recorded in every brigade war diary – only the 42nd Battalion advancing to the north of Hamel on the left flank of the attack seem to have completely escaped this tragic circumstance – with C Company of 13th Battalion taking particularly heavy casualties even before they had moved from their jumping off positions and throughout the entirety of their advance to the south of Vaire Wood.

The plan for the taking of Pear Trench fell apart: the creeping artillery barrage managed to miss this trench system entirely, as did the three tanks deployed to assist the infantry in its capture.[5] A Company of 15th Battalion was therefore forced to mount an unsupported assault on an intact defensive trench system that included 10 machine guns. Taking the redoubt in 'the old way' cost the battalion most of its 240 casualties.[6] Waiting for it to be bypassed by neighbouring units, thereby rendering it untenable, could have been a viable alternative.

It cannot be denied that tanks played a vital part in the attack. Why none was allocated to 25th Battalion on the right wing of the assault remains a mystery: this battalion suffered excessive casualties in trying to neutralise a German strongpoint. The presence of even one tank could have swung the situation in favour of the Australian infantry.

The question also has to be asked as to whether the 257 casualties suffered in the diversionary assaults to the north of the Somme were worth it. Evidence might suggest that the 'feints' and the artillery barrage alone were enough to convince German commanders in that sector that they were about to be attacked, the possibility of supporting their embattled compatriots south of the river effectively negated.[7] There is evidence that German reserve troops were sent to the battlefield north of the Somme: units of *IR 201* were moved forward on the afternoon of 4 July, and were sent to defend the heights facing Elliott's 58th and 59th Battalions, but they were only deployed as darkness fell, too late to have any meaningful effect on events.[8]

In the aftermath of the battle, Monash was deservedly able to bask in the reflected glory of innumerable congratulatory telegrams and messages, and the instructional pamphlet was quickly issued, citing Hamel as the correct way to conduct an 'all-arms' battle. In *Amiens to the*

5 Most contemporary accounts written by tank personnel do not admit this failure. The report on tank operations produced by 5th Tank Brigade, written on 23 July, does, however, comment, but concludes that 'this action did not materially affect the attack as owing to its proximity to the infantry starting line, it was not expected that tanks would arrive in time to participate in the attack.' This is nonsense: Captain Scott's No. 1 Section of A Coy was tasked specifically with attacking Pear Trench, and their non-appearance cost many infantry lives.

6 Pedersen, *Battleground Europe: Hamel, Somme*, p.77.

7 See Peter Fitzsimons, *Monash's Masterpiece* (London: Constable, 2018), pp.325–326.

8 Bergeder, *Das Reserve-Infanterie-Regiment Nr. 202*, p.145.

Armistice, Harris and Barr conclude that Hamel was 'a model for a future operation',[9] and John Terraine, in *To Win a War. 1918, The Year of Victory*, describes it as 'a little masterpiece, casting a long shadow before it.'[10] On 12 August, four days after Monash's Australians had once more proven their worth, this time at the Battle of Amiens – arguably Hamel writ large – he was knighted 'in the field'[11] at the Chateau de Bertangles by King George V.

The Australian Corps was heavily involved in the further successes of the Hundred Days Offensives, but Monash's fears of excessive casualties resulting in the need to reorganise units and formations came true: they fought their last engagement of the war at Montbrehain on 5 October. The Corps had suffered heavy casualties: between 8 August and 5 October, these amounted to losses of 1,317 officers and 22,845 other ranks.[12] The Australians were a spent force:

> Their work had been exhausting. Furthermore, the steady drain on resources after sixty days of almost continuous battle activity had so reduced their fighting strength that a very drastic re-organization had become necessary. This could only be effected by a complete withdrawal from the fighting zone… and before they were again called upon for further front-line service, hostilities had ended.[13]

Sir John Monash's position on the pedestal at the centre named in his honour is secure, and deservedly so. One might suspect, however, that had he himself commissioned it, it would have been a slightly taller pedestal.

The Australian Memorial on the site of the Wolfsberg. (Author)

9 J.P. Harris with Niall Barr, *Amiens to the Armistice* (London: Brassey's, 1998), p.57.
10 John Terraine, *To Win a War. 1918, The Year of Victory* (London: Macmillan, 1986), p.85.
11 Fitzsimons, *Monash's Masterpiece*, p.350.
12 Bean, *The Official History*, vol.VI, p.1044, footnote 19.
13 Monash, *Australian Victories*, p.270.

Appendix I

Battle of Hamel, 4 July 1918

Order of Battle

Fourth Army: General Sir Henry Rawlinson
Australian Corps: Lieutenant General John Monash
Chief of Staff: Brigadier General Thomas Albert Blamey.

4th Division: Major General Ewan George Sinclair-MacLagan
Chief of Staff: Lieutenant Colonel John Dudley Lavarack.

4th Brigade: *Brigadier General Charles Henry Brand*
13th Battalion: *Lieutenant Colonel Douglas Gray Marks*
Adjutant: Captain A.W. Davis
A Company – Captain. George Marper
B Company – Lieutenant William Henry Merifield
C Company – Captain. Robert Alexander McKillop
D Company – Captain John Govett Geary (kia 8.8.18)
14th Battalion: *Lieutenant Colonel Henry Arnold Crowther*
Adjutant: Captain John Arthur Mitchell
A Company – Captain Norman Wilson
B Company – Lieutenant William Jacka
C Company – Captain William Robert Wadsworth
D Company – Captain William Robert Moody Beamond
15th Battalion: *Lieutenant Colonel Terence Patrick McSharry*
A Company – Captain Ernest Kenneth Carter
B Company – Lieutenant Simon Fahey Porter
C Company – Captain Robert Glasgow
D Company – Captain Ernest Martin Bradley
16th Battalion: *Lieutenant Colonel Edmund Alfred Drake-Brockman*
A Company – Major Ross Harwood
B Company – Captain Harold Arthur Faulkner Wilkinson
C Company – Captain Frederick Frank Woods

D Company – Captain William James Dalton Lynas MC & 2 Bars.

11th Brigade: ***Brigadier General James Harold Cannan***[1]
Brigade Major: Major George Alan Vasey
41st Battalion: *Lieutenant Colonel Alexander Robert Heron*
Adjutant: Lieutenant Kenneth Adrian Murdoch
X Company – Captain George Thomas
B Company – Captain William Uren
C Company – Temporary Captain Reginald Rhodes Wood
D Company – Lieutenant John James Hanley
42nd Battalion: 'Australian Black Watch', *Major Edward John Dibdin*
Adjutant: Lieutenant Arthur Coleman Dibdin.
A Company – Temporary Captain Stanley Richard Warry
B Company – Lieutenant Frederick George Lewis
C Company – Captain Thomas Jack
D Company – Captain Richard DeBurgh Falkiner O'Bryen
43rd Battalion: *Lieutenant Colonel John Farrell*
Adjutant: Captain Eustace James Colliver
A Company – Captain John Thomas Moran
B Company – Captain Henry Samuel Cope
C Company – Captain Richard Clarence Sexton
D Company – Major Adolph Walter Lott
E Company (US) – Captain Luke
44th Battalion: 'Old Bill's Thousand', *Lieutenant Colonel James Purcell Clark*
A Company – Captain Wilfred James Stables
B Company – Lieutenant James Seabrook Everett
C Company – Captain Hugh Lionel Fowler
D Company – Captain Edgar Copley Adams

6th Brigade: ***Brigadier General John Paton***[2]
21st Battalion: *Major Alfred Effingham Reed*
A Company – Lieutenant William Holman Roberts
B Company – Lieutenant Harry Neville Garton MC
C Company – Captain Monkton Bowes Kelly
D Company – Lieutenant Percival Toomey Hurrey
23rd Battalion: *Lieutenant Colonel William Brazenor*
A Company – Captain Richard George Moss
B Company – Captain George Leslie Hinchcliffe
C Company – Lieutenant William Alexander Martin
D Company – Lieutenant Sydney Joseph Hodgson

1 11th Brigade was attached from 3rd Australian Division, (Major General J. Gellibrand)
2 6th Brigade was attached from 2nd Australian Division: (Major General C. Rosenthal)

7th Brigade: *Brigadier General Evan Alexander Wisdom.*
25th Battalion: *Lieutenant Colonel William MacIntyre Davis*
Adjutant: Captain George Carroll

5th Division: Major General Sir Joseph John Talbot Hobbs

14th Brigade: *Brigadier General James Campbell Stewart*
55th Battalion: *Lieutenant Colonel Percy William Woods*
Adjutant: Captain. Norman Ewart Franklin Pinkstone.

15th Brigade: *Brigadier General Harold Edward 'Pompey' Elliott*
57th Battalion: *Major Roderick McLean Campbell Aitchison*
58th Battalion: *Lieutenant Colonel Charles Vincent Watson*
Officer Commanding Operation 4 July – Captain Forbes Campbell Dawson MC, D Company.
59th Battalion: *Lieutenant Colonel John Joseph Scanlan*
A Company – Captain Akeroyd
B Company – Captain K.G. McDonald
60th Battalion. *Lieutenant Colonel Herbert Thomas Christopher Layh*
Adjutant: Lieutenant James D. Haddow.
C Company – Captain Jennings
D Company – Lieutenant M.D. Knight

Artillery

Southern Group: *Lt-Col H.M. Ballingale DSO,*
23rd Army Brigade RFA, 179th Army Brigade RFA, 14th Army Brigade RFA.

Right Group: *Lt-Col T.I.C. Williams DSO,*
10th Aust. F.A. Bde, 189th Army Bde RFA, 78th Brigade RFA (17th Div), 79th Brigade RFA (17th Div), 236th Bde RFA (47th Div).

Centre Group: *Lt-Col H.O. Caddy DSO,*
11th Aust. F.A. Bde, 13th Aust. F.A. Bde, 14th Aust. F.A. Bde, 150th Army Bde, RFA.

Left Group: *Lt-Col H.V. de Satge DSO,*
298th Army Bde RFA, 4th RHA Bde (3rd Cavalry Div), 235th Bde RFA (47th Div).

Detached for Special Purpose: 16th Army Bde RHA – ***Lt-Col J.G.B. Allardyce DSO,*** A, Q & U Batteries.

Trench Mortar Batteries
4th Australian Light Trench Mortar Battery: Captain A. Martin
7th Australian Light Trench Mortar Battery: Captain F. Brand.
8th Australian Light Trench Mortar Battery: Captain Walker

11th Australian Light Trench Mortar Battery: Captain C.W. Couchman
15th Australian Light Trench Mortar Battery: Lieutenant H.S. McColl

Machine Gun Battalions
2nd Australian Machine Gun Battalion: Lieutenant Colonel Ralston
3rd Australian Machine Gun Battalion: Lieutenant Colonel A.C. Blacklow
4th Australian Machine Gun Battalion: Lieutenant Colonel Murray
5th Australian Machine Gun Battalion: Lieutenant Colonel T.R. Marsden

Engineers

4th Division C.R.E.: *Lieutenant Colonel R.J. Dyer DSO.*
Adjutant: Lieutenant G.F.S Donaldson
4th Field Company Australian Engineers: Major H.G. Tolley DSO
12th Field Company Australian Engineers: Major C.C. Riddell DSO
13th Field Company Australian Engineers: Major R.B. Carr

5th Division C.R.E.: *Lieutenant Colonel A.E. Mather*
8th Field Company Australian Engineers: Major W.G. Farquhar
14th Field Company Australian Engineers: Major J. Coghlan
15th Field Company Australian Engineers: Major Greenway

5th Tank Brigade: Brigadier General Anthony Courage
13th Battalion: *Lieutenant Colonel. Philip Lyon*
  C Company – Captain Henry Edward Morritt
    No. 9 Section: Captain Lockhart Henry Larkins, with 23rd Battalion
    No. 10 Section: Captain Thomas Percival Patterson Walker, with 23rd Battalion
  C Company – Major Edward Foster
    No. 11 Section: Captain Hywel Lewis, with 42nd Battalion
    No. 12 Section: Captain Alexander Fletcher, with 42nd Battalion
  B Company – Major F. N. Griffin, in support behind B & C Companies of 8th Tank Battalion
    No. 5 Section: Lieutenant Wilfrid Ernest Baker
    No. 6 Section: Captain Donald Fullerton Nicol
    No. 7 Section: Captain Basil Benjamin Hill
    No. 8 Section: Captain James Donald Willard
8th Battalion: *Lieutenant Colonel. C.Y.D. Bingham*
  A Company – Major E.D. Blackburn
    No. 1 Section: Captain C.E. Scott, with A Company, 15th Battalion
    No. 2 Section: Captain A. Rogerson, liaison between 4th & 11th Brigades
    No. 3 Section: Captain P.W. Batten, in support
    No. 4 Section: Captain J. McFarland, in support
  B Company – Major G.A. Grounds
    No. 5 Section: Lieutenant I.C.A. Glanville, with 15th Battalion

No. 6 Section: Captain W.H. Viveash, with 16th Battalion
No. 7 Section: Captain A.E.H. Jones, with 16th Battalion
No. 8 Section: Captain W.N. Edwards, with 13th Battalion
C Company – Major J.A. Bennewith
No. 9 Section: Captain W.C.D. Miles, with 44th Battalion
No. 10 Section: Captain W.L.S. Hindhaugh, with 43rd Battalion
No. 11 Section: Captain J.L. De Thierry, with 43rd Battalion
No. 12 Section: Captain J.A. Rogers, with 44th Battalion

Appendix II

Allied Fatalities 4–6 July 1918

4th Australian Division

4th Brigade

13th Battalion
4 July 1918
Bailey, Charles Reginald Pte 5655. Adelaide Cemetery III.O.8.
Blunden, William Henry Pte 4150. Crouy British Cemetery III.B.25.
Butler, William Thomas MM L/Cpl 2113. Villers-Bretonneux Military Cemetery XII.A.7.
Copas, Arthur Trevor Pte 3614. Villers-Bretonneux Memorial.
Davis, Arthur Leslie Pte 3625. Villers-Bretonneux Military Cemetery III.D.8.
Deane, Robert Patrick Pte 319. Villers-Bretonneux Military Cemetery XII.E.7.
Fairbairn, Norman Stanley Bathurst Cpl 3759. Villers-Bretonneux Military Cemetery III.D.10.
Ford, Arthur Thomas Pte 3638. Villers-Bretonneux Memorial.
Foster, Harold Pte 6514. Crucifix Corner Cemetery Sp. Mem. 2.
Grace, Frank Cecil Pte 6256. Crucifix Corner Cemetery IX.E.1
Hall, Arthur James MM 2/Lt. Villers-Bretonneux Memorial.
Lawson, Harold Pte 5064. Villers-Bretonneux Memorial.
Leeder, Reginald Gordon Pte 284. Villers-Bretonneux Memorial.
Lewis, Charles Horace Sgt 51. Crouy British Cemetery III.B.4
Parrish, Thomas Pte 3770. Villers-Bretonneux Memorial.
Pike, William Thomas Pte 2632. Villers-Bretonneux Memorial.
Robinson, Joseph Pte 3693. Villers-Bretonneux Memorial.
Rogers, John Bowen Pte 85. Villers-Bretonneux Military Cemetery VIII.C.3.
Wholohan, Michael Joseph Pte 3731. Villers-Bretonneux Memorial
Wolff, David Ernest Pte 7609. Villers-Bretonneux Memorial.

5 July 1918
Byrne, Michael Ambrose L/Cpl 3246. Crouy British Cemetery III.D.2.
Nolan, Frank Pte 4241. Crouy British Cemetery III.B.13
Roach, Michael Joseph Cpl 7063. Crouy British Cemetery III.D.1.

6 July 1918
Fitzgerald, Joseph Francis Pte 4185. Villers-Bretonneux Memorial.
Hathaway, Frederick Pte 3756. Crouy British Cemetery III.D.19.
Holt, Marsden Cpl 1956. Villers-Bretonneux Memorial.

14th Battalion
4 July 1918
Cochrane, Harry Stanley Cpl 5762. Crucifix Corner Cemetery V.E. 18.
Fisher, William Thomas Sgt 1709. Crucifix Corner Cemetery V.E.4.
Floyd, David William Pte 317. Daours Communal Cemetery Extension III.D.27.
Hawksbee, Leonard Howard Pte 6859. Villers-Bretonneux Cemetery XII.C.5.
Hughes, William Leslie Pte 5394. Crucifix Corner Cemetery X.C.10.
Wood, Ramsay Lt. Crucifix Corner Cemetery X.C.5.

5 July 1918
O'Shea, Alfred Edward Pte 6331. Crouy British Cemetery III.D.16.
Thomas, Claude Edison Pte 1262. Villers-Bretonneux Cemetery III.C.7.

15th Battalion
4 July 1918
Allason, Sidney Ernest Pte 7681. Villers-Bretonneux Memorial.
Baker, Bert Henry Pte 338. Crouy British Cemetery III.D.7.
Banks, William James Cpl 2432. Crouy British Cemetery III.B.11.
Bolck, Robert Pte 5985. Crucifix Corner Cemetery IX.B.12.
Bowring, Albert Pte 2727. Villers-Bretonneux Military Cemetery XII.C.3.
Bromfield, Jack Mawdsley Pte 7199. Crucifix Corner Cemetery IX.B.7.
Cobbett, Alan Lewis Pte 557. Crucifix Corner Cemetery X.B.2.
Cradock, Lance Edgell Pte 7217. Daours Communal Cemetery Extension III.D.39.
Dawes, Thomas Baden Pte 7844. Villers-Bretonneux Memorial.
Elliott, Richard George Pte 7082. Villers-Bretonneux Military Cemetery XV.E.1.
Fewster, George Edward Lt. Crucifix Corner Cemetery X.C.13.
Fisher, William Archibald Pte 3292. Villers-Bretonneux Military Cemetery II.B.2.
Fraser, James MC Lt. Crucifix Corner Cemetery X.C.15.
Gall, Frederick Pte 5405. Villers-Bretonneux Memorial.
Hollamby, Charles Sgt 1706. Villers-Bretonneux Memorial.
Hopton, Henry Pte 6277. Crucifix Corner Cemetery X.B.6.
Humphreys, Edward Cpl 4821. Villers-Bretonneux Military Cemetery XII.E.4.
Laws, Robert Eland Pte 3333. Crucifix Corner Cemetery IX.B.19.
Lindsay, Herbert Arthur Cpl 3789. Villers-Bretonneux Memorial.
McBride, James Gordon Pte 7801. Crouy British Cemetery III.B.27.
McKenzie, William Archibald Pte 7018. Villers-Bretonneux Memorial.
McKiernan, Jack Murray Pte 6318. Villers-Bretonneux Military Cemetery III.B.4.
Miller, Francis Macdonald Pte 7515. Crucifix Corner Cemetery X.B.3.
Nash, George Henry Pte 7850. Crucifix Corner Cemetery X.B.7.
New, Arthur Henry Cpl 4567. Crucifix Corner Cemetery X.B.1.

Oates, Robert Pte 7327. Villers-Bretonneux Military Cemetery XII.E.4.
Pelissier, Arthur Henry Pte 6329. Villers-Bretonneux Memorial.
Penn, Charles Arthur Pte 938. Villers-Bretonneux Memorial.
Pinion, Stanley Pte 7843. Crucifix Corner Cemetery X.C.14.
Ryan, Reginald Joseph Andrew Pte 7859. Villers-Bretonneux Military Cemetery XII.E.4.
Spencer, William James Lt. Villers-Bretonneux Military Cemetery II.C.8.
Stuart-Russell, Aubrey Beverley L/Cpl 6571. Crouy British Cemetery III.B.12.
Thomas, Charles Llewelyn Pte 7788. Crucifix Corner Cemetery X.C.17.
Vogler, John George Pte 4609. Villers-Bretonneux Memorial.
Watson, Alfred Pte 92. Crucifix Corner Cemetery IX.B.13.
Watterson, Percy Gordon Pte 7326. Crucifix Corner Cemetery IX.B.16.
Williams, Henry George Pte 6588. Crucifix Corner Cemetery X.B.8.
Wilson, James Barnes Pte 3929. Crucifix Corner Cemetery X.B.5.
Worthington, George Herbert Pte 7832. Crucifix Corner Cemetery IX.B.14.

5 July 1918
Crowley, Patrick Pte 7614. Crouy British Cemetery III.D.3.
Grant, Robert John MM Pte 1611. Crouy British Cemetery III.D.8.
Peacock, Ernest Charles Pte 7824. Crucifix Corner Cemetery X.C.16.
Penny, Francis Robert Pte 2265. Crouy British Cemetery III.B.23.
Wheeldon, Errol Ray Pte 7841. Crucifix Corner Cemetery X.B.4.
Wilson Henry Pte 7789A. Villers-Bretonneux Military Cemetery XII.E.4.

6 July 1918
Basing, Walter Henry Cpl 2341. Crouy British Cemetery III.D.23.
Gnatz, John Henry Pte 2314. Crouy British Cemetery III.D.25.
Gordon, Alexander L/Cpl 6975. Crouy British Cemetery III.D.27.
O'Sullivan, James George Pte 6123. Crucifix Corner Cemetery X.C.18.

16th Battalion
4 July 1918
Ball, George MM Cpl 650. Villers-Bretonneux Military Cemetery XII.A.5.
Beaver, Joseph George Pte 8070. Villers-Bretonneux Military Cemetery XIII.F.6.
Blee, Horace Edgar 2/Lt. Daours Communal Cemetery Extension III.D.38.
Blinman, Harold Goldie CSM 1457. Daours Communal Cemetery Extension III.D.36.
Buckingham, Hugh Pte 3416. Villers-Bretonneux Military Cemetery XII.F.5.
Gibson, Horace William Pte 6822. Crucifix Corner Cemetery IX.A.17.
Hennerty, Joseph Leonard Pte 5332. Villers-Bretonneux Military Cemetery XII.B.4.
Hill, Thomas Henry Pte 7753. Villers-Bretonneux Military Cemetery XIII.E.1.
Newell, Bernard Edward Sgt 213. Crouy British Cemetery III.B.16.
Rushby, George Edward MM Cpl 2521. Villers-Bretonneux Military Cemetery XII.C.7.
Scott, Alexander Paterson Cpl 7191. Villers-Bretonneux Military Cemetery XII.F.7.
Storey, Colin Charles Pte 7140. Villers-Bretonneux Military Cemetery XII.F.6.
Taylor, Charles John Pte 3056. Villers-Bretonneux Military Cemetery XII.F.3.
Watson, John Leonard Pte 8037. Villers-Bretonneux Military Cemetery II.D.1.

Weir, John Bryce Pte 4937. Villers-Bretonneux Military Cemetery XI.D.7.
Woods, Frederick Frank Capt. Daours Communal Cemetery Extension III.D.37

5 July 1918
Barrass, John James Pte 7213. Crouy British Cemetery VI.D.18.
Ward, Alfred Willoughby Pte 6351. Crouy British Cemetery III.B.15.

11th Brigade

41st Battalion
4 July 1918
Pickering, William David Pte 256. Villers-Bretonneux Military Cemetery VIII.B.10.

6 July 1918
Warren, Thomas Pte 2893. Crouy British Cemetery III.E.6.

42nd Battalion
4 July 1918
Cocks, Harold Reginald Sgt 3281. Crouy British Cemetery III.B.19.
Holley, John Thomas Cpl 1138. Daours Communal Cemetery Extension III.D.40.
Sessarago, Frederick Harold Lt. Villers-Bretonneux Military Cemetery VIII.B.9.

5 July 1918
Young, Claverhouse Pte 2003. Villers-Bretonneux Military Cemetery III.B.5.

43rd Battalion
4 July 1918
Blucher, Charles Robert Cpl 631. Villers-Bretonneux Military Cemetery XI.C.7.
Bowes, Joseph L/Cpl 2288. Villers-Bretonneux Military Cemetery XII.B.5.
Brook, Frank Richmond Lt. Villers-Bretonneux Military Cemetery III.C.3.
Burford, Leo Alston Pte 3025. Villers-Bretonneux Military Cemetery III.C.2.
Carragher, Matthew Pte 4771. Crucifix Corner Cemetery VII.C.23.
Cole, George James Pte 3031. Villers-Bretonneux Military Cemetery VII.E.2.
Davidson, Edgar Robert 2/Lt. Villers-Bretonneux Military Cemetery XII.D.10.
Eschner, Lawrence Cpl 4783. Crouy British Cemetery III.B.22.
Garnham, Edward Maurice Pte 2326. Villers-Bretonneux Military Cemetery III.B.1.
Gillon, William Pte 2570. Crucifix Corner Cemetery IX.D.17.
Hansen, Maurice Nicholas Pte 2822. Crucifix Corner Cemetery IX.B.17.
Knight, Robert Henry Pte 4810. Crucifix Corner Cemetery IX.D.12.
Lawlor, Alfred John Pte 2594. Crucifix Corner Cemetery IX.D.20.
Luscombe, Kingsley Howard Pte 509. Villers-Bretonneux Military Cemetery III.B.8.
Matthews, Arthur Frederick Pte 4822. Villers-Bretonneux Memorial.
McCann, Jack Stewart Sydney L/Cpl 1059. Crucifix Corner Cemetery IX.D.4.
O'Brien, Leslie Victor L/Cpl 4489. Crucifix Corner Cemetery IX.D.21.

O'Donnell, Richard Pte 2429. Daours Communal Cemetery Extension III.D.41.
Ramsay, James Richard Pte 4842. Villers-Bretonneux Military Cemetery III.B.2.
Rosewarne, Victor Frayne Pte 362. Crucifix Corner Cemetery IX.B.5.
Tormay, Francis Connolly MM Pte 3324. Crucifix Corner Cemetery IX.D.19.
Townsend, Percival Seymour Pte 1713. Daours Communal Cemetery Extension III.D.25.
Tubel, Samuel Pte 3722. Villers-Bretonneux Memorial.
Young, Kenneth Jack Pte 614. Daours Communal Cemetery Extension III.D.34.

5 July 1918
Brereton, Edward Herbert Charles Cpl 1806. St Sever Cemetery Extension, Rouen Q.II.E.19.
Roach, Douglas Peter Pte 5850. St Sever Cemetery Extension, Rouen, Q.IV.A.1.

44th Battalion
4 July 1918
Adam, Robert Pte 3017. Adelaide Cemetery III.S.14.
Atkins, William Pte 2530. Villers-Bretonneux Military Cemetery I.F.10.
Ayre, William Charles Pte 3379. Villers-Bretonneux Military Cemetery III.B.3.
Barnard, James Thomas Pte 3568. Villers-Bretonneux Military Cemetery III.A.1.
Bournes, Frederick Pte 2300. Villers-Bretonneux Memorial.
Comben, Charles Thomas Pte 402. Villers-Bretonneux Military Cemetery I.F.9.
Duckham, Horace Pte 3278. Villers-Bretonneux Military Cemetery XIII.F.4.
Duty, John William Pte 2322. Villers-Bretonneux Military Cemetery I.F.8.
Grace, Stephen Pte 2575. Villers-Bretonneux Memorial.
Hodgkinson, Oliver William Pte 2108. Crouy British Cemetery III.B.26.
Kelly, Ernest Roger Pte 7492. Villers-Bretonneux Memorial.
Kemp, Peter Pte 3301. Crucifix Corner Cemetery VII.C.22.
Lynch, James Joseph Pte 638A. Villers-Bretonneux Military Cemetery I.F.7.
MacLennan, Dougal Pte 642. Crucifix Corner Cemetery IX.B.4.
Morley, George William L/Cpl 3412. Crucifix Corner Cemetery IX.D.13.
Moyle, Robert Pte 6334. Villers-Bretonneux Military Cemetery XI.E.4.
Niesler, George Pte 642A. Crucifix Corner Cemetery IX.B.18.
Parker, Alfred Sgt 2032. Villers-Bretonneux Military Cemetery III.C.1.
Turner, Henry Newton Pte 7494. Daours Communal Cemetery Extension III.D.29.
Walmsley, George Oscar Harden Cpl 2043. Crucifix Corner Cemetery IX.D.3.
Walton, Rupert Pte 2657. Villers-Bretonneux Military Cemetery XI.B.5.
Wise, William Herbert Pte 2169. Villers-Bretonneux Memorial.

5 July 1918
Clark, Norman Thomas Pte 1896. Villers-Bretonneux Military Cemetery I.F.12.
Holman, Victor Pte 2112. Crouy British Cemetery III.D.9.
Moyle, John Willie L/Cpl 3394. Villers-Bretonneux Military Cemetery XII.D.9.

6 July 1918
Baker, Edward Pte 1894. Villers-Bretonneux Memorial.
Connolly, Mark Francis L/Sgt 123. Crouy British Cemetery III.D.15.

Hughes, Clarence Edgar Cpl 2346. Villers-Bretonneux Memorial.
Moran, John Pte 3426. Villers-Bretonneux Memorial.

6th Brigade (attached to 4th Division, from 2nd Division, for 4 July attack)

21st Battalion
4 July 1918
Gilbert, David Charles Pte 6808. Crouy British Cemetery III.B.8.
Green, Oswald Roger Sgt 6922. Crouy British Cemetery III.B.9.
Hart, John Thomas Pte 6812A. Crucifix Corner Cemetery IX.A.24.
Haysey, Norman Pte 6813A. Crucifix Corner Cemetery III.B.3.
Hogan, Arthur Moore Pte 5029. Villers-Bretonneux Military Cemetery XX.C.9.
Hunt, George Campbell DCM CSM 153. Crucifix Corner Cemetery IX.A.22
Johanson, Gustaf Pte 4446. Villers-Bretonneux Memorial.
McSweeney, John Francis Pte 3891. Longeau British Cemetery IV.A.4.
Oke, Norman Richard L/Cpl 3979. Crucifix Corner Cemetery IX.A.23.
Smith, Frederick Pte 6131. Crucifix Corner Cemetery IX.A.21
Snell, William Sherman Pte 5444. Villers-Bretonneux Military Cemetery XX.C.7.

5 July 1918
Farries, Richard Pte 6800. Crucifix Corner Cemetery IX.A.19.

6 July 1918
Garland, Eugene Loftus MM Cpl 1545. Crouy British Cemetery III.D.20.
McEachen, Alan Neil Pte 5881. Villers-Bretonneux Memorial.
Rochstein, Karl Sainsbury Pte 2038. St Pierre Cemetery, Amiens XIII.E.7.
Woods, Richard Charles Pte 6909A. Longeau British Cemetery IV.A.6.

23rd Battalion
4 July 1918
Batten, Bertran Leslie Pte 6955. Crouy British Cemetery III.B.10.
Breen, Gordon MM 2/Lt. Villers-Bretonneux Military Cemetery X.E.5.
Ellis, Wilfred Charles MM Cpl 5815. Villers-Bretonneux Military Cemetery IX.F.10.
Fynney, Rupert Snowden Pte 6141. Villers-Bretonneux Military Cemetery XX.B.1.
Grohs, Reinhardt Herman Pte 5984. Crucifix Corner Cemetery III.B.15.
Jones, Ernest Pte 6873A. Crucifix Corner Cemetery V.E.11.
Kelly, William Peter Pte 2895. St Pierre Cemetery, Amiens XIII.E.4.
McGrath George Reginald Pte 1242. Villers-Bretonneux Military Cemetery XX.E.5.
McGuire, John Pte 2194. Crucifix Corner Cemetery III.B.12.
McIntyre, William Murray Pte 6905A. Villers-Bretonneux Military Cemetery X.E.4.
Ryan, Denis Pte 6165. Villers-Bretonneux Military Cemetery X.A.6.
Shugg, James Pte 6945A. St Pierre Cemetery, Amiens XIII.E.5.
White, Joe Pte 6973. Crucifix Corner Cemetery V.E.9.

5 July 1918
Beckman, John Henry Pte 6285. Crouy British Cemetery III.D.6.
Kent, Edgar Ford Pte 2894. Villers-Bretonneux Military Cemetery XX.E.9.
Mackie, Leonard Augustus Pte 5638. Crucifix Corner Cemetery III.B.14.
Taylor, Vivian George L/Cpl 2811. Villers-Bretonneux Military Cemetery VII.A.5.

6 July 1918
Bell, Charles Ralph Douglas Pte 4531. Crouy British Cemetery III.D.21.

2nd Australian Division

7th Brigade

25th Battalion
4 July 1918
Beanland, Charles Henri 2/Lt. Crouy British Cemetery III.B.21.
Bowman, Frank Alexander Pte 677A. Crucifix Corner Cemetery IX.E.8.
Buhmann, Herman Ernest Otto Pte 6784. Crucifix Corner Cemetery IX.E.9.
Cain, John Henry Pte 6050. Crucifix Corner Cemetery IX.E.21.
Campbell, David Fleming L/Cpl 715A. Crouy British Cemetery III.B.18.
Chadwick, Norman Pte 5552. Crucifix Corner Cemetery IX.A.4.
Cossar, Alexander McDonald Pte 6302. Crucifix Corner Cemetery IX.A.2.
Dixson, Edwin Pte 4789. Crucifix Corner Cemetery IX.A.6.
Doorey, Alfred Stanley Hodgson Pte 3613A. Villers-Bretonneux Memorial.
Evans, Herbert L/Cpl 6545. Crucifix Corner Cemetery VII.C.13.
Frederick, James Henry Pte 685A. Crucifix Corner Cemetery VII.C.14.
Groves, Alexander Pte 6563. Villers-Bretonneux Memorial.
Hall, Walter Pte 386. Crucifix Corner Cemetery IX.E.12.
Hanneysee, Percival John Pte 7072. Crucifix Corner Cemetery VII.D.2.
Hawes, Norman Brill Sgt 384. Villers-Bretonneux Memorial.
Heather, Wylde Sgt 884. Villers-Bretonneux Memorial.
Hooke, George Edward Pte 5351. Crucifix Corner Cemetery IX.A.1.
McIntyre, Archibald Maltman Pte 7089. Crucifix Corner Cemetery VII.C.15.
Norvill, Alexander Roy Pte 4193. Villers-Bretonneux Memorial.
Penny, Charles Pte 5735. Crouy British Cemetery III.B.7.
Toft, Cecil George 2/Lt. Crucifix Corner Cemetery IX.E.19.
Vickers, Edgar Stanley Pte 536. Villers-Bretonneux Memorial.
Warner, William Edmund Pte 5664. Villers-Bretonneux Memorial.
Yapp, Thomas Pte 3259. Crucifix Corner Cemetery IX.E.22.

5 July 1918
Allport, Frank Pte 3456. Crouy British Cemetery III.D.10.

6 July 1918
Hughes, Archibald Herbert Pte 36575. Crouy British Cemetery III.D.14.

5th Australian Division

14 Brigade

55th Battalion

4 July 1918
Allen, Walter Otto Herbert Cpl 1612. Villers-Bretonneux Memorial.
Brown, Francis Cecil Pte 3212. Franvillers Communal Cemetery Extension I.G.6.
Hamilton, Ernest Cpl 1665. Franvillers Communal Cemetery Extension I.G.7.
Hart, William Barker L/Cpl 2674. Franvillers Communal Cemetery Extension I.G.8.
Harvey, William Raymond Pte 2684. Franvillers Communal Cemetery Extension I.G.9.
Holliday, Sydney Charles Cpl 2152. Villers-Bretonneux Memorial.
Ireland, George Pte 1658. Franvillers Communal Cemetery Extension I.G.5.
Isedale, Harold Richard Pte 5478. Franvillers Communal Cemetery Extension I.G.4.
MacDonald, John Pte 3186. Franvillers Communal Cemetery Extension I.G.12.
McPherson, Leonard Donald Pte 2470. Franvillers Communal Cemetery Extension I.G.10.
Piddington, William Thomas 2/Lt. Franvillers Communal Cemetery Extension I.G.11.
Ruse, Samuel Boley Pte 3211. Villers-Bretonneux Memorial.
Simmonds, Edward Ernest Pte 2982. Daours Communal Cemetery Extension III.C.14.
Sinclair, Charles Robert Pte 5182. Villers-Bretonneux Memorial.
Stafford, Louis Norman Lt. Villers-Bretonneux Memorial.

5 July 1918
Byrnes, Cecil John Pte 2617. Vignacourt British Cemetery II.E.11.
Dixon, Benjamin Pte 4677. Vignacourt British Cemetery II.E.7.
Whittaker, Thomas Pte 2514. Vignacourt British Cemetery II.E.12.

6 July 1918
Burnaby, Ernest Arthur Pte 5330. Franvillers Communal Cemetery Extension I.G.3.
Dalton, Michael George Pte 1908. Vignacourt British Cemetery II.E.16.

15th Brigade

57th Battalion

4 July 1918
Bray, Edwin Lander, Cpl 5044. Franvillers C.C.Ext. I.G.16.
Dean, Leslie, Pte 4798. Villers-Bretonneux Memorial.
Jarman, William, Sgt 6749. Franvillers C.C.Ext. I.G.15.
Silcock, Edwin John, Pte 3103. Villers-Bretonneux Memorial.
Steet, Arthur, Pte 3229. Vignacourt British Cemetery II.E.6.

58th Battalion
4 July 1918
Day, Arthur John Pte 3131. Villers-Bretonneux Memorial.
Evans, Alfred John Pte 3139. Villers-Bretonneux Memorial.
Flett, Arthur Callaway Pte 2411. Villers-Bretonneux Memorial.
Thompson, Ivo Garfield Lt. Ribemont Communal Cemetery Extension II.AA.2.

5 July 1918
Middleton, Wilfred Pte 2712. Vignacourt British Cemetery II.E.13.
Sellars, Robert Charles Pte 3223. Villers-Bretonneux Memorial.
Skinner, Edwin Charles Cpl 4642. Villers-Bretonneux Memorial.
Tredgett, Edwin James Pte 3321. Villers-Bretonneux Memorial.
Tyler, Frank Henry Sgt 3274. Villers Bretonneux Memorial.

59th Battalion
4 July 1918
Brand, Bert Pte 2865. Méricourt-L'Abbé Communal Cemetery Ext. III.E.9.
Cherry, John Howard Cpl 2144. Méricourt-L'Abbé Communal Cemetery Ext. III.G.1.
Coulson, Harold Pte 3369. Méricourt-L'Abbé Communal Cemetery Ext. III.E.8.
Facey, Stephen George DCM 2/Lt. Méricourt-L'Abbé Communal Cemetery Ext. III.E.1.
Fynch, Andrew Roy Sgt 1707. Querrieu British Cemetery C.34.
Gouge, Richard Edmund Pte 5386. Villers-Bretonneux Memorial.
Grenfell, James Henry Pte 4793. Méricourt-L'Abbé Communal Cemetery Ext. III.E.16.
Harris, James Gordon Pte 3533. Villers-Bretonneux Memorial.
Healey, Arthur John Pte 2915. Méricourt-L'Abbé Communal Cemetery Ext. III.E.17.
Langdon, William Thomas Pte 4237. Méricourt-L'Abbé Communal Cemetery Ext. III.E.7.
Leckie, Sidney Pte 4155. Méricourt-L'Abbé Communal Cemetery Ext. III.F.2.
Morrisey, Percy William Pte 3424. Villers-Bretonneux Memorial.
Nairn, William John Pte 3217. Méricourt-L'Abbé Communal Cemetery Ext. III.D.9.
Oliver, George William Douglas L/Cpl 2619. Villers-Bretonneux Memorial.
Rule, Albert Michael Cpl 5760. Méricourt-L'Abbé Communal Cemetery Ext. III.E.11.
Rusden, Arthur Stewart Keylock Cpl 5215. Méricourt-L'Abbé Communal Cemetery Ext. III.E.6.
Stanford, Charles Trevor L/Cpl 3622. Vignacourt British Cemetery II.E.10.
Wason, Thomas Matthew T. Pte 6131. Villers-Bretonneux Memorial.

5 July 1918
Rawson, James Gerald Lt. Vignacourt British Cemetery II.E.14.

60th Battalion
4 July 1918
Clayton, George Seth, Pte 3710. Méricourt L'Abbé C.C.Ext. III.D.13
Farley, Stanley Edward, Pte 3144. Villers-Bretonneux Memorial
Greville, Clifford Thomas, Pte 3395. Méricourt L'Abbé C.C.Ext. III.E.2.
Jordon, Dudley Samuel, Cpl 5115. Méricourt L'Abbé C.C.Ext. III.F.6

Moynihan, Charles David, Pte 2546. Méricourt L'Abbé C.C.Ext. III.E.10.
O'Bree, Stanley Pierpoint, Pte 6139. Méricourt L'Abbé C.C.Ext. III.F.8.
Penglase, Percival Roy, Pte 2230. Méricourt L'Abbé C.C.Ext. III.F.7.
Teasdale, Cecil Giles, Pte 3605. Méricourt L'Abbé C.C.Ext. III.E.5.
Williams, Herbert Lewis, Sgt 5238. Méricourt L'Abbé C.C.Ext. III.E.4.

6 July 1918
Knight, M.D., MC, Lt. Méricourt L'Abbé C.C.Ext. III.D.12

Australian Field Artillery

2nd Brigade
Dunn, Harry Walter MM Gnr 17187. Longuenesse Souvenir Cemetery V.C.42.

10th Brigade
Brunton, Lawrence MC Lt. Villers-Bretonneux Military Cemetery XIX.F.8.
Moxham, Robert Leslie Dick Gnr 32912. Crouy British Cemetery III.B.24.
Rogers, Harry Lelean Bdr 1822. Ribemont Communal Cemetery Extension IV.M.4.

Australian Light Trench Mortar

7th Battery
Cable, James Troy Gnr 1764. Crucifix Corner Cemetery III.B.19.
Lawson, George Thomas Gnr 20968. Crucifix Corner Cemetery III.B.22.
Whiley, William Thomas Cpl 2289. Adelaide Cemetery III.L.12.

8th Battery
Ranson, Joseph Robert Lt. Méricourt-L'Abbé Communal Cemetery Ext. III.E.2.

11th Battery
Robertson, Max Oscar Pte 270. Crouy British Cemetery III.B.17.

15th Battery
Moore, John Charles Lt (attchd from 60 Bn). Méricourt – L'Abbé Comm. Cem. Ext. III.E.3.

Australian Machine Gun Corps

2nd Battalion
Anderson, William Thomas Pte 426. Adelaide Cemetery III.G.24.
Cleland, Harold Myles Pte 6732. Adelaide Cemetery III.G.22.
Du Bois, Alfred Bernard Gordon Cumming Pte 1894. Crucifix Corner Cemetery V.E.10.
Dunn, William Wallace Robert Pte 996. Adelaide Cemetery I.B.12.

Everard, William Inns Cpl 2355. Crucifix Corner Cemetery IX.E.10.
Fisher, Thomas Pte 2331. Crucifix Corner Cemetery V.E.13.
Jones, Sydney Pte 3556. Adelaide Cemetery I.B.13.
Shelley, Robert Parker Lt. Longueau British Cemetery IV.A.5.

3rd Battalion
4 July 1918
Blamey, William James Pte 455A. Villers-Bretonneux Military Cemetery III.C.8.
Duff, Reginald Herbert Pte 608. Bonnay Communal Cemetery Extension C.18.

6 July 1918
Binnie, Daniel McNie Pte 322. Villers-Bretonneux Memorial.

4th Battalion
Davis, Percy Cpl 740. Villers-Bretonneux Military Cemetery IX.E.7.
Dovey, Reginald Walter Lt. Villers-Bretonneux Military Cemetery VIII.E.3.

Australian Engineers

4th Field Company
Davidson, Eric Sinclair 2/Lt. Villers-Bretonneux Military Cemetery XII.C.9.

7th Field Company
5 July 1918
Porter, John Watson MM Cpl 2711. Adelaide Cemetery I.B.21.

15th Field Company
McLennan, Oliver Keith Spr 6024. Ribemont Communal Cemetery Extension Spec. Mem.

5th Division Signal Company
Conlon, Patrick John Spr 2866. Méricourt-L'Abbé Communal Cemetery Ext. III.E.13.

Australian Pioneers

2nd Battalion
4 July 1918
Harris, Robert William Matthews Pte 3130. Blangy-Tronville Communal Cemetery.
Martin, Gilbert Pte 2251. Blangy-Tronville Communal Cemetery.

5 July 1918
Box, John Daniel Pte 4382. Daours Communal Cemetery Extension III.D.28.
Dynes, Phillip Pte 2857. Villers-Bretonneux Memorial.
Felton, Thomas Edward Pte 1533. Villers-Bretonneux Memorial.

Jenkins, Bertram Hewett L/Cpl 3161. St Sever Cemetery Extension, Rouen Q.II.E.20.
Pigdon, Albert Whonam Pte 2696. Daours Communal Cemetery Extension III.D.26.
Sadler, Frederick Archer Pte 1821. Villers-Bretonneux Memorial.

4th Battalion
5 July 1918
Anderson, Peter Pte 3794. Villers-Bretonneux Military Cemetery III.D.1.
Armour, Edgar William Pte 4956. Villers-Bretonneux Military Cemetery III.C.5.
Bowness, Robert Oliver Pte 2383. Villers-Bretonneux Military Cemetery III.B.10.

6 July 1918
Cartledge, Albert Pte 4766. Crouy British Cemetery III.D.12.

Australian Army Medical Corps

7th Field Ambulance
Ball, James Percival Pte 17081. Beacon Cemetery, Sailly-Laurette I.I.9.
Coutts, George Gordon MM L/Cpl 3575. Beacon Cemetery, Sailly-Laurette I.I.8.

Tank Corps

5th Brigade

8th Battalion
5 July 1918
Norman, William Sgt 91731. dow. Crouy British Cemetery III.D.4.

13th Battalion
4 July 1918
Atack, Percy 2/Lt. Villers-Bretonneux Military Cemetery XIX.B.8.
Berry, John Leslie Lt. Villers-Bretonneux Military Cemetery XIX.E.5.
Billington, A.V. Pte 304427. Villers-Bretonneux Military Cemetery XIX.E.9.
Gannon, F. Pte 301630. Villers-Bretonneux Military Cemetery XIX.A.8.
Larkins, Lockhart Henry Capt. Villers-Bretonneux Military Cemetery XIX.D.8.
Sullivan, T.J. Cpl 300450. Villers-Bretonneux Military Cemetery XIV.E.10.
Walker, Thomas Percival Patterson Capt. Villers-Bretonneux Military Cemetery XIX.E.7.

5 July 1918
Allison, William Pte 301626. Crouy British Cemetery III.D.13.
Hulton, Benjamin Wright 2/Lt. Crouy British Cemetery III.D.11.

6 July 1918
Haydock, E. Pte 300208. Crouy British Cemetery III.D.17.

No. 3 Squadron, Australian Flying Corps

Harris Lt (Pilot) RE8 C4580. Villers-Bretonneux Military Cemetery XV.A.7
Knowles Lt (Observer) RE8 B5073. Villers-Bretonneux Military Cemetery XVII.B.8

131st Infantry Regiment, 33rd American Division

4 July 1918
E Company
Bell, Leo, Pte 1387337. Original burial: Hamel Communal Cemetery, then American Cemetery Vaire -sur Somme Grave I.D.14. Repatriated to Chicago 30.12.20.
Heap, Harold R. Pte 1387309. Original burial: Crucifix Corner Cemetery, Grave V.A.2. Reburied 16.11.20 at Somme American Cemetery, Bony, B.32.1
Huston, Chester I., Cpl 1387311. Original burial: Crucifix Corner Cemetery, Grave V.A.5. Repatriated and buried Braceville-Gardner Cemetery, Braceville, Illinois, USA.
Ludtke, Richard P. Pte 1387411. Original burial in isolated grave, map reference 62D P.11.b.7.6. Reburied Beacon British Cemetery, Grave III.A.1, then on 2.3.21 at Somme American Cemetery, Bony, D.3.15.
Meyer, Joseph, Pte 1387420. Original burial in Hamel Communal Cemetery, then Crucifix Corner, grave II.D.21, repatriated to Belleville, Illinois 1.12.21.
Schmidt, Herman A. Pte 465544. Original burial in Vaire Wood British Cemetery, grave 8, then Crucifix Corner, grave V.A.8. Repatriated to East St Louis, Illinois, 27.3.21.
Teunones, Carl J. Pte 2078813. Original burial in Hamel Communal Cemetery, then Vaux-sur-Somme American Cemetery, grave I.D.18. Repatriated to Chicago, Illinois 21.10.20. reburied 30.12.20 in Arlington National Cemetery, USA. Section 18, Site 736.
Treadman, William W. Pte 1387474. Original burial in Hamel Communal Cemetery, then Vaux-sur-Somme American Cemetery, grave I.D.7. Repatriated to Joliet, Illinois 30.12.20.
Urbanski, Joseph A. Pte 1387475. Original burial in Crouy British Cemetery, grave 7. Repatriated to Norwood Park Station, Illinois 13.1.21.

D Company
Hawkins, Charles F. Pte 1387061. Original burial in Crucifix Corner Cemetery, grave V.D.17. Repatriated to Ford, West Virginia 16.11.20. Reburied 7.4.21 in Arlington National Cemetery, USA, site 1206.

K Company
D'Avolio, Guerino, Pte 2061198. Original burial in Crucifix Corner Cemetery, grave V.A.3. Repatriated to Chicago, Illinois 29.7.21.

M Company
Boswell, Harold, Pte 1388628. Original burial in Crouy British Cemetery, American Plot Grave 4. Repatriated to Chicago, Illinois 31.3.21.

132nd Infantry Regiment, 33rd American Division

4 July 1918

A Company

Ducabage, Adam J. Pte 2072765. Original burial in Crouy British Cemetery, American Plot A.2. Reburied 26.8.22 in Somme American Cemetery, Bony, A.11.14.

Glemzer, Charles. Pte 1389626. Somme American Cemetery, Bony, Tablet of Missing. Recorded as Charles Glemzia.

Hunsaker, George R. Sgt 2057600. Original burial in unspecified 'Australian' Cemetery, then Vaux-sur-Somme American Cemetery, grave II.B.20., re-assigned grave I.C.5 on 26.1.21. Reburied 17.10.22 in Somme American Cemetery, Bony, C.11.15.

Johnson, Sidney N. Pte 1390438. Somme American Cemetery, Bony. Tablet of Missing.

Kokoszka, Paul Pte 1389644. Somme American Cemetery, Bony. Tablet of Missing.

McKibben, Robert R. Pte 2077746. Original burial in Adelaide Cemetery, grave D.15. Repatriated to Freeport, Illinois 31.12.20.

Metzen, William J. Pte 2057640. Original burial in Hamel Communal Cemetery, then Vaux-sur-Somme American Cemetery, grave I.A.3. Repatriated to Howard, Illinois 4.10.21. Reburied 12.1.22 in Arlington National Cemetery USA, grave 4030.

Oberto, Dominick. Pte 1390420. Original burial in Hamel Communal Cemetery, then Vaux-sur-Somme American Cemetery, grave I.D.8. Repatriated to Springvalley, Illinois 31.12.20.

G Company

Coduti, Philip. Pte 1391027. Somme American Cemetery, Bony. Tablet of Missing.

Duckworth, Elijah Pte 1975976. Original burial in Hamelet Communal Cemetery, grave A.29, then Vaux-sur-Somme American Cemetery, grave I.D.9. One of two bodies found in grave 9 on 26.5.21, Duckworth was repatriated to Parks, Illinois and reburied on 25.7.21 in Arlington National Cemetery, USA. Sect. 18, Site 3142

Engelhardt, Henry Pte 1976170. Original burial in Vaire Wood British Cemetery, grave 2. Moved to Crucifix Corner Cemetery, grave V.A.6 on 16.11.20. Reburied 22.8.22 in Somme American Cemetery, Bony, B.21.15.

Gadbois, Edward J. Pte 1391033. Original burial in Vaire Wood British Cemetery, grave 4. Moved on 15.11.20 to Crucifix Corner Cemetery, grave V.A.11. Repatriated to Chicago, Illinois on 24.3.21.

Hanson, George M. Pte 2159873. Original burial in Vaire Wood British Cemetery, grave 3. Moved to Crucifix Corner Cemetery, grave V.A.14. Repatriated to Spring Valley, Minnesota on 8.4.21.

Harris, Edward Pte 1391038. Somme American Cemetery, Bony. Tablet of Missing.

Hogan, John J. Cpl 1391006. Original burial in Vaire Wood British Cemetery, grave 1. Moved to Crucifix Corner Cemetery, grave V.A.9. Reburied 26.8.22 in Somme American Cemetery, Bony, A.10.14

Jaski, John Pte 1391127. Somme American Cemetery, Bony. Tablet of Missing.

Kranzmeyer, Henry Pte 1391132. Original burial Tincourt British Cemetery, grave 19. Moved to Vaux-sur-Somme American Cemetery, grave II.A.10. Repatriated to Chicago on 24.3.21.

Lyng, Alfred E. Pte 1391139. Original burial in St Sever Cemetery, Rouen, grave I.A.5, renumbered I.A.1 on 31.3.21. Reburied 18.8.22 in Somme American Cemetery, Bony, grave

B.15.6. His headstone, and entry in the National Archives Catalog, the 'Card Register of Burials of Deceased American Soldiers' give his date of death as 14.7.18. In Abel Davis' history of the 132nd Regiment, he is described as dying of wounds on 4.7.18. The discrepancy remains unsolved.

Perri, Luigi Pte 1391161. Original burial in Vaire Wood British Cemetery, grave 6. Moved to Crucifix Corner Cemetery, grave V.A.10. Repatriated to Cosenza, Italy on 19.10.22.

Reninger, Arnold S. Cpl 1390985. Original burial in an isolated grave at Bois de Failvox (?) near Hamel. Moved to Vaux-sur-Somme American Cemetery, grave III.A.23 on 17.6.19. Repatriated to Chicago, Illinois on 30.12.20.

Sobanski, John Pte 1391177. Somme American Cemetery, Bony. Tablet of Missing.

Taylor, Lee A. Pte 1391073. Somme American Cemetery, Bony. Tablet of Missing.

L Company

Blasius, John Jr Pte 1390218. Original burial in Crouy British Cemetery, grave 5. Repatriated to Chicago, Illinois on 10.1.21.

M Company

Papovasilupulos, James Pte 1390791. Original burial in Vaire Wood British Cemetery, grave 7. Moved to Crucifix Corner Cemetery, grave V.A.7. Repatriated to Kalamota, Greece, on 25.6.22.

Company Unknown

Eddy, Charles L. Pte. Somme American Cemetery, Bony. Tablet of Missing.

5 July

Wesolowski, Jozef Pte 1391196. Original burial in Crouy British Cemetery, American Plot grave 3. Reburied 22.8.22 in Somme American Cemetery, Bony, B.12.9. Wesolowski's mother was resident in Poland.

6 July

A Company

Vidal, Arthur Pte 1390302. Original burial in St Sever Cemetery, Rouen, H.I.A.3. Repatriated to Chicago, Illinois on 21.7.21.

American Total – 39

Appendix III

Overall Casualty Figures Reported by Battalions for 4 July 1918[1]

	Killed		Wounded		Missing		Total	
	Off	OR	Off	OR	Off	OR	Off	OR
4 Bde								
13 Bn	2	24	6	93	-	1	8	118
Attchd US	-	7	4	42	-	4	4	53
14 Bn	1	4	1	49	-	-	2	53
15 Bn	3	41	6	190	-	-	9	231
Attchd US	-	13	2	44	-	12	2	69
16 Bn	2	11	3	62	-	-	5	73
4 Bde Total	*8*	*100*	*22*	*480*	-	*17*	*30*	*597*
6 Bde								
21 Bn	-	6	2	32	-	8	2	46
23 Bn	1	9	4	61	-	-	5	70
6 Bde Total	*1*	*15*	*6*	*93*	-	*8*	*7*	*116*
7 Bde								
25 Bn	2	19	1	71	-	-	3	90
7 Bde Total	*2*	*19*	*1*	*71*	-	-	*3*	*90*
11 Bde								
41 Bn	-	1	1	8	-	-	1	9
42 Bn	2	1	-	48	-	-	2	49
Attchd US	-	-	2	6	-	-	2	6
43 Bn	2	17	4	74	1	1	7	92
44 Bn	-	22	5	113	-	13	5	148
11 Bde Total	*4*	*41*	*12*	*249*	*1*	*14*	*17*	*304*
14 Bde								
55 Bn	1	8	1	58	1	1	3	67

1 57 & 60 Bns only reported casualties for the whole of July 1918, so are not included in the table. 57 Bn casualties overall for the month were 2 officers and 37 other ranks, 60 Bn reported 5 officers and 58 other ranks.

	Killed		**Wounded**		**Missing**		**Total**	
	Off	**OR**	**Off**	**OR**	**Off**	**OR**	**Off**	**OR**
15 Bde								
58 Bn	1	9	1	30	-	-	2	39
59 Bn	2	15	5	46	-	-	7	61
15 Bde Total	*4*	*32*	*7*	*134*	*1*	*1*	*12*	*167*
Total	**19**	**207**	**48**	**1,027**	**2**	**40**	**69**	**1,274**
Grand total	**226**		**1,075**		**42**		**1,343**	

Appendix IV

Map References for Original Trench Maps & How to Interpret Them.

The method for using map references is explained below, allowing the reader to locate locations on the maps referred to in the text using First World War-style coordinates.

The areas shown on the maps are divided into large rectangles, each identified by a capital letter of the alphabet. These are, in turn, divided into smaller squares (1,000 yards by 1,000 yards on the ground) identified by a number.

Each numbered square is divided into four quarters, referred to as a, b, c & d, though only rarely marked as such on the maps. Each side of these 500-yard by 500-yard 'sub-squares' are considered to be divided into 10. Examples will now serve best:

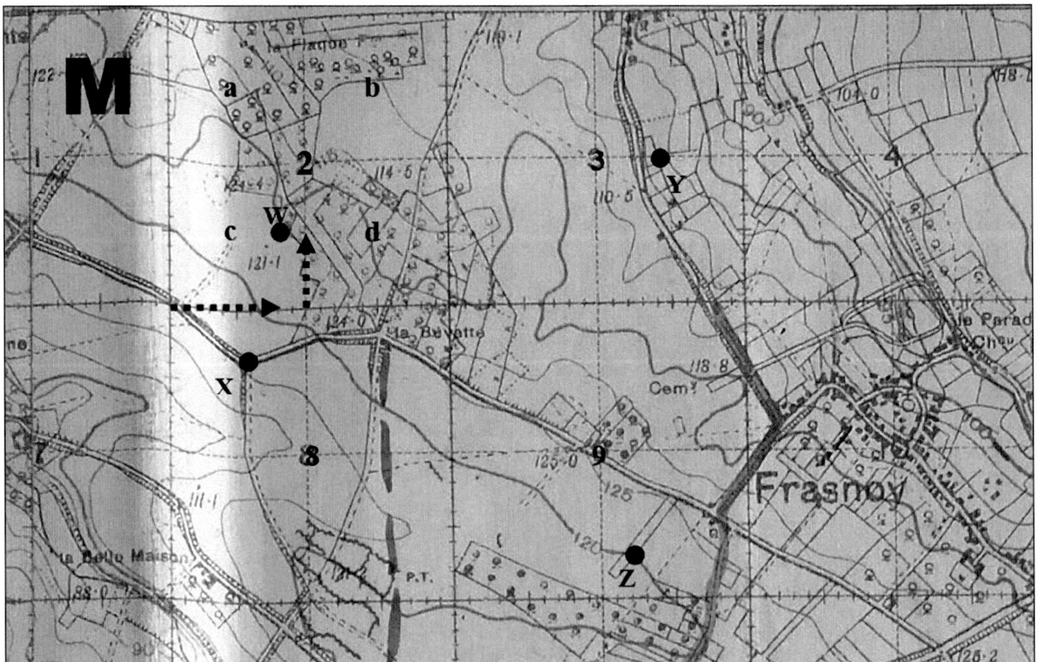

The dot marked 'W' is in square M.2. It is in sub-square c, therefore M.2 c. Count from left to right along the southern horizontal boundary of that sub-square – the red dot is above the eighth division. Count upwards along the eastern vertical boundary, and the dot is adjacent to the fifth division. Therefore, this point can be described as being at M.2 c 8.5. Similarly, the dot marked 'X' is at M.8 a 6.7. The dot marked 'Y' is at M.3 b 4.0, and the dot marked 'Z' is at M.9 d 2.3.

Any point on the map can therefore thus be identified to within 50 yards on the ground. On larger scale maps, each side of a sub-square is divided not into 10, but 100, therefore M.2 c 82.51 locates the centre of 'W' to an accuracy of five yards. This notation is not often used in the text of this work.

Bibliography

Archival Sources

Australian War Memorial (AWM)
1DRL/0428 Australian Red Cross Society Wounded & Missing Enquiry Bureau Files
26 361/2 Australian Corps General Staff Diary June 1918
26.487.6 Historical Section A.W.C. Memorandum for Colonel Bach
28 1/236 Recommendation File for Honours and Awards, AIF 1914-18 War
2018.19.35 Diary of 165 Private Eric Giles Miller, 43/Bn
2018.19.46 Letters of Captain Lionel Gordon Short, 23/Bn
361/2 Australian Corps General Staff Diary. July 1918
3DRL 2316. Monash Collection 4 – 24 June 1918
3DRL 2316. Monash Collection July 1918
DRL 2316 War Letters of General Monash. Final Typed Copy 1934, Vol. 11
38 3DRL 606/116/1 Records of C.E.W. Bean, Official Historian
38 3DRL606/190/1 Official History, 1914-1918 War: Records of C.E.W. Bean, Official Historian. Diaries and Notebooks
315 419/099/002. Papers of James Campbell Stewart
4 1/48/27 War Diary 4th Australian Division General Staff. June 1918
4 1/48/28 War Diary 4th Australian Division General Staff. July 1918
4 13/13/26 War Diary HQ 4th Australian Divisional Artillery. July 1918
4 1/48, Roll 832. 4th Australian Divisional Intelligence Summary No. 304
4 23/4/33 & 34 War Diary 4 Australian Infantry Brigade HQ
4 23/6/35 War Diary 6 Australian Infantry Brigade HQ
4 23/7/35 War Diary 7 Australian Infantry Brigade HQ
4 23/11/19 War Diary 11 Australian Infantry Brigade HQ, June 1918
4 23/11/20 War Diary 11 Australian Infantry Brigade HQ, July 1918
4 23/14/27 War Diary 14 Australian Infantry Brigade HQ, June 1918
4 23/14/28 War Diary 14 Australian Infantry Brigade HQ, July 1918
4 23/15/28 War Diary 15 Australian Infantry Brigade HQ, June 1918
4 23/15/29 War Diary 15 Australian Infantry Brigade HQ, July 1918
4 23/30/45 War Diary 13th Australian Battalion
4 23/31/45 War Diary 14th Australian Battalion
4 23/32/40 War Diary 15th Australian Battalion

4 23/33/32 War Diary 16th Australian Battalion
4 23/38/35 War Diary 21st Australian Battalion
4 23/40/34 War Diary 23rd Australian Battalion
4 23/42/35 War Diary 25th Australian Battalion
4 23/58/21 Part 1. War Diary 41st Australian Battalion
4 23/59/21 War Diary 42nd Australian Battalion
4 23/60/23 War Diary 43rd Australian Battalion
4 23/61/22 War Diary 44th Australian Battalion
4 23/72/29 War Diary 55th Australian Battalion
4 23/75/30 War Diary 58th Australian Battalion
4 23/76/30 War Diary 59th Australian Battalion
4 23/77/30 War Diary 60th Australian Battalion
4 14/10/30 War Diary 4th Australian Divisional Engineers HQ
4 14/27/35 War Diary 8th Field Company, Australian Engineers, July 1918
4 13/120/4 War Diary 7th Australian Light Trench Mortar Battery
4 8/6/18 War Diary 3 Squadron Australian Flying Corps. June 1918

Other Archives
Churchill College Archives, University of Cambridge. Rawlinson Papers (CCA)

The National Archives, Kew (TNA)
WO95/112-1 War Diary 5th Tank Brigade July 1918
WO95/115/2 *'The History of the 13th Tank Battalion.'*
WO95/112-5 8th Tank Battalion War Experiences
WO95/114-3 War Diary 8th Tank Battalion
WO95/114-5 8th Tank Battalion War History

Bovington Tank Museum Archives
E2012.4678. Papers of Sergeant Edwin Bond
WW1/Hassell 8.Doc. Papers of J. Gordon Hassell
E2006.478. Tank Actions 1918, Hamel
E1974.44. Papers of Sergeant Wynn Dixon

Secondary Sources

Bean, C.E.W., *The Official History of Australia in the War of 1914-1918* (Sydney: Angus & Robertson, 1920–1942) Vol. VI.
Bergeder, Dr Fritz, *Das Reserve-Infanterie Regiment 202 auf den Schlachtfeldern des Weltkrieges 1914-1918.* (Berlin & Wilmersdorf: Verlag Tradition, 1927)
Biggs, Donald F. (ed.), et al, *Illinois in the World War. An Illustrated History of the Thirty-Third Division. Volume 1.* (Chicago: States Publication Society, 1921)
Bishop, *The Hell, The Humour, The Heartbreak* (Kenthurst: Kangaroo Press, 1993)
Chataway, Lt T.P., *History of the 15th Battalion Australian Imperial Forces War 1914-1918,* revised and edited by Lt-Col. Paul Goldenstedt (Brisbane: William Brooks & Co Ltd, 1948)

Cook, Timothy J., *Snowy to the Somme. A Muddy and Bloody Campaign, 1916-1918* (Newport: Big Sky Publishing Ltd, 2014)

Davis, Abel, *The Story of the 132nd Infantry A.E.F.* (1929)

Edmonds, Sir James, *Military Operations France and Belgium, 1918. Vol. III* (London: Macmillan, 1939)

Fitzsimons, Peter, *Monash's Masterpiece. The Battle of Le Hamel and the 93 Minutes that Changed the World* (London: Constable, 2018)

Griffith, Paddy, *Battle Tactics of the Western Front. The British Army's Art of Attack 1916-18* (London: Yale University Press, 1994)

Groos, Carl & von Rudloff, Werner, *Infanterie-Regiment Herwarth von Bittenfeld (1. Westfälisches) Nr. 13 im Weltkriege 1914-1918* (Oldenburg & Berlin: Verlag Gerhard Stalling, 1927)

Huidekoper, Frederic L., *The Story of the Thirty-Third Division, 'The Prairie Division'* (Chicago: reprinted from the Chicago Daily News, 1919)

Longmore, Capt. C., *Eggs-A-Cook! The Story of the Forty-Fourth. War – as the Digger Saw it* (Perth: The Colortype Press Ltd, 1921)

Longmore, C. *The Old Sixteenth. Being a Record of the 16th Battalion AIF during the Great War 1914-1918* (Perth, W.A.: The History Committee of the 16th Battalion Association, 1929)

Monash, Sir John, *Australian Victories in France in 1918* (London: Hutchinson & Co. 1920)

Pedersen, Peter, *Battleground Europe: Hamel, Somme* (Barnsley: Pen & Sword, 2003)

Poetter, Capt., *Infanterie-Regiment Nr. 55* (Oldenburg/Berlin: Druck und Verlag von Gerhard Stalling, 1922)

Riebensahm, Gustav, *Infanterie-Regiment Prinz Friedrich der Niederlande (2. Westfälisches) Nr. 15 im Weltkriege 1914-18* (Minden: Selbstverlag des Bundes ehemaliger Angehöriger des Infanterie-Regiments Nr.15, 1931)

Sanborn, Col. Joseph B., *The 131st U.S. Infantry (First Infantry Illinois National Guard) in the World War Narrative – Operations – Statistics* (Chicago: 1919)

Schultz, Walter, *Infanterie-Regiment Graf Bülow von Dennewitz (6. Westfälisches) Nr. 55 im Weltkriege* (Detmold: Verlag der Meyerschen Hofbuchhandlung (Max Staercke), 1928)

Sheffield, G. & Bourne, J., (eds), *Douglas Haig. War Diaries and Letters 1914-1918* (London: Weidenfeld & Nicolson, 2005)

Terraine, John, *To Win a War. 1918, The Year of Victory* (London: Macmillan, 1986)

Ulrich, Herbert, *Reserve-Infanterie-Regiment 52 im Weltkriege. Zusammengestellt aus Berichten, Tagebüchern und eigenen Erlebnissen.* (Cottbus: Lausitzer Verlagsanstalt, 1925)

Wanliss, Newton, *The History of the Fourteenth Battalion AIF* (Melbourne: The Arrow Printery, 1929)

White, Thomas A., *The History of the Thirteenth Battalion AIF* (Sydney: Tyrells Ltd. 1924)

Index

A page number in italics denotes a photograph.

PEOPLE

PLACES

UNITS & FORMATIONS

Wolverhampton Military Studies

WOLVERHAMPTON
MILITARY STUDIES SERIES

www.helion.co.uk/wolverhamptonmilitarystudies

Submissions

The publishers would be pleased to receive submissions for this series. Please contact us via email (info@helion.co.uk), or in writing to Helion & Company Limited, Unit 8 Amherst Business Centre, Budbrooke Road, Warwick, CV34 5WE